Life, Psychotherapy and Death

of related interest

Not Too Late
Psychotherapy and Ageing
Ann Orbach
ISBN 1 85302 380 9

Wholeness in Later Life
Ruth Bright
ISBN 1 85302 447 3

The Social Symbolism of Grief and Mourning
Roger Grainger
ISBN 1 85302 480 5

Spirituality and Ageing
Edited by Albert Jewell
ISBN 1 85302 631 X

Past Trauma in Late Life
European Perspectives in Therapeutic Work with Older People
Edited by Linda Hunt, Mary Marshall and Cherry Rowlings
ISBN 1 85302 446 5

Music Therapy in Palliative Care
New Voices
Edited by David Aldridge
ISBN 1 85302 739 1

Life, Psychotherapy and Death

The End of Our Exploring

Ann Orbach

Jessica Kingsley Publishers
London and Philadelphia

For permission to reprint copyright material the editors gratefully acknowledge the following:
Extract from *Peter Pan* by J.M. Barrie reproduced with the kind permission of Great Ormond Street Hospital Children's Charity, London; extract from *Last Orders* by Graham Swift reprinted with the kind permission of Macmillan Publishers Ltd, London; extract from *Cries Unheard* by Gitta Sereny reprinted with the kind permission of Macmillan Publishers Ltd, London; excerpts from 'Little Gidding' in *Four Quartets*, Copyright © 1992 by T.S. Eliot and renewed 1970 by Esme Valerie Eliot, reprinted by permission of Harcourt Brace and Company, Florida, USA and Faber and Faber Ltd, London; excerpts from *Murder in the Cathedral* by T.S. Eliot, copyright © 1935 by Harcourt Brace and Company and renewed 1963 by T.S. Eliot, reprinted by permission of Harcourt Brace and Company, Florida, USA and Faber and Faber Ltd, London; extract from *Wasted: A Memoir of Anorexia and Bulimia* by Marya Hornbacher, copyright © 1998 by Marya Hornbacher-Beard, reprinted by permission of HarperCollins Publishers, Inc, New York, USA and HarperCollins Publishers Ltd, London; extract from *Modern Nature: The Journals of Derek Jarman* (Hutchinson) by Derek Jarman reprinted with the kind permission of Random House UK Ltd, London; extract from *Anam Cara: A Book of Celtic Wisdom* by John O'Donohue, copyright © 1997 by John O'Donohue, reprinted with the kind permission of HarperCollins Publishers, Inc., New York, USA and Transworld Publishers Ltd, London.

First published in the United Kingdom in 1999 by
Jessica Kingsley Publishers Ltd,
116 Pentonville Road,
London N1 9JB,
England
and
325 Chestnut Street,
Philadelphia, PA 19106,
USA.

www.jkp.com

Copyright © 1999 Ann Orbach

Library of Congress Cataloging in Publication Data
Orbach, Ann.
Life, psychotherapy and death : the end of our exploring / Ann Orbach.
p. cm.
Includes bibliographical references and index.
ISBN 1 85302 553 4 (pbk. : alk. paper)
1. Death--Psychological aspects. 2. Psychotherapy. 3. Counseling. I. Title.
BF789.D4073 1999
155.9'37--dc21
98-32272
CIP

British Library Cataloguing in Publication Data
Orbach, Ann
Life, psychotherapy and death : the end of our exploring
1. Death 2. Death - Psychological aspects 3. Death - Social aspects 4. Psychotherapy
I. Title
306.9

ISBN 1 85302 553 4

Printed and Bound in Great Britain by
Athenaeum Press, Gateshead, Tyne and Wear

Contents

We shall not cease from exploration...

T.S. Eliot, *Little Gidding*

To die will be an awfully big adventure

J.M. Barrie, *Peter Pan*

Acknowledgements

I would like to thank the friends and colleagues whose advice, information and personal stories have made this book possible, especially: Stephen Adams-Langley, Susana Amez, Penelope Bide, Jackie Brookfield, Perry French, Margaret Garland, Rosamund Kirby-Johnson, Marina Lister, Bernard McDonagh, Elizabeth Reisz, Ann Saltwell, Mary Scott, Mona Schaanning, Josefine Speyer. My special thanks also to those patients whose experiences have greatly enhanced my understanding of both life and death.

CHAPTER I

All Must Die

'All who live must die. Passing through nature to eternity.'

Shakespeare, *Hamlet*, I, 2

No Escape

In thinking about death, we come up against two inescapable truths: certainty and unknowing.

Our bodies are visible entities. We watch what happens to them and have evidence that they are not made to last more than, at most, a century, usually less. When their functioning comes to an end, we bury or burn them and, perhaps, that is the end of the story. But our immaterial selves are less easily defined or pinned down. There are many beliefs about their destiny but no facts. As Hamlet tells us in his most famous speech, 'no traveller returns' with news from beyond the grave.

As children, unless obviously deprived, we look to our homes and, especially, our mothers for stability and reassurance. Even though not idyllic, the world of our expectations is, on the whole, a safe place to be. But, sooner or later, disillusion hits us. Life turns out to be risky, disappointing, even tragic. We need look no further than our television screens to be aware that people of all ages keep dying. Suddenly, or slowly, it dawns on us that eventually death will be our fate also, and from this certainty there can be no escape.

In mythology, almost invariably, there are descriptions of a golden age before death arrived in the world, a time in which there was no separation of man from God. Out of man's carelessness, but also sometimes through choice, the cord that joined earth to heaven was cut. Left to themselves, humans began to procreate. They also died. In our own culture the story goes that it was Adam and Eve's sin that cut them off from God. But it was also their choice. With the begetting of children, each generation, for ecological reasons, has to die.

In an African legend it was the women who chose children and death rather than living for ever with God. The men opted for immortality but the women won the day. According to Eskimo myth, 'There was no death: people were periodically rejuvenated. But eventually the population became dangerously large, threatening to tip up the land and plunge it into the sea. Then an old woman, seeing the danger, used magic words to summon death and war. So the world was lightened, and universal catastrophe was averted' (Willis, 1993, p.23).

The world's mythology is reflected in individual lives. At first, there is no separation of child from parent; yet each of us makes our bid for freedom and the taste of forbidden fruit. There is no adventure in paradise. Sameness becomes boring and, in choosing life rather than stagnation, we are, with the Africans, Eskimos, Adam and Eve and all adventurous humans, choosing death as our goal.

Dying is a process. But death is a state which has been defined and redefined by scientists as they observe loss of function in the human body, which cells are able to renew themselves and which, once destroyed, are irreplaceable. 'From a physiological point of view, the definition of death should be "the permanent disappearance of every sign of life" ... or more clearly "death has occurred when *spontaneous vital functions* have ceased permanently"' (Ivan and Melrose, 1986, p.14).

Until fairly recently, doctors would register the moment of death as when the heartbeat and breathing stops. But, with modern techniques of life support, both these functions can be re-established and kept going. So a more complicated definition is needed and, for the last few decades, we have become familiar with a new concept, that of brain death. It seems harder, these days, to catch the *moment* of death. But here is a description of the process:

> Today the law defines death, with appropriate blurriness, as the cessation of brain function. Though the heart may still throb and the unknowing bone marrow create new cells, no man's history can outlive his brain. The brain dies gradually ... Gradually, too, every other cell in the body dies, including those newly alive in the marrow. The sequence of events by which tissues and organs gradually yield up their vital forces in the hours before

and after the officially pronounced death are the true biological mechanisms of dying. (Nuland, 1994, p.42)

Some scientists may be looking ahead to the possibility of brain transplants. If this should ever happen, what, one wonders, will become of individual personality. To live on with another person's brain seems to me a kind of death – depending, of course, on how much separation there turns out to be between brain, as physical organ, and mind, as a state of thought and feeling. Whose memories would this newly manufactured person retain? But that is science fiction. As things stand today, it is still true to say 'the irreplaceable brain is the final obstacle to physical immortality' (Ivan and Melrose, 1986, p.39).

So much for definitions. Experience of death is pretty well impossible to describe, except objectively, when confronted with a corpse. In the days of big families and less medical expertise, children and young adults were likely to have some familiarity with the sight of death, often in their own homes. After 1900, fewer of us died in youth (except in war) and it was quite usual to grow up and become middle-aged without this experience. In my own childhood, too much curiosity about dead bodies would have been considered morbid. I remember being told, as a joke, that a passage in an early-nineteenth-century children's book went as follows:

'Have you ever seen a corpse, my child?
No Mama, but I should dearly love to.'

The book is long since out of print but that is how I remember it. I laughed, of course, and yet I was fascinated. How would it feel, I wondered, to look on the face of the dead. Although frightened, I had a frisson of excitement, a feeling that, indeed, I would 'dearly love to'.

I was 45 when my father died, and this was my first experience of death. Looking at his unmoving body, I was aware only of absence. Where ever he was now, he had left his body behind like a suit of old clothes. There was no fear, only sorrow at such a final departure.

Those cultures in which death is surrounded by rituals may help the individual to accept what is happening as a recognisable and natural process. The family gathers around the deathbed to say goodbye: there may even be a wake, a public send-off the night before the funeral, with the body still in the house, almost, it seems, participating. The funeral itself is elaborate and a communal grief expressed through the wearing of sombre clothes. A fixed period may be set aside for mourning, according to the closeness of the dead relative. Bouquets and wreaths are welcomed rather than considered a waste of money, their flowering and withering experienced as a powerful symbol of living and dying. There can be no argument against the common sense of 'no flowers by request' and donating the equivalent sum to a chosen charity, but, perhaps, the mourners are not in the mood to be sensible, preferring to deck the coffin with as much beauty as they can. If religious convictions are shared, the official patterns are easily accepted but with the breakdown of churchgoing in today's questioning society, the influx of Moslems, Jews, Sikhs, Buddhists and new sects, as well as scientific discoveries and increasing agnosticism, the old patterns wear out and lose their symbolic power.

A century ago the unmentionable subject was sex. Then followed a taboo on death. Death was hospitalised and hidden away. The dying, although they often knew their fate, were not told. Relatives, who also knew, were advised not to talk about it. Doctors and nurses kept up a pretence of recovery. Mourners were expected to control their feelings. When I was a child, I heard my parents describing a funeral they had just attended. The widow had 'made an exhibition of herself' in that she cried right through the service. They spoke as though she should feel ashamed. How awful, I thought, to be an adult and never allowed to cry, even over a husband's death.

As we head for a new century, the taboo has lifted. It may have something to do with the arrival of AIDS and so many youthful deaths from a sexually transmitted illness, whose victims are refusing to observe either of the taboos. Death is fast becoming the 'in' subject. When I asked the secretary of our local Alzheimer's society if she would talk to me about the sufferers and their relatives, she responded with enthusiasm: 'I'm *into* death!'

Talking about death and making it ordinary may take away its numinosity. Over-familiarity becomes like denial, a way of talking without feeling. Clinging to our own philosophies of comfort, we may stop listening to each other's.

At a weekend workshop, individuals were encouraged to voice their beliefs about death. One had attended a spiritualist church and received a message from his dead brother – 'So of course there's a spirit world'. Others described 'near death experiences' as moving down a tunnel towards a light. Or, there was comfort in a life well lived and in being able to say one had done one's best. Some were consoled by having children and grandchildren to live after them or they spoke of a cycle of deaths and births; at each death there is birth and life begins for someone else. Our bodies would be recycled and made into compost to enrich the physical world. There might be a part of us called 'soul' but most of the participants did not think of it as immortal; souls died when bodies died. To each of these statements the facilitator would say: 'that's your truth, but listen to the others'. So each made a contribution and there was no argument. If there were traditional Christians in the room, they kept quiet.

What, then, have I, as an ageing psychotherapist (but also a frightened child), to say about death?

To my patients I say very little, but I do a lot of listening. Sometimes, they air their doubts and beliefs. I am seldom tempted to tell them mine. Often, they express their fears, which usually have more to do with life than death, although the two fears tend to go together.

Ernest Becker (1973) depicts very clearly the human condition. Our problem is that we have both an animal body and what he calls a symbolic self, and these two ways of being are not easily compatible:

> The neurotic tries to cheat nature. He won't pay the price that nature wants of him: to age, fall ill or be injured, and die … We can see that neurosis is par excellence the danger of a symbolic animal whose body is a problem to him. Instead of living in the part way that nature provided for he lives in the total way made possible by symbols. One substitutes the magical all-inclusive world of the self for the real fragmentary world of experience. (p.183)

He points out the value of repression. It is impossible to live with the totality of life: 'Men aren't built to be gods, to take in the whole world: they are built like other creatures, to take in the piece of ground under their noses' (p.178).

The psychotic shuts out even the fragments and withdraws into his fantasies, making his own world in his head. The rest of us are all, to some extent, neurotic. We have to protect ourselves from being swamped by endless possibilities. So we tend to bite off only what we can chew. Some bite off more than they can digest. At the other end of the spectrum are those who are so fearful of life that they become almost incapable of action and look for safety in obsessions and phobias. Through their symptoms, they are trying hard to live, as if to step outside their well-organised rituals would be to risk death. But, in fact, both fears come together in the symptom.

The failure to live fully and realise one's potential induces guilt. I knew a patient whose fear of death was not for herself but for everyone in the world whom she might unwittingly have injured, not only by her actions but also through the power of her thoughts. On the one hand, she had bitten off a lot more of the world than she could comfortably chew – she saw herself as having to save mankind – while, on the other, her life was crippled by rituals of checking possible impediments (such as, for instance, broken glass in the streets), which, once noticed, she felt compelled to clear away. Not to perform such 'duties' brought on agonising guilt. She was the eldest in her family and felt sure that her inexperienced mother had bungled the task of caring for her, either by smothering or inappropriate handling. She was also sure that, as an infant, she had had murderous fantasies towards her mother, for which, throughout her life, she had to atone.

This is one illustration of the narrowing of experience brought about by fear of both life and death. Others are likely to emerge in the course of writing this book. On the theme of fear, a lot more needs to be said.

In so far as we are all neurotic, it goes without saying that therapists are no more immune to resistance than their patients. Most of us immerse ourselves in the business of living, but always with an undercurrent of knowing that death will get us in the end. Whether this end will be violent or peaceful is not something that we can foresee, only that an end of some sort is inevitable. In the face of such stark certainty, neurosis seems the only sanity and indifference the Janus face of denial. We are reminded at funerals that 'in the midst of life we are in death', but, for daily living, the reminder is repressed. Nevertheless, the unconscious psyche 'knows' about death as well as life and, provided there is not a total split with the conscious ego, there may be some hidden preparation.

A patient came for therapy, having given himself a year to get ready for retirement. He attended regularly and worked hard but, in fact, talked hardly at all about having to retire. Only once did we touch on the subject of death, which he dismissed as not of much concern. He put this down to his 'non-attachment'. An older colleague had said to him, with some passion: 'Make sure you die before you have to retire'. Together, we looked for (and, to some extent, found) his own passion and also what he called his 'earthiness', hiding behind the pleasant but sometimes rather flippant persona that he showed to the world.

A few weeks after ending therapy (without being quite convinced that he wanted to end), he had a heart attack and died. Unconsciously, perhaps, he knew that retirement was not what he had come into therapy to talk about.

Similarly, a couple, who shared a house with the wife's mother, thought they wanted to talk about where to live when the old lady died. But every time the subject came up, the conversation drifted to other topics and no decisions were made or even discussed. It was only when the husband got cancer and died five years before his mother-in-law that the wife began wondering about their unconscious knowledge of this unforeseen death.

According to Jung (1977):

> Willynilly, the ageing person prepares himself for death. That is why I think nature herself is already preparing for the end. Objectively it is a matter of indifference what the individual consciousness may think about it. But subjectively it makes an enormous difference whether consciousness keeps in step with the psyche or whether it clings to opinions of which the heart knows nothing. (p.410)

Nature – or biology – certainly imposes an end, that is unless with organ transplants and new genetic developments we succeed in postponing it indefinitely. But what matters more to our symbolic selves is whether we can accept and co-operate with nature's imposition.

Seeking Therapy on the Way to Death

One of the hard things about therapy with dying people is how seldom the opportunity arises to go through the dying process with them to its inevitable end and, sometimes, not even to hear about the death when it occurs. It is the therapist's lot to stay quietly behind the scenes, an anonymous presence that does not intrude on the patient's family and relationships.

If death occurs unexpectedly during the course of therapy, the next and subsequent sessions will have to be cancelled and a reason given, but, in some cases, the relatives are quite unaware of the therapist's existence, only that there is a telephone number in the patient's diary and appointments that will not now be kept. Funerals need no invitation but, if we decide to go, it is to sit discreetly at the back and remain anonymous to the end.

What is more likely is that the therapy finishes when the patient becomes too ill to attend and, although the therapist may hope for further contact, other professionals are taking responsibility and future meetings may be discouraged. Endings in therapy, like the end of life, are, in these cases, unplanned and the therapist is left stranded, wanting to know the mode of that person's dying but feeling one has no right to ask.

A patient, whom I will call Anita, was in her twenties and newly married. A malignant brain tumour, only partially operable, had resulted in mild epilepsy and near blindness, so she came to me by taxi or, sometimes, her husband brought her. When, reluctantly, she agreed to an operation, I saw her in hospital and then visited her at home.

She believed in alternative medicine, treating the whole person, eating pure food and using only natural remedies. She was disappointed that she could not fit me easily into this pattern. She put a lot of pressure on me to see cancer as more to do with the mind than the body and wanted me to take sides with her against conventional doctors. She felt that she had been forced by her mother to go through surgery and radiotherapy, whereas she would have preferred the way of diet and meditation. I told her that I was open to all possibilities but did not have enough knowledge to come down on one side or the other. To most of her questions I could only reply 'I don't know'. She wanted a charismatic healer and was attending lectures and meditation classes as well as seeing me. The leader told her that she could not die of cancer, only of fear. He gave her a special diet needing long and complicated preparation, which boosted her morale in that she felt she could do something to help herself and at least control what she took into her body. I said that I thought it was worth trying to find out how much, as individuals, we could be in charge of our lives, but whether enough to conquer cancer was not something I was qualified to speak about. I commended her positive approach, rather than just resigning herself to expecting the worst, but could only see my job as enabling her to face the truth of her illness. Her guru, or one of his followers, had gone so far as to encourage her to get pregnant, as if the growth of the tumour could be channelled into new life. I must have looked startled. 'Oh', she said, 'you don't agree'. I said that I couldn't speak for myself but could only say that I was fairly sure that general medical opinion would be against pregnancy in her case, seeing it as highly dangerous.

I felt a lot of compassion, but refused to be pushed by her into saying what she wanted to hear, and I couldn't help noticing that her *petits mals* used to occur as interruptions when I was saying something that was not to her liking.

Therapy with Anita gradually petered out. She chose the guru, who gave her hope rather than what she called my down-to-earth attitude. We left it that she would call me if she wanted to continue, but that was more than twenty years ago and she never did, nor did I hear what became of her. If she died, I hope she was not too much afraid. I believe she chose the glamorous male guru, instead of me, as the one who could take away her fear – and, perhaps, he could.

Jill was in her early thirties, but feelings of doom had been with her since childhood, when she first had Hodgkin's Disease. I knew about her from her mother, who was a patient of mine. When Jill said that she wanted to see me, I felt, at first, that I must refuse, so I referred her to a colleague. This was her third therapist and she felt that all of them expected a lot from her, which she felt too weak to give. With me, she was relieved at not having to explain everything as I knew so much of her story already. After considerable hesitation, I agreed to give her a session – I didn't feel that I could refuse what might be her dying wish. Her mother was keen that I should take her on, even though we talked at some length of the possible threat to her own therapy.

Jill arrived looking frail and waif-like, and also very tired. She felt rejected by the doctor/therapist who treated her before going to my colleague. This was someone whom she had particularly wanted to see, because of his high reputation, but he had seemed reluctant to take her on for any length of time. He said that her problems were deep and her spirit broken but underestimated her physical symptoms, which were gradually getting worse. She recognised insomnia and itching skin as symptomatic of the Hodgkin's she had suffered years ago, although, at the time of our first meeting, she was still waiting for a diagnosis.

She described to me her almost total inability to sleep and her dread of silence and being alone at night; once morning came and she was aware of other people's activity, it felt safer to relax and allow herself the sleep she both longed for and dreaded. She kept feeling that 'something awful would happen' if she wasn't always on the watch. She had a habit of turning away from me with her voice trailing off, as though her hope was getting fainter. She wanted rescuing and she wanted me to do it. I said gently that she might have to face the possibility of there being no rescuer. But I knew it was important that I should not refuse to go on seeing her, which I agreed to do on a weekly basis.

I was always careful not to overload her with interpretations and, in fact, to do almost nothing at all except to go on being there and stay awake. At our second meeting she lay down and felt protected by my wakefulness. There was a silence and she drifted off to sleep, looking peaceful. Towards the end of the hour she woke up, startled, and said that she had found herself fighting to keep awake with her mind moving very fast; then there was a dream of running and being chased. I told her that she had been lying quite still. She said: 'But I mustn't go to sleep here'. I said: 'Why not? It's what you need most'. So she felt that I was giving her permission. After that, we arranged two-hour sessions and she could sometimes manage to spend nearly half that time asleep. This felt like a gift that I was giving her.

She talked of not being at home in her body, hating it for being weak and for the hole that was left when, on recovering from her childhood illness, the doctors decided to give one last dose of chemotherapy, 'to make sure', and destroyed her ovaries. Since then, she had been very wary about people doing things to her. She had a boyfriend, Freddie, who was kind and gentle, but there was no sexual involvement. Sex would have meant having something done to her. She tried to break off the relationship as not being fair to him, but Freddie stayed with her. She described him as staid and passive and wished sometimes that he would show the sort of initiative she longed for but could not manage herself. But she was grateful for his kindness and loyalty.

On better days she wondered what to do with the rest of her life. Being well was as frightening as being ill, and less familiar. If well, so much more would be expected. Her brother urged her to leave home – it was high time – but she was getting on better with her mother than ever before and they had fun together. In her childhood, her mother had been depressed and sent her away to boarding school. Then she got ill. It was hard now to remember what it was like to be well.

Eventually, the diagnosis of Hodgkin's (which she already knew) was confirmed and she was given chemotherapy. She committed herself to going through with it, though she said that it felt, to her, both mechanical and depersonalising. Between treatments she was tempted just to stay in bed, covered up and protected. She said it was like hanging on to a cliff edge and she was terrified of falling.

We had long silences, which were comfortable in that she knew I would not necessarily expect her to talk, but she also saw it as an example of not being able to sustain anything she did, not being able to concentrate on reading more than a few pages and not being able to sleep. I commented that she did not seem to believe in her own continuity.

She found the treatment increasingly hard to bear. When she had to go back after a two-week break, it felt like going to her execution. She said that she was quite unsure about trusting doctors and her instinct was beginning to say 'no more'. However, she persevered to the end of the course. Then she had to take steroids and disliked the way they made her feel. Her itching symptom returned and made her anxious. She said that the steroids had the effect on her of not knowing who she was. A fellow patient died and she talked of an inexorable fate which no one could stop. She remembered her 'doomed to die' feelings as a child and knowing there was something very wrong before anyone else noticed. It had always been hard to believe in a future. I found myself sharing her hopelessness and being much affected by this dying girl, who, it seemed, had never really had a chance to live.

Our last session was mostly silent. She said something about being on steroids for ever and that she had been told her depression was 'chemically' induced and, therefore, out of her control. Some sentences started with 'at the moment', others with 'it seems eternal'. When she got up to go I had the feeling that she was disappointed and, quite likely, blaming herself. We neither of us knew this was to be our last meeting.

She died several months later and I heard the rest of her story from her mother. She had relapsed and become very ill. There had been one last attempt at extra-intensive chemotherapy, which affected her lungs. So, in the end, it was the treatment that killed her. She insisted on coming home to die and had been sensitively looked after by both parents. Her father was with her when she died. She had sent me a card only a month before because she heard that I had been in hospital. All she said about herself was that she wished her breathing would get better so that she could walk more easily and climb stairs.

Her parents chose words of John Donne to put on her gravestone:

> All other things to their destruction draw,
> Only our love hath no decay;
> This no tomorrow hath, nor yesterday,
> Running it never runs from us away,
> But truly keeps his first, last, everlasting day.

> *The Anniversary*

To Be or Not To Be – Is There a Death Instinct?

Consciously, and most of the time, provided outside circumstances are not too threatening or the body in too much pain, human beings want to stay alive. Unconsciously, the life instinct must be enormously strong for the organism to survive the 'slings and arrows of outrageous fortune', not least the trauma of birth itself. The two glimpses I have given of patients dying young are poignant because they show so much fear (in one case denial) and a longing for life. But there is also a hint in both that they welcomed unconsciousness. Anita's epilepsy was not willed, but sometimes it served in warding off unbearable reality. And, through meditation, she strove for

Nirvana as a blissful cessation of conscious desire. Jill yearned for sleep and the end of suffering. She submitted to invasive treatments with no real hope of being made well, while, in her own words, 'instinct' cried out 'no more'.

Freud played with the idea of a death instinct, notably in *Beyond the Pleasure Principle*, in which he explored what he called the 'compulsion to repeat', both as a phenomenon in the behaviour of children and of adults in psychoanalysis. Children often demand exact repetitions of the games and stories which they most enjoy, but sometimes they need also to repeat unpleasant experiences in order to master them. Patients in analysis get drawn again and again to painful childhood events and need to regress in the transference, even though they may feel 'an obscure fear – a dread of rousing something that, so they feel, is better left sleeping – what they are afraid of at bottom is the emergence of a compulsion with its hint of possession by some "daemonic power"' (Freud, 1984, p.308). Freud goes on to suggest that there may be an instinct inherent in all organic life to return to an earlier state: 'If we are to take it as a truth that knows no exception that everything living dies for *internal* reasons – becomes inorganic once again – then we shall be compelled to say that *"the aim of all life is death"*' (p.311).

Later, in a letter to Einstein dated 1932, he writes: 'As a result of a little speculation, we have come to suppose that this instinct is at work in every living creature and is striving to bring it to ruin and to reduce life to its original condition of inanimate matter' (Freud, 1991).

The death instinct, when directed outwards, turns into destructiveness. 'The organism preserves its own life, so to say, by destroying an extraneous one' (Freud, 1991). It can also be directed towards self-destruction.

Freud acknowledged that these ideas were speculative, rather than scientific, and most of his immediate successors were luke-warm about the death instinct, seeing no evidence for the concept. Melanie Klein, however, had no such doubts. From the beginning of life, Kleinians maintain that the infant is caught in a struggle between life and death forces, as it experiences contrasting feelings of being comforted or abandoned, fed or left hungry. In this ambivalent state everything bad is projected onto the mother's breast, which becomes both needed and persecutory. The good is also projected but kept separate, as though there are two breasts, one good and one bad. This splitting is called the paranoid-schizoid position. Only gradually, with ongoing introjection of good-enough mothering, can the split be mended and love/hate, life/death accepted as parts of a whole experience. This achievement, called the depressive position, is never finished for good.

Throughout life we are haunted by loss, fear of death and guilt at our own destructiveness, as well as the capacity to make amends, to love and to create.

Some time later, Jacques Lacan re-established Freud's death instinct (or death drive, depending on how we translate the German 'trieb'), as the most fundamental issue of Freud's metapsychology. With the expressed intention of returning to the master, Lacan developed the theme with his own elaborate variations. But, whereas Freud writes with clarity, Lacan is famously elusive.

Even the three 'orders' on which his theories are based are not quite what we expect. Of these, the most important must be the Real, but this is unknown and unknowable. It has to do with 'organic need, the unconsciousness of the body' (Boothby, 1991, p.19). Unlike the Imaginary and the Symbolic, the Real has no bounds.

The ego does not belong to the Real but to the Imaginary. Lacan stresses the 'prematurity' of human birth. The infant comes into the world as a '*corps morcelé*' – that is, as a fragmented body. 'It is through the image of another person that the human infant gains the first inkling of its bodily integrity and the first measure of control over its movements' (Boothby, 1991, p.24). It is from the *gestalt*, seen in the mirror or in the other person, that the imaginary ego is formed and it has no *reality outside the imagination*:

> The question of the death instinct in Lacan is closely related to the notion of imaginary alienation ... Alienation in the Imaginary is first and foremost an estrangement of oneself from oneself. The imaginary formation of the ego is alienating not just because it is modelled on an other outside the subject but because imaginary identification somehow splits the subject from itself. (Boothby, 1991, p.47)

The human child is also born into language, the order of the Symbolic: '...the subject inhabits the world of symbol, that is to say a world of others who speak. That is why his desire is susceptible for the mediation of recognition' (Lacan, 1988, p.171). The desire comes from lack. In language the being of the individual is '*only represented* ... caught up in language's function of representing something inaccessible, the margin beyond life and the ultimate, inaccessible experience of death' (Bienvenuto and Kennedy, 1986, p.17).

But this inaccessible something also has to do with joy, or, in French, '*jouissance*', which is not translatable and lies beyond the 'pleasure principle': *Jouissance*, like death, represents *something whose limits cannot be overcome*. In Lacan's thought the "other" of life, the negativity to be overcome, non-being (in Freudian terms the death drive) paradoxically becomes the centre of life' (Bienvenuto and Kennedy, 1986, p.179).

Jouissance means orgasm and also mystical ecstasy. Lacan advises us to go to Rome and look at Bernini's statue of St. Theresa: 'And what does she enjoy? It is clear that the essential testimony of the mystics consists in saying that they experience it but do not know anything about "it"' (Lacan, 1975, p.71). The Real is what we can neither imagine nor symbolise. It is where we meet death and that inexpressible enjoyment that the French call *'jouissance'*.

Jung (1977) believed that life, as an energy process, is irreversible and directed towards a goal. That goal is a state of rest: 'In the long run everything that happens is, as it were, no more than the initial disturbance of a perpetual state of rest, which for ever attempts to establish itself' (p.405). In this, he seemed to agree with Freud that the aim of all life is death:

> Like the sun, the libido also wills its own descent, its own involution. During the first half of life, it strives for growth; during the second half, softly at first and then ever more perceptibly, it points towards an altered goal. And just as in youth the urge for limitless expression often lies hidden under veiling layers of resistance to life, so that 'other urge' often hides behind an obstinate and purposeless cleaving to life in its old form. (Jung, 1990, p.438)

For Jung, life and death are inseparable, both actually and in the mind. The ecological necessity for death, already mentioned, has been present since time immemorial, embodied in ancient myth. Death, transformation and resurrection are psychic facts, the stuff of religion and poetry.

There is also a conscious pull towards death, not only in suicidal desperation or even weariness, but in the longing for an end to separate existence and merging with a lover or God. This has found its expression through the centuries in music, painting and poetry.

Keats, listening to a nightingale, wished:

> to cease upon the midnight with no pain,
> Whilst thou art pouring forth thy soul abroad
> In such an ecstasy!

Teilhard de Chardin, in his *Hymn of the Universe*, gives us a hint, I think, of *jouissance* as he pushes the frontiers of language for the Real to break through:

> In death we are caught up, overwhelmed, dominated by that divine power which lies within the forces of inner disintegration, and above all, within that irresistible yearning which will drive the separated soul on to com-

plete its further predestined journey as infallibly as the sun causes the mists to rise from the water on which it shines. Death surrenders us completely to God; it makes us pass into God. (Teilhard de Chardin, 1979, p.136)

CHAPTER 2

Out of Season

Matthew, Mark, Luke and John
Bless the bed that I lie on.
Four angels round my bed,
One at foot and one at head,
One to guard me while I pray
And one to bear my soul away.

Nursery Rhyme

The Angel that presided o'er my birth
Said 'Little creature, formed of Joy and Mirth,
Go, love without the help of any Thing on Earth'.

William Blake (1977, p.141)

Fragile Beginnings

There is probably a temptation in all of us to look back on early childhood as
a time when we partook of that lost paradise spoken about in mythology, a
time before death came into the world. Most children, even if unlucky
enough to be bereaved, have only the vaguest concept of what the word
'death' means. But babies, long before we attribute to them thought or imagination, have had to face what Winnicott called 'primitive agonies' (Kohon,
1986), even, in the sense of annihilation, the experience of death itself.
Erikson (1974), who lists eight stages of human development, describes the
first years as conflict between 'basic trust and basic mistrust':

> But even under the most favourable circumstances, this stage seems to in-
> troduce into psychic life (and become prototypical for) a sense of inner di-
> vision and universal nostalgia for a paradise forfeited. It is against this

powerful combination of a sense of having been deprived, of having been divided, and of having been abandoned that basic trust must maintain itself throughout life. (p.241)

With modern technology, many babies torn out of the womb before their time can survive the traumas of their births and the transfer from mother to incubator. Through neurophysiological, psychoanalytic and ultrasonic studies, it is increasingly possible to observe physical and emotional development and to pick up clues through the baby's crying of just how much pain the necessary therapeutic procedures can cause. It used to be thought that the newborn lacked capacity for suffering and its crying was no more than a reflex. Dr Romana Negri (1994), working in Italy, respects these miniature humans as individuals and encourages her staff to attend to both the body and mind of the infant. She writes of baby Giacomo:

> He is always immobile, supine, with legs and arms spread out. A hiccup shakes him, and his face shows frequent grimaces. He is very irritated by the bronchial suctioning manoeuvres: he reacts by kicking, when an electrode is removed from his abdomen. I feel almost paralysed by anxiety at the sight of such a distressed baby. (p.90)

She describes herself as 'painfully constrained by a clash with primitive and obscure mental processes of my own' but has to find the strength to encourage the nurses, who would find it much easier to go on seeing the child as a textbook case rather than a person. She also works with the parents, fathers as well as mothers, and shows them the importance of their presence beside the incubator, their touch, their voices and the relationship that begins to form with their baby.

These are situations where death is always on the horizon, and anxiety is intense. Sometimes, the parents find it difficult to stay by the incubator, so close to the danger. Giacomo survived but some of these babies, despite all the technology, all the love lavished on them and, not least, their own heroic efforts, do eventually give up and die. What is amazing is the resilience of those who manage to live.

What Children Know and What They Can Talk About

A three-year-old said to her grandmother: 'My other Nanna isn't going to die'. 'How do you know?' 'She tells me so. Are *you* going to die?' 'Yes, I am'. 'Why?' 'Because everything dies. Flowers die'. 'You're not a flower'. The grandmother wanted to explain that, although she was not a flower, she felt herself to be part of nature, part of everything that lives, but she realised that this concept was too abstract for a three-year-old mind. The child, meanwhile, had switched her thoughts away from death to the garden outside and was busy picking up pebbles and watering the plants, happily talking to herself – or the flowers – while she played.

A four-year-old boy announced: 'Flowers die and we die, don't we Mummy? Who kills us in the night? Does Jesus?' (Anthony, 1971, p.25). Perhaps, this shows that the nursery rhyme quoted at the beginning of this chapter is not always comforting. Religious teaching may be helpful, provided the parents believe what they are saying, yet a lot of the imagery can be confusing to a child's very concrete thinking, in which fact and metaphor are not differentiated. I remember being taught what was supposed to be a simple prayer: 'Jesus, tender shepherd hear me, bless thy little lamb tonight'. I formed a rather grey mental picture of sheep on a dark hill and wondered why I had to pray for them. I never realised that the little lamb was me. I was much happier when introduced to the majestic language of the Lord's Prayer.

A week after his grandfather's death, a little boy attended the funeral and wanted to know what was in 'that box'. When they told him, he shook his head. 'Oh no, that's not Grandad. He rose again on the third day'. His theology was muddled but the episode is typical of the young child's tendency to see death as a temporary state. Grandad died. He lay down and stopped moving but is he still dead today?

Sylvia Anthony (1971), in her book about children's discovery of death, gives examples at various ages of what death means, and does not mean, to the very young. For example:

> 'I killed the black cat. I cut it in half in the coal shed with a chopper.'
> Mother: 'Oh why did you do that?' Richard: 'I thought we didn't want it anymore.' Mother: 'Could I see the body?' Richard: 'No, it isn't there now. I stucked it together again and it walked away.' (p.108)

This child, at four years old, had clearly not seen death as permanent and was still at a stage of grandiosity, cherishing the fantasy of his own power over life and death. I say 'fantasy' because his mind probably operated on two levels and he may not have sorted out (or wanted to sort out) the difference between play and objective reality. At five, I remember imagining that my stuffed dog was ill and might die. Only I could save him. So I held him close and cuddled him until my arm hurt. I was prepared to suffer pain for his sake, yet, at the same time, I knew that I was playing a game, testing out, I suppose, my coping mechanisms for use in later life. In the same spirit, on having to leave our family cat when returning to England from another country, I presented him with one of my toys, a woolly lamb, which I was prepared to sacrifice because I loved the alive cat more than the toy lamb. But I mourned the lamb because I knew that the cat would tear it apart and 'kill' it.

Playing with death excites children because of the solemnity surrounding the subject and, although more openly talked about today than formerly, there must be a lingering sense of a grown-up secret which, like sex, is not suitable for children. My son, at the age of seven, had begun to understand death's permanence but he got cross and walked away when told about a real person's death. On television, he could accept that most of what he saw was 'only a story' but got upset when he discovered that the 'News' was real. When I took him to the play of *Treasure Island*, the stabbing and bleeding seemed real enough for him to assume that a whole lot of people (criminals, perhaps) were put to death every day by the actors. Some years later, when we were living in Italy, he discovered that the ancient Romans did, in fact, use disposable criminals for their dramas.

In their games, children can experience the excitement of being powerful enough to kill. In play, they identify with heroes and victims, allies and enemies, 'goodies' and 'baddies', and, depending on upbringing, are able to know the difference and also to *make* a difference between play and life. If there has been a failure on the part of parents and teachers, either by example or inadequate setting of boundaries, this difference may get confused, so that, when the child has developed the strength to harm people, he may actually use this power. The ten-year-old murderers of the toddler, James Bulger, were old enough in years and intelligence to know what they were doing but were, nevertheless, unable to restrain either themselves or each other from fatally acting out whatever aggressiveness and frustration they were feeling. Less deprived children might have found a satisfying outlet in play or sport rather than venting their rage on someone more helpless than themselves. Adolescents sometimes play dangerously with death, through drugs, excessive speed, truanting and showing off to their peer group.

Researchers have defined ages and stages that children go through in their knowledge of death and most would agree that concepts of finality and irreversibility are unlikely below the age of five, when 'why' questions are added to questions of what death looks like and is (Anthony, 1971). But, as mentioned already, before the intellect reaches this level of understanding, there has been an experience. Both infant observation and regression in adult psychotherapy show how 'the young infant registers the possibility of death through a sense of the danger of death ... one could say that there is a primitive awareness of death as part of a survival pattern, and that fear of separation and loss is, in origin, a fear of being totally abandoned and left to die' (Judd, 1989, p.18). In that sense, awareness of death comes with birth, our first experience of separation-anxiety.

Answering Children's Questions

Separation is a dependent child's greatest dread. Long before the intellect can grasp what death means, there is an instinctive knowledge that survival would not be possible without good enough parenting. It is this anxiety that we need to address when children ask us questions about death. Provided there has not been a bereavement and the child has no life-threatening illness, the subject will not need to be tackled until the questions actually get asked. We only need to be ready and not disconcerted at the spontaneity and lack of inhibition that the child may show: 'you're very old Mummy. When are you going to die?', or, 'does dying hurt?', or even, 'what's it like being dead?', and, perhaps most difficult of all, especially for non-believers, 'where do all the dead people go?'

Children are looking for straight answers and are not easily fooled if we speak without conviction or show discomfort. If they don't like our answers, they will quite likely change the subject: 'let's play something else', or, as in one of Sylvia Anthony's examples, 'now I will go on with my tea'. It is probably wisest to let the child set the pace rather than burdening him (or her) with too much indigestible information. An easy way out is to reassure – for instance: 'you won't die till you're old' – which is unsatisfactory in that it is not necessarily true and, perhaps, it is not the child's own death which he fears as much as the death of the parent, who he knows is getting older and likely to die before he does. In fact, any adult seems immeasurably old to the young child.

Bruno Bettelheim (1987), writing about fairy tales, stresses their value in addressing problems of sibling rivalry, loneliness, isolation and existential anxiety:

> The fairy tale offers solutions in ways that the child can grasp on his level of understanding ... 'And they lived happily ever after' does not for a moment fool the child that eternal life is possible. But it does indicate that which alone can take the sting out of the narrow limits of our time on this earth: forming a satisfying bond to another. The tales teach that when one

has done this, one has reached the ultimate in emotional security of existence and permanence of relation available to man: and this alone can dissi-
pate the fear of death. (pp.10–11)

He advises telling rather than reading the stories, so that the child can participate in what has been told and retold from one generation to another:

> Thus the narrator let his unconscious understanding of what the story told
> be influenced by that of the child. Successive narrators adapted the story ac-
> cording to the questions the child asked, the delight and fear he expressed
> openly or indicated by the way he snuggled up to the adult. (pp.150–1)

If children are not satisfied with the way a story is told, they will often add to
it or leave out details and so adapt it to their own emotional needs. One
should never explain the story but allow the child's imagination to play with
the images that it presents. I made the mistake of trying to explain a story
when, many years ago, I read the very popular Narnia books to my son.
Reaching the final story in the series *The Last Battle*, I realised that it was all
about death, the end of the world, judgement, heaven and hell. It even
described a stable that 'had something inside it bigger than our whole world'
(Lewis, 1966, p.128). 'Does it remind you of anything?' I asked. My son took
no notice and I saw that it was useless to describe one story in terms of
another but, as in the best fairy tales, let the images speak for themselves,
more to the child's unconscious than conscious thinking.

So, what about the stories in the Bible and the Christian gospels? A lot
depends on what the stories mean to us and what we believe about God.
Committed Christians will probably convince their children, at least for the
time being, and give them the consolation of going to heaven when they die.
And yet not all children like the idea of such enormous change, nor do they
necessarily want to go and live with Jesus, who seems a shadowy figure
compared with their flesh-and-blood parents. Eternal life may seem too big a
concept to take in. But the unbelieving parent faces a more daunting task and
it is not surprising that many of them try to avoid telling their children that
death is the end of everything and a final separation. So they find themselves
talking glibly about what, to them, is a purely imaginary heaven, a game of
'let's pretend'.

Another evasion tactic is the euphemism. Those who die are described as
'passing away', 'passing over', 'laid to rest'. Or a child had 'lost' her father or
little brother. How careless of her! If lost, why can't he be found? And will
she too get lost?

We should be careful what we say to children. They take us literally. A child of six was told that if she had an electric shock, she would die. One day she fiddled with a plug and had a slight shock. She told her mother, who probably made sympathetic noises but no more than seemed necessary. The child decided it was best to meet death sitting tidily in a chair, so she sat still, waiting for it to happen. She was not afraid but hurt and disappointed that her mother appeared not to mind. It was not death but being unloved that upset her. We would do well to remember that if our children are assured that we love them, they can face most hardships at least as well as we can. Winnicott (1986) once commented that 'healthy children are rather better at death than healthy adults' (p.62). Erikson (1974) gives us the other side of the coin: 'Healthy children will not fear life if their elders have integrity enough not to fear death' (p.251). The two fears usually go together.

The First Bereavements

Animals

'Dear Slipper,' wrote a boy of six, 'I'm sorry you are dead. Love from Christy.' His brother, aged four, seemed unaware of what had happened to the family dog and his reaction was to laugh. Knowing Christy's grandmother and the various dogs she has mourned, I am sure that Slipper had a funeral. Losing animals, performing a ritual and having a good cry – all these are useful rehearsals for coping with future bereavements of *people* we love. The death of a pet may even feel worse at the time but will probably have fewer long-term effects.

Animal funerals can be therapeutic, especially if the child has a hand (literally) in burying the favourite pet, preferably in a familiar plot of earth among the seeds from which flowers will grow in the spring. What is hard to take in is that the animal, unlike the flowers, has gone for good. Perhaps Christy's letter was addressed to heaven.

Siblings

Children love their brothers and sisters, but they also hate them. Jung (1954) reports a conversation between a father and his four-year-old daughter: Father: 'What would you say if you got a little brother tonight?' Anna: 'I would kill him'. Jung continues: '*Kill* is a perfectly harmless expression on the lips of a child, only meaning to get rid of...' (p.10). Sylvia Anthony (1971) comments: 'The adult tendency to exonerate the child may appear sentimental. *Kill* may be, as Jung says, a harmless expression, but babies may need to be protected from children not much older than themselves who may actually injure them' (p.109).

We have all observed (and if we have younger siblings, actually experienced) intense feelings of rejection when a new baby absorbs the mother's attention, and the jealousy that ensues. The older child has the power to damage the baby and, if not watched, may try out his (or her) strength. Whether or not feelings of aggression are acted on, the impulse is strong and, if the baby does get hurt, the older child may be convinced that his own magical thoughts were enough to cause the disaster.

But there is love mixed with hate. Isobel sulked beside her sister's pram, muttering 'horrid baby'. A friend, who came up to have a look, suggested that if Isobel wanted to get rid of her sister, she was willing to take her away. As she spoke, she gave the pram a push. Isobel cried out in desperation: 'No, no, its not *your* baby, it's my little sister'.

Elizabeth's brother, David, died on St. David's Day. He was six months old. By a strange coincidence, his Uncle David had died at the same age and on the same day. Both Davids were the first sons of their mothers. Elizabeth remembers the day very well, although she was only two. She was playing in the garden and David was asleep in his pram. She was told not to come into the house as the pram was blocking the doorway. She wanted to fetch something and thought she could move the pram, but it was higher than she could reach. The pram tipped over and she ran away. David neither moved nor cried, and was never seen alive again.

Elizabeth's feeling was not so much guilt for being naughty as fear of adult anger. She has no memory of the moment that she knew he was dead, nor of how she was told, but remembers the sight of her mother walking down the path with David in her arms, a shawl covering his face. She asked where they were taking David but cannot now remember whether they said it was to her grandfather or to Jesus. Her grandfather was the Rector and it was he who buried David. She knew what death was: it was going away and never coming back.

Nobody talked about David's death and she felt shut out for ever, knowing that her mother would rather it had been she, not David, who had died. These feelings have never changed. She tried many times to talk about what happened but the subject was always avoided. At six, she gave up trying. When she was 15 she told her mother that it was she who had tipped the pram, but this was not accepted: her mother insisted that nobody had been there. Elizabeth went on believing that she had killed her brother. She found herself writing a long poem – it was as though her hand just wrote. She thought the poem came from David and that he had forgiven her. In her early twenties, Elizabeth traced the coroner who had presided over the inquest and wrote to him for information. He replied with a factual letter. No cause of death had been discovered.

Thinking about it long afterwards, she realised how unlikely it was that, if she had tipped her brother out of the pram, he would have made no sound. It now seems probable that it was a cot death and that he was already dead before his fall.

What is striking about this account is how much the child knew without being told and that, at such an early age, she had formed a clear concept of death and recognised its permanence. Individual children do not always fit the categories which researchers make for them, so I am not arguing with Elizabeth's memories, nor doubting the severity of their impact on her inner world.

Children find it hard to cope with silence and no explanations. If a sibling dies and the parents mourn, the child's sorrow sometimes gets overlooked. Rosemary Mander (1994), writing about the loss of a baby, gives us some recollections of a fifty-year-old, forty years after the stillbirth of her brother: 'We got the cot out. Mummy knitted vests. We cleaned her bedroom so it would be OK for when the midwife came. Everybody said I was "a proper little midwife"'. But there was no baby '...nobody told me what was happening. It was obvious I wasn't meant to ask ... They probably thought I'd forgotten about the baby'. Her sister took her shopping and one of the shopkeepers asked about the baby. It was then that she heard about the brother who was born dead. But, realising that she was not meant to talk about it, she said nothing. 'I think I was being protected by not being told directly. I'm sure they thought it best' (p.102). She was left wondering. In a big family, like hers, perhaps it didn't matter if one child died. Or was dying too awful to talk about? Nobody cried and life went on as though nothing had happened.

Twins

To lose a twin, especially one that is identical, is like losing a part of oneself. The companionship of being in the womb together and, after birth, to have shared the same mother's love, despite all the rivalry that this situation is bound to entail, must be the closest human relationship imaginable. To understand the seriousness of this loss, it is worth looking at what it is like to be in such close partnership.

I have, more than once, found myself seeing a twin sister in therapy and been struck by how each one was differentiated in her family. In one case the twins were labelled 'helpful' and 'pretty', and felt the need to live up to their titles. I saw the 'pretty' one, who also sounded the stronger of the two but relied on her sister to help her out of practical difficulties. These were fraternal twins, so it was not difficult to tell them apart, but being conceived and born at the same time had resulted in a passionate love-hate relationship.

Identical twins have an even closer bond, their genetic make-up being exactly the same, yet we do not experience them as clones. A twin who came to me for therapy, although married and a mother, could not envisage a more satisfying relationship than the one she had with her twin sister. But each relied on the other to complement herself. They shared qualities between them. One was stronger, more active and said to be the favourite. Her sister held the memories and was better at relating to people. 'My' twin told me that, in infancy, she had been slow in starting to talk, and that was because she only wanted to communicate with her sister and, for that, they had their own language. Sometimes they looked at each other and wondered why there had to be two of them, rather than one person holding their divided qualities. As it was, neither felt complete without the other and when one got ill the other also suffered.

In therapy I felt that I was being treated like a twin sister – on one occasion she paid me with a cheque and signed it with my name! The emphasis was on my sameness rather than my difference. I could manage empathy but no surprises. After a year, I referred her to a male colleague, who could never be treated as a twin sister. I trusted him to surprise her, and I believe he did.

Another patient was the youngest in a family of eight. As a child, she had always felt that something or someone was missing. When she managed to put this in words, her mother admitted that she was a surviving twin. Her sister had died at birth. After that, she found a spot in the churchyard which she thought might be where her sister was buried. She picked flowers to put on the grave and felt comforted by this ritual. One of her older sisters disillusioned her. There was no grave; stillborn babies were not buried. So she was left with her survivor guilt.

A male patient told me that, right through his childhood, he had imagined a twin brother who played with him. He knew that no such twin existed but the fantasy had been strong.

There is an awareness these days, through ultrasound early in pregnancy, that sometimes one twin does not survive the first stage of being in the womb, possibly as a result of placental malfunction. The 'vanishing twin' gets re-absorbed and the mother never knows that more than one child was conceived (Mander, 1994).

Or does she? When Mary was pregnant for the third time, she had a haemorrhage which the doctor said was a miscarriage. Mary insisted that she was still pregnant and that her baby would be born in February. The doctor then agreed but said the birth would be in April. A daughter, Jane, was born in February. But Mary was sure she had lost a twin. An African friend told Mary that when one twin dies, he calls the other to follow. Jane died at 31.

Parents

Marina lost her father when she was eight. He was already retired when she was born and it was her mother who went out to work, so her father was a close companion, interested in her school work and proud of her achievements. There were three grown-up sons in the family but Marina was the only girl and she must have been aware that he thought her very special. Carrying so much of his hope for a radiant future might, but had not yet, become a burden. He died suddenly of a heart attack. Both mother and daughter shared their grief and there was no question of not allowing the child to mourn. Her mother asked my advice about whether Marina should go to the funeral. My reaction was 'ask her'. She was there, looking bewildered and frail. He was buried in a snowstorm and, standing by the grave, I remember her looking down at the coffin and up at the sky. Her feelings and her questioning were expressed in a poem that she wrote soon after his death:

Pa, dear Pa
hasn't gone far,
only into the next room,
and it isn't full of gloom.
Oh dearest Pa,
please come back.
There is something that we lack.
It's your love, it's your care.
You were always there

when we needed you.
Just give us a tiny clue
where you have gone.

She cried herself to sleep every night but was able to get on with her life, make friends and do well at school. Her mourning was never blocked but evident for all to see. When, several months later, I visited the cemetery with mother and daughter, Marina picked daisies and made a chain to hang over the gravestone, on which there were some words by Emily Bronte: 'What thou art may never be destroyed'. When I gave Marina a book token for her fifteenth birthday, she told me that she wanted to buy a book of poetry, mentioning poems that she could have found at home among her father's books. But she wanted a poetry book for herself. I saw this wish as both separating and staying with her father and I thought that was just as it should be.

Coping with a parent's death is not always so straightforward. Tom, at eight, was referred to a counsellor for behavioural problems. His father had died three years before whilst playing squash. Tom had shown no grief at the time but now he was angrily hitting other boys and being rude to teachers. The counsellor faced him with this inappropriate behaviour and tried to explore its cause, but Tom would not talk directly of his father's death. The counsellor played with him a game of 'squares', which involved marking out one's territory. Tom was highly competitive and got bored with the game if he failed to win. Playing 'squiggles' produced a tennis racket (reminiscent of father's death), a crocodile, a bird eating a worm, lightning and a hot air balloon. Afterwards, he drew a peaceful scene of trees and sunshine, labelling it 'this picture is dun'. Eventually, he talked about Dad and cried, then, 'what shall we play now?'

A psychotherapist who works with children told me about Amy who, at three and a half, was in a car crash while on holiday in France. Her father and one of her grandmothers were killed. She and her mother were injured and had to be in intensive care. Her other grandmother came at once and was at Amy's bedside when she came round from coma. A year later, her mother was in therapy. Amy was full of fears and had nightmares. This was a Catholic family and Amy was told that her father was 'up there' with Jesus, rather than in a cemetery, which was described as a garden. Amy was in therapy for two years. At first she was cautious, then gradually relaxed and was able to be angry about Dad not coming back. Her fantasy was that her mother would not let him come. She blamed both Jesus and Mum for keeping him away. She could also be controlling and angry with her therapist, afraid of holiday breaks and any sudden disappearances. She played games of car crashes and hospitals. Her patients always recovered. Amy knew that her mother would not have any more children and thought that was her fault for giving her 'such a bad tummy ache' when she was born. But, most of all, she blamed Jesus.

When therapy ended, her fears had gone. She sent a card saying 'goodbye – you will always remember me', which sounds rather like a command!

This therapist also told me about children who had known violence and death close at hand. These were refugees who were likely to be deported, so she never knew how long she would be able to work with them. In the case of one adolescent, the father, a member of the Mafia, had disappeared and the family did not know if he were dead or alive. The girl had started therapy at 12. She was now 16. She had recurring nightmares, somatic symptoms, enuresis and long bouts of crying. She could not contain her feelings and felt herself to be uncontained. She had a bad relationship with her mother but had idealised her father, with whom she communicated in her dreams. In fact, he had been a gangster who beat up his wife and deserted his children. Gradually the idealisation and unresolved Oedipal issues were worked through: she stopped wetting her bed, her emotions became more contained and she could face the probability of her father's death. She also began dating boys and leading a normal adolescent life. She was able to cut down her therapy from three times to once a week but had to live with the uncertainty of her possible deportation.

It is probably true to say that most bereaved children are not seen as needing therapy. What they do need is a chance to talk, ask questions and share their grief with other family members. I have already mentioned Mary's daughter, Jane, who died of cancer aged 31. She left a husband and two boys of seven and four. Their father did his best. They saw their mother's body and went to her funeral, which he insisted must be secular. This was hard on the grandmother who believed in God. The older boy, William, told her he was not allowed to pray. 'Never mind', said Mary, 'I'll do it for you'. Jane had done what she could in preparing the boys for her death, but their father's way of coping was to put away all photographs and reminders and get on with his life. In less than two years he married the au pair girl. This made for continuity, but the boys still remembered their mother. William said to Mary: 'I think, so far, I've had a tiring life'. The younger boy, Samuel, said he had a pain in his tummy. 'What's the matter, Sammy?' 'I've got cancer!'

Mary is making an album of her daughter's life, which she will keep at her house for when the boys come to stay.

Rose worked as housekeeper and nanny in a bereaved household. She was a trained counsellor. The children were five, four and two. The father was struggling to get back into his profession, feeling he had lost ground during the year that his wife had been dying of leukaemia. The children had been shuttled between various households. They had not been allowed to say goodbye to their mother, nor had they gone to the funeral. They felt 'left out' with nothing explained to them. They talked to Rose about digging up their mother, bringing her home in a taxi, keeping her in a glass case – this last turned out to have more to do with Egyptian mummies than 'Snow White'. The concept of heaven was not helpful – 'why can't we take an aeroplane and rescue her? She belongs with us not Jesus. Why does he want *our* mother?'

Rose listened, helped them express their anger and work through their fantasies. She explained about Egyptian burial customs. The school psychologist had confidence in her ability to help them and she felt she had the school's support. After about six months she persuaded their father and the vicar to take the children to the burial plot for a 'Farewell Service'. A local convent let them pick whatever flowers they liked from its garden. A florist gave ribbons and let them choose the colours. So they had their goodbye ceremony and felt better for it.

Alison Hargreaves, mother of two children, was killed descending K2, the second-highest peak in the Himalayas. A film was made of a pilgrimage organised by her husband Jim to visit the mountain where she died. The initiative had come from six-year-old Tom.

> After a twelve day trek, the father and his two children (the four year old carried by a craggy porter and the six year old legging it with enviable toughness) were with eighty porters, a television crew, a doctor, an altitude sickness specialist and a bereavement counsellor, arriving within sight of K2. (Fox and Gill, 1996, p.147)

The film, called *Alison's Last Mountain*, was shown on BBC1 and served as an unusual 'memorial service' for a huge congregation of viewers. We saw the children drawing trees with falling leaves and pictures of the mountain. A cairn was built on which to leave their various offerings. Kate asked if she could 'put a sweetie there, too, for Mummy'. She saw a cloud just above the peak and wondered if that was Mummy. 'Her spirit is climbing in these mountains' said Jim. This family was able to choose what seemed to all three an appropriate ceremony. It was a giving-back of Alison to the mountains she loved. Being together in the place where she died must have given their mourning a specially clear focus.

Jonathan's Story

Jonathan came into therapy in his late thirties to help him in his work and to understand himself better. His father had died of a heart attack when he was nine, after which everything changed. He remembers his mother screaming and crying in the night and a neighbour, who was a nurse, coming in to comfort her. His father was 56. He was headmaster of the local primary school and Jonathan, who was a bright boy, felt special in being his son. Outside school they had fun together. His paternal grandmother had died a year before his father, and his grandfather a year after, so three important members of the family were wiped out when he was between seven and ten. In his family it was not usual for women and children to attend funerals, so neither he, nor his mother and two younger sisters joined the men in burying his father. There is still no headstone on the grave, though Jonathan has talked with one of his sisters about the possibility of putting one up.

After this loss, the girls got steadily closer to their mother but Jonathan was left out. His sister said, long afterwards, that she remembered him as a 'big boy crashing about'. His mother seemed unable to cope with him, perhaps because he looked too like his father. He acted out his mourning, and, perhaps, hers too, in that he got angry and 'smashed things up'.

His mother took a teacher-training course and, on weekdays, the children had to live with a child-minder. Two years later, Jonathan was sent to boarding school. This was supposed to be a wonderful opportunity. The school sounded like paradise, which, of course, it was not, but his mother never bothered to find out. He felt betrayed. She very seldom wrote and hardly ever came to see him. At the end of term he usually had to find his own way home by a complicated route. He never felt welcome at home. His mother and sisters had made a life without him.

Looking back at his time at school, he is always ambivalent, appreciating the good things but also hating its strictness and almost military discipline. For the first year he continued to be a bright little boy, then gradually floundered and, in his early teens, became anorexic, refusing food, both actual and metaphorical, in that he responded less and less to what was being taught. It was only when he got too weak to play rugby (at which he excelled) that he began to eat again. Usually, he loves his food. In his home there had always been an emphasis on good cooking but, after his father's death, no one laid the table and the family never ate together. There was food in the kitchen and they helped themselves. His mother taught him to cook but not to eat.

Jonathan still needs to think and talk again and again about his time at school. He is aware of a change inside him and sometimes feels as though he is back to being 18, on the brink of adult life but making different choices. The more he mulls over the past, the more aware I become of his paralysing depression after his father's death. I am not saying that, in being anorexic, he wanted to die but that part of him was dead and letting himself be hungry reflected a terrible inner emptiness. There seems to have been no guidance, although, perhaps, some of the masters tried, but he could not ask for help. Playing rugby was, and continued to be, a life-line.

Rebelling (though passively) against the school's authority, he turned his back on opportunities to go to university, preferring work on a building site, where he managed to earn good money. At 21 he married a disabled girl and felt that he took on her disability. Eventually, in the face of enormous criticism, he had the courage to leave her. He now has a promising career and a healthy wife. But he is still sensitive in situations where she gets together with her women friends and he re-experiences his mother and sisters shutting him out of their cosy, feminine life.

When we started working together, he used to have fantasies of my not being there when he came. I warned him, at the first session, that I was about to go away for six weeks. His wife pointed out that of all the therapists that might have been available, he chose the one who was going to leave him and that he kept repeating being sent away to school by his mother. When I got back, I was disoriented about time and place and, although there was no question of not seeing him when he turned up, I showed on my face that I had got muddled and was not expecting him just then. I apologised, saying I was not yet quite 'down to earth' and he realised that I had gone somewhere a long way off. Once I was safely back, he let himself feel closer to me and had a dream that I was showing him photographs of my son with his rugby team. I seemed to be the mother who took an interest in his successes and affirmed him. Later, when we agreed to meet twice a week, he again found it hard to believe that I would actually be there for him at the second session. Much later still, he left me for a year. This had a lot to do with money, but perhaps that was not the only reason, and I had to respect his decision. We are now working again but with a planned end in view.

Jonathan's story shows how the trauma of losing a parent in childhood becomes reactivated in later life, especially if not properly mourned at the time. Listening to him, I felt I was sharing his lonely adolescence and feelings of disability and how hard it had been to free himself from the imprisonment of that harsh school and choose a life for himself. Now, in his new marriage, he has become very much more alive and has been able to do some healthy mourning. But he has come to accept that, although his mother enjoys her grandchildren, he is never going to entirely repair his own relationship with her or talk with her about his father.

He says he is still changing.

Children Who Die

What could be more emotive than a child's death? To the adult, it seems an outrage, a reversal of the natural order of things. For parents, it is one of the hardest bereavements – 'it should have been me'. But, before exploring parental loss, it is important to try and understand the mind of the dying child. The question we are likely to ask ourselves is: how much do these very sick children know of what is going on inside them?

Awareness alternates with denial, just as it does in the case of dying adults. Being alive is the only state we know and it is hard to think beyond the final breath. We have already seen how a young child puzzles over the concept of death and its finality. As long as one is healthy, one's own death remains unreal and children are often consoled in expecting not to die until they are old. But, if they get ill and have to be treated – often painfully – in hospital, the possibility of dying earlier in life may arise:

> The young child, in a way that is developmentally appropriate, is curious about the distinction between being alive and being dead. There may not be any form of self-reference explicitly expressed … However, at a funda- mental level, consciously or not, the child is grappling with the concepts that have become salient with the onslaught of the illness. The theme of 'alive-dead' may recur in an almost ritualised form as the child attempts to work through his or her comprehension. (Sourkes, 1995, p.109)

The child may begin to understand dead by comparing it with living:

> Together, Ricky and the therapist listed and played out different actions; for example, walk, talk, look, sing, jump on the bed. The activities were done with great enjoyment and elaboration. At the end, the therapist con-

cluded: 'these are all the things we can do when we are alive. When we are dead, we can't do them anymore'. (Sourkes, p.110)

Ricky, who was himself terminally ill, was trying to understand the death of another child on his hospital ward. He was not yet applying the word 'dead' to his own situation. He stated that three things were necessary for life – food, toys and love – and he had all three.

Whether or not a child has been told his diagnosis, he has an intimate relationship with his body and what goes on inside it. In Winnicott's (1960) language, his psychosomatic existence has taken on a personal pattern, which he calls 'the psyche indwelling in the soma'. With his skin as 'a limiting membrane', the child experiences an inside and outside, a 'me' and 'not me'.

Any change in the body's function must affect individual experience, whether consciously or unconsciously. Treatment, involving needles and catheters, is very likely perceived as an invasion of that private territory which 'me' inhabits. Dorothy Judd (1989), who works as a psychotherapist with dying children, draws our attention to the way cancer is often described:

> The patient's body is considered under attack, or 'invaded' by leukaemia. The language is therefore one of warfare and of military terminology … we talk about the body's 'defences' in its attempt to obliterate, wipe out or fight the cancer … the patients are 'bombarded' with radiotherapy; chemotherapy is chemical warfare using toxins. (p.40)

Even if not told directly, the child can hardly be ignorant of the battlefield inside him.

If parents and carers cannot bear to talk about the severity of the illness, the child feels isolated, perhaps distrustful. Attitudes are slow to change and, until quite recently, awkward truths have been avoided. Death was hidden behind screens and there was a lot of whispering among nurses. Since the other children on the ward were afflicted by the same illness as the friend who had secretly died, some of them were bound to link what was happening with their own likely fates. But they found it hard to ask questions when the staff appeared to be too busy or unwilling to stop and talk to them, or, if they did, only evasively or with an unconvincing brightness. Sometimes, it seemed that death was shameful; one had to pretend it never happened.

However, we must not forget that these situations are distressing for the adults as well as the children. Professionals often feel the need to switch off their feelings. They may even be encouraged not to get emotionally involved, just to concentrate on the technicalities of treatment without causing undue pain or discomfort. But, these days, there is increasing frankness on the wards. A recent television documentary (*Brief Lives*, Thames TV, 1996) took us inside the Great Ormond Street Children's Hospital to hear what doctors and nurses had to say about how it felt to treat children with life-threatening illnesses. Now that the prognosis for children with cancer and leukaemia is so much better than formerly, they know that not all the children in their care will die, but there is still a lot of uncertainty for both staff and patients. This seems to be what it is hardest to bear – not knowing which of the children will come through.

The film showed a doctor who made a point of sitting with a child and her mother, looking at photographs in the family album and trying to pick up clues that would make it possible to talk about death. He commented on a dog, who was present in some of the pictures and not in others. The child told the doctor that the dog had died. The doctor said that that was sad and went on to say how sad it was when people died. The child said nothing in response, but she did not change the subject and seemed at ease with the doctor and appreciative of his friendly interest.

Children need explanations and to be told the truth. But, most of all, they need to be listened to. The listener may be surprised at how much some of these children know without being told. Outside the big cities, child psychotherapists tend to be thin on the ground. But, sometimes, lay volunteers can at least listen and try to answer a child's questions. In my locality a trust (called 'Snowdrop') has been set up to raise money for respite care for families of life-threatened children. It also provides volunteers to visit these families in their homes. I spoke to one of them, who said that she found it an advantage to be seen as a lay person and not medical. She asks the families to talk to her rather than being spoken at. The children are very open with their questions and she, in her turn, brings up or encourages some of the questions that the family might be afraid to ask: 'what does it feel like?'; 'what happens if…?' She usually says: 'I don't know. What do *you* think?' She finds that parents try and protect their children and the children protect the parents. The children usually have an attitude of acceptance and talk easily once they know that she is listening. The parents are the ones who prevaricate.

Writing as a psychotherapist, the Canadian author, Barbara Sourkes, reminds us that sick children come into therapy because they have a serious physical disease rather than being psychologically ill-adjusted in the first place. Whether the trauma of having such a disease will affect the child in later life is not particularly relevant in this context because one is treating a child who, most probably, has no future. The task may not be to help that child to live but to help him or her to die. Within the framework that therapy provides, 'the child seeks to reintegrate the shattered facets of his or her life. Through words, drawings and play, the child conveys the experience of living with the ever present threat of loss, and transforms the essence of his or her reality into expression' (Sourkes, 1995, p.3).

In some cases the trauma of illness does not hit suddenly when a child has been healthy until that time, but has been there from the beginning. Sophie, who has come into therapy aged ten, was born with a rare and incurable condition. The prognosis is steady deterioration and shortened life-expectancy. It has taken a long time to find helpful medication and her early development was disturbed, so that, at ten, she presents as a five-year-old, physically small and babyish in behaviour. Her parents collude with each other in their denial of her possible death but the family is loving and mutually supportive and the child well cared for. Sophie is filled with persecutory anxieties and needs to perform pacifying rituals. Her own fear has been projected outward and she is afraid that her mother may die; she can hardly bear to let her out of her sight. She can never leave the house without saying 'I love you' to both parents and demands repeated reassurances and expressions of love from them. For the sake of peace and quiet, her parents give her what she asks. Sophie is obsessionally tidy and afraid of anything new. She made a fuss about entering the therapist's room and her father had to carry her in, but, now that she has got used to regular sessions, she enjoys coming. She finds she can tell her therapist about worries that she is unable to share with her parents. She knows there is something wrong with her but denies having bodily organs. The therapist has decided that the consultant should explain her illness to her in language that Sophie can understand and tell her what she has got inside her. This is a doctor whom she has known all her life, someone to whom she will listen and whom she trusts. The therapist has spoken to Sophie's mother about this and has got her agreement. Sophie has drawn pictures of ghosts taking her away, but also sunny landscapes, a rainbow and a beautiful cat. Everything good is separated from what is bad. The therapist is now idealised but hopes the child can bring good and bad together and get into the real sadness of her situation, so that both she and her parents can face the truth without despairing. This is a child who seems not to feel at home in her body, her psyche *not* 'indwelling' in the soma. Or, in

Kleinian language, she is still in the paranoid schizoid stage and needs to reach the depressive position.

Piers is a ten-year-old boy with Cystic Fibrosis. He is not expected to live beyond adolescence. He has been referred by his consultant paediatrician to a psychotherapist, who sees him for weekly sessions. Piers was abandoned by his mother and did not see her at all for a year. He lives with his grandparents and his mother now visits him once a month. When his mother left, he refused medication. He also missed a good deal of school through arriving late after daily physiotherapy. Now it has been arranged that he can attend school all day.

In a typical session, Piers went striding into the room and straight to the wet sand box. 'This', he said, 'needs more water'. He filled some buckets and poured the water, filling one end of the sand box and leaving wet sand at the other end. From the toy cupboard he chose an ambulance, a helicopter and a box of people. He flew the helicopter into the water and said it had crashed. He put some of the people in the helicopter and others on a 'stretcher' that floated in the water. Then he collected a 'cage' and put some men inside it, saying that they had been caught by gunge and would drown inside the cage, which he submerged. He added more gunge, which he made out of wet sand.

'When the gunge gets you', he said, 'it attacks the back of your neck. It numbs and controls you and you don't know it has you'. He brought out more men and put them in the ambulance, which he moved further into the water, declaring: 'All these people are caught'. He collected a green Lego dragon. 'This monster is going to kill them. He has captured them and keeps them here'. He picked up another man, wearing a helmet and knapsack. 'This is me', he said, but described what 'me' did in the third person. This man (me) attacked the monster and rescued the people but said that they were still caught by the gunge, even though he had let them out of the cage.

The gunge kept coming and covered all the people floating in the water. Piers made a fortification out of the helicopter and ambulance, which he placed in the corner of the sand box. But he said that the people were dead: 'They have gone to a watery grave'. He continued to dam the water and bury the people. He talked to his therapist about the strength of the sea. Meanwhile, he went on trying to rescue the people and said that one of the men was buried with a hose to breathe through.

Piers went on playing till the end of his session and had difficulty in ending the game. The gunge that he had made out of sand, no doubt, showed his preoccupation with the gunge in his lungs and his need to get it out. He told his therapist: 'When we are alive, we eat plants, but when we are dead, the plants eat us. And that's it.'

Having to conduct therapy in a hospital setting inevitably includes interruptions, often with staff members trying to join in the 'play'. Sometimes, the child has to be 'barrier nursed' – anyone coming into the room, including the therapist, has to put on a mask, gloves and a plastic apron to reduce any possibility of infection. This must be a very isolating experience for both patient and therapist.

It is important to explain to the child the therapist's special function. Dorothy Judd, who kept a diary about treating a dying boy, Robert, aged seven and a half, told him that she was neither a doctor nor a nurse but someone to talk to and that on each visit she would bring a box of toys specially for him. She explained that she would not be leaving the toys with him between visits but neither would any other child be playing with them. Taking them away each time was part of what made them special. Robert acquiesced, saying 'if you have a toy or something *all* the time, you get bored with it' (Judd, 1989, p.86). She wondered what he was feeling about her own coming and going, in and out of his precarious life. The box included plasticine, a miniature hospital set and various small figures, both human and animal. Robert played with them and she interpreted not only what he did with the toys but also what he felt about the constant interruptions, some of which were cheerful, irrelevant remarks – a doctor correcting his calling a rhinoceros a hippo, or a head poking round the door saying 'come on, smile!'. 'There seems to be a need, on the part of the staff, for him to be happy, even though there is much more for him to be angry about' (Judd, 1989, p.91).

Barbara Sourkes included stuffed animals among the child's special toys. Her patient, Ricky, came into hospital with a menagerie of animals of his own, each with their own names. His favourite was Poly Polar Bear, the one which was to have most significance in his therapy and which his parents gave to the therapist after his death for her to use with other children. Several months later, Poly was chosen by a girl called Karen and pictures of him featured in a little book, *My Life is Feelings*, which she wrote as part of her therapy. This was a way of expressing her own fears and sadness by describing Poly's dislike of needles, tubes and spinal taps, how Poly was upset at losing all his fur in chemotherapy and how glad he was when it grew again.

These stuffed animals become very important and fulfil some of the functions of Winnicott's 'transitional objects', special possessions that act as bridges between child and mother and between the inner and outer world of the child:

> Within the psychotherapy, the stuffed animal 'lives' in the relationship between the child and the therapist. The animal belongs to the therapist; yet by naming it and sharing identical experiences, the child comes to 'own' it ... Through the authority of actual ownership, the therapist can impute feelings or comment more assertively than if the animal were the child's. (Sourkes, 1995, p.16)

In Ricky's case, the bear originally belonged to him. We have seen how it came to be owned by his therapist and was then special to another sick child.

The question remains: how much do dying children know?

Sometimes, they tell us: 'I know I'm going to die very soon and just have to talk to somebody about it' (Kübler-Ross, 1983, p.21). This child was aged eight. Kübler-Ross believes that in all terminally ill children there is some awareness that they are dying, even if the knowledge is below the threshold of consciousness. This awareness is often communicated indirectly through dreams or through drawing and painting. Rachel was an American child dying of leukaemia. Her therapist has written a detailed description of her pictures (Bertoia, 1993).

A lot of the pictures, looked at casually, seem bright and cheerful but more careful study hints at something not quite right with the world. In the first picture of the series the central figure has oddly bent legs and her bright yellow hair is not properly attached to her head. She stands under a cloud beside a tree with an enormous trunk but very few leaves. On each of her arms there is a spider. Next, she drew a wolf and the scared faces of children hiding in trees.

Rachel's mother kept a journal and recorded some of the child's surprising statements – for instance, 'children are closer to God than adults'. A little later, the sentence was repeated and she was asked how she knew: 'Because they haven't been here so long'. A drawing, about this time, was of a bed of tulips. One of the flowers had an X in the centre, as though it was crossed out. A close friend had just died of the same illness. Towards the end of her life, the pictures became less disturbed. Some of them were about journeys. One of the last before she died showed a car heading into the sunset.

Before her final hospitalisation, Rachel told her mother that she could hear God but could not see him. She wanted to know what he looked like. Another day, she ran out of her room in great excitement to tell her mother about heaven, claiming to have been there: 'It is beautiful, everything is so colourful there, the green colours are so clear, the trees and grass. It is because there is no pollution'.

She was nine years old when she died.

Rachel's paintings were interpreted along Jungian lines and her drawings were seen as showing:

> death/separation images interspersed with those of rebirth ... On a conscious level she had to progress slowly with her understanding, resistance and tolerance ... Once she could no longer deny her prognosis ... she continued to work at tolerating her pain-riddled experience emotionally and physically ... she also gained spiritual insights to both her physical end and what was beyond ... there is a profound sense of hope in her legacy. (Bertoia, 1993, p.91)

Parents Whose Children Die

Death Before Birth

Miscarriage is a secret death, known only to the couple concerned and a few friends. Whether or not we think of the foetus as a person, there is a death of potential and also a death of hope, the parents' hope for a particular child, conceived at a certain time, and on whom the mother – and, perhaps, the father – will have begun to focus their fantasies. A series of miscarriages brings a sense of failure. For other women, pregnancy seems effortless. The mother asks herself: why should it be different for me?

In her desire to prove there was nothing wrong with her body, a disappointed mother went out of the way to get herself pregnant by a man who was not her husband. She succeeded. This was nearly, but not quite, the death of her marriage. Her husband accepted the child as his own and they stayed together.

A friend of hers, whom I will call Kate, found herself quite envious. She was not able to conceive at all, let alone miscarry. She and her husband spent an anxious time submitting to tests and waiting for results. Kate was first to hear that it was her husband, Charles, and not she, who was infertile. The doctor warned her that the news would have to be broken to him carefully. Some men, he told her, would feel their virility to be threatened. They might even become impotent. Charles felt no such threat. He minded more for

Kate's sake than his own, sensing that her longing for children was stronger than his. Kate did her best to convince him that her maternal instinct was not specially strong, but she felt as though a door had been shut in her face. The doctor told her that there was still some slight possibility of a child being conceived but was not too hopeful as the sperm count was very low. There was nothing the medical profession could do to help. This was 40 years ago. Kate was told that there was such a thing as insemination by donor, which was then called AID, but she only wanted Charles' child. Eventually, they managed to adopt. It seemed to them fairer to have a child who genetically belonged to neither of them. They loved their adopted child, although he was unlike the son and daughter of Kate's fantasies. Secretly, she went on hoping to conceive. Every month she was disappointed.

What, for a woman, is lost is the childbearing experience and, for the man, being present at his child's birth. For both, there is the loss of genetic continuity. Charles' father never accepted the adopted child as his grandson and left his money to his other son's children, who, as carriers of his genes, ensured for him a sort of immortality.

Stillbirth

Before birth, the mother has a relationship with the real baby inside her and the future child of her imagination. Rosemary Mander (1994), writing for midwives, has this to say:

> The baby's image is a composite of those she loves and admires, including herself, partner, parents and other children ... Inevitably the mother's fantasies involve wishing for and dreaming of a perfect baby, but lurking in the background is the fear of a baby being born with a disability. (p.15)

Kate, as just mentioned, had the fantasy relationship but never had the real baby inside her. Probably, every pregnant mother has the 'lurking' fear of disability. Some mothers, nowadays, with modern techniques of scanning, may be faced with a difficult (almost impossible) decision as to whether to keep the disabled foetus or end the pregnancy. But, perhaps worst of all, it happens sometimes that after a full-term pregnancy the baby dies, either just before or at birth.

The mother will be the first to realise that her active and kicking baby has stopped moving and that her body has become a coffin. At this point there will be a decision to induce labour as soon as possible so that she can see and hold the dead baby before too much physical change adds to the horror of the situation. At this point a sensitive midwife, unless too traumatised herself, may be the best counsellor.

Sometimes, no one knows about the death until the actual birth. Things go badly wrong and the baby dies and cannot be resuscitated. Here, too, the midwife may be the person best able just to 'be there' for the mother. It is a delicate job to find the right balance of empathy and detachment in trying to help the parents in their acceptance and mourning.

At one time, the stillborn baby was treated rather like the aborted foetus but with the difference that, legally, the birth had to be registered. The midwife now encourages the mother to hold her child and, perhaps, have a photograph taken, and it is important that there should be a funeral as a focus for the family's mourning. The parents may choose a white wooden coffin, a 'Moses' basket or just a shroud for the burial. An archaeological dig in Cumbria revealed a baby buried in a swan's wing – 'a gentle, loving and caring image, resonating with a mysterious poetry all its own. Enveloping wings, protecting, soft and warming, yet strong and powerful...' (Fox and Gill, 1996, p.48). It is as though the child were being got ready for a journey, perhaps a flight.

Mourning a child who never managed to live, except in the restricted world of the mother's womb, must be quite unlike remembering shared experiences, however short that person's life:

> If there is loss in childbearing, these memories do not exist. The mother may have memories of her baby's movements or she may recall imaginary 'conversations', perhaps willing her baby to quieten down to sleep or pleading with the baby to be born in order to end an interminable pregnancy. The baby's father has even less by which to remember that baby. (Mander, 1994, p.33)

For the larger family, and the parents' friends, it is as though the baby never existed. And we have already seen what it was like for a baby's sister when her stillborn brother was never talked about.

Termination of Pregnancy

What most of us call 'abortion' has for some time been legal, both in cases of abnormality and for 'social' reasons. The practice engenders extreme emotions. Some say it is a woman's right to decide what happens to her body. Others take the side of the unborn child, whom the mother decides to kill.

Religious people, especially Catholics, who believe in the sanctity of all life, usually take the latter view.

If the pregnancy is terminated because of an abnormality, the mother will probably be relieved, but this is bound up with quite different emotions, especially if the child has been much wanted and if, on account of her age, or for other reasons, the mother's hope of a normal baby in the future is diminished. She is likely to feel guilt, a sense of failure and a narcissistic wound. If the termination was performed for so-called social reasons, the guilt may be more intense, though if she is an unmarried teenager, she may have persuaded herself, or been persuaded, that the baby is better off unborn than brought up inadequately by her as a single parent. But I doubt whether all doubt can be successfully avoided.

Before the days of legal termination and the 'pill', Rosemary became pregnant twice by boyfriends whom she knew she would never marry. Twice she managed what we used to call a 'back-street' abortion. When, eventually, she married a husband she loved – and she had a Catholic wedding – she was determined, as an act of reparation, to have two children to replace the two she had lost. After successfully giving birth to a son, she was diagnosed as having ovarian cancer. Although only one ovary was affected, her doctor urged her to have both removed. But she insisted on retaining one of them in order to conceive a second child. This happened, but during pregnancy the cancer spread. This time, the doctor wanted her to agree to a termination. She refused and it became a race between the baby's birth and her death. Because of the pregnancy she could not be given adequate pain-killing drugs, so she suffered, but managed to hang on to life just long enough for her daughter to be born. Two weeks later, Rosemary was dead.

Giving up Babies for Adoption

Although there is no physical death, mothers who have surrendered their children have had to face a parting that precludes ever getting in touch with them again. Customs are changing fast, but, in the past, although the adopting parents were told the mother's name, the natural mother did not know the identity of her child's new family. She was told the date of the court hearing and would not have been stopped if she wanted to attend, but this was not encouraged.

Because of legal abortion, and the lessening of social stigma, there are now fewer unwanted babies, which is bad news for would-be adopters, but easier for the mothers. The stigmatisation used to be merciless, not least from hospital staff:

> I think that a hospital is there to give care to people, not a court room where you are judged for what you have or have not done. The midwife did this, because when she read my notes her attitude to me changed. She had been kind and welcoming when I came into the labour ward, but after she read them she was chilly. (Mander, 1994, p.51)

We may think this attitude is quite out of date, but, in a book published as late as 1994, a mother is quoted as saying:

> I think secrecy's important for certain people, yes … because for some people, unmarried mothers are still, especially in the country, it seems to be very much frowned upon. Yeah. I don't think we are as permissive as all that. I think people like to think we are, but I don't think we are. (Mander, 1994, p.51)

Relinquishing a child is like a death without a funeral. There is no rite of passage for these mothers. In the past most of them just had to get back to work, with no one to help them mourn. These were the days before trained counsellors were available in almost any situation. Even now, perhaps because fewer mothers give up their babies, it needs to be emphasised that relinquishment is a form of bereavement and grief is both natural and necessary.

Slaughter of the Innocents

One of the saddest stories in the New Testament tells us that King Herod was 'exceeding wroth, and sent forth and slew all the children…' (Matthew 2, v.16). The scene has often been painted by the old masters, sometimes with painful realism. What shocks us is the random killing of so many helpless children and the anguish of the mothers as their babies are torn from them. The gospel reminds us of an earlier story in which Rachael was infertile for many years while her husband slept with her sister and had many sons. There was 'lamentation and weeping and great mourning, Rachael weeping for her children, and would not be comforted, because they are not' (v.18). Similarly, in Greek myth, Niobe's daughters are killed and she cannot stop weeping, even after she is turned to stone. It is often said that a mother whose child dies never gets over it. She will not be comforted, though hatred and envy of other mothers may indeed turn her heart to stone.

Dunblane

In a television documentary a year after the Dunblane massacre we were shown the self-help group that brought the parents together to help each other with their mourning. They described the morning of that fateful day, 13 March 1996, when they were summoned to the school to hear which children had been killed. They were all stunned with shock – how could such a thing happen 'in a wee village like Dunblane?' – and the first thought: 'I hope it's not my kid'. 'The brain shuts down', said one of the fathers. They described the awful waiting for news and how they were aware that the police, clergy and medical staff were there with them and had the knowledge they were waiting for but, for each family, there had to be a formality. The names were called and they were shown into another room to be told. They went on hoping to the last minute, wondering who the lucky ones would be. The tension was almost unbearable. When they knew the worst, the bereaved parents found themselves angry with the families who had survived. Then there was guilt about their anger.

The father of five-year-old Emily thought that the death of a child was the worst thing that could happen to anyone. Then he became aware of Mick, whose wife had died a year before. Now he had lost his daughter, who was Emily's friend, and he thought of how Mick's whole life had been taken away. All of them looked to Mick's 'awesome' strength to support them in their pain.

A mother said how much she had looked forward to her daughter growing up, hoping she would continue to be a friend and companion and they could go on having fun together. She wondered what this beautiful five-year-old would be like, about boyfriends and her wedding. Would she still be beautiful? Although they had been thrown together by this horrific happening, they said that they were not a closed group but quite approachable if outside people wanted to talk to them. They didn't spend all their time crying. On the other hand, it was important that they should be able to cry when they wanted to without embarrassment. It was understood between them that the families could call on each other at any time of the day or night without being turned away.

Emily's father spoke of his daughter as messy, wild, noisy, determined and 'driving him nuts', but how he missed coming home tired from work and being irritated! Mick said that bereaved people could function well if their feelings were respected. There was not just one stereotyped way of coping with grief but many, and this needed to be understood by other people. 'The memories will always be there', said a mother, 'It takes a long time, but it does get easier'.

People outside were beginning to say they should move on. Move on? Where to? None of them wanted to arrive at a time of forgetting.

On 13 March 1997 the group had a party and Emily's father proposed a toast to the group and to the children. He spoke for everyone present when he described how special the group had become and he drew comfort from knowing that the children were together 'wherever they are' and that the parents, too, were happy together. A mother kept repeating 'Talk about your children. Don't try and pretend they never existed.'

The Story of Two Mothers

Harriet

Meeting Harriet in her seventies, one is aware of enormous energy. Her husband is calm, whereas Harriet is fiery. They complement each other and there is mutual dependency. They have two successful sons and three grandchildren. At 67, Harriet achieved a degree, at 70 an MA, and she is now working for an MPhil. She has the status of both pensioner and student. She is also politically active, fighting for her ideals with a single-mindedness more often associated with youth than age. She is always too busy to think about slowing down.

Harriet is not my patient and I am not in the habit of analysing my friends but, sometimes, meeting people late in life and talking about the past brings surprises. Although I knew there had been a tragedy, I hesitated to ask questions and it was not until I talked to her about this book that she opened up. She says now that I 'squeezed' the story out of her.

Originally, she had a family of three – the youngest a girl, called Ruth. One summer they had a boating holiday with the children. The boat was moored. The parents were busy. The children, aged twelve, ten and eight, were fishing over the side. The two boys left Ruth alone and went to look for the shops. Harriet assumed the three of them had gone together. When they got back it was discovered that Ruth had disappeared. Later, the police retrieved her body. There was a bruise on her head as if she had hit the bottom and been knocked out, rather than slowly drowning.

It was a painful story to tell and Harriet was vague about what happened next. She was hysterical, she said, and cried for days. She leaned hard on her husband, who calmly supported her. Both were overcome with guilt at their negligence. This was not neurotic guilt but, even if exaggerated, quite rationally based. The self-blame must have been acute. Harriet found herself hating mothers who were happy, and hating their children. The hating brought on more guilt.

Eventually, Harriet coped by throwing herself into work. Like so many mothers, who need to be there for their children during the holidays, she trained as a teacher. The tragedy was never talked about in the family. I thought of the Dunblane mother and her plea: 'talk about your children'.

Years later, Harriet went into therapy, not ostensibly to mourn Ruth's death but because of vague feelings of what she called 'unease'. The therapist undoubtedly helped but Harriet finds it hard now to explain how. It was not only to do with Ruth, though she found she had many tears still to shed. This not remembering seems to me healthy. If therapy 'works', it must be all right to let it go.

I asked what Ruth was like. 'Bright', she said, 'full of life, intelligent, often naughty. But sometimes it is hard to remember.' There is a photograph of Ruth at eight years old, which Harriet had put away. At last, she can bear to look at her again as she was just before she died.

Looking at Harriet's need to plunge herself in work, it strikes me that she is doing what her intelligent daughter was never able to do – going to university and achieving academic recognition. Perhaps, writing her thesis is like giving birth.

Having a Jungian inclination, I am more interested in where a person is going in life rather than exploring reasons from the past to establish why people are as they are. This is the teleological view, whereas Freud was reductive. I see Harriet, despite her tragic loss, as on her way to individuation, fulfilling not only her own potential but also that of the child who died and lives inside her.

Mary

Mary's daughter, Jane, was grown-up when she died, so her mother was able to tell me that she had always made the most of life and, as I have already mentioned, she bequeathed to the world two sons.

Unlike Ruth's sudden death, Jane's was agonisingly slow. Mary says that she knew her daughter was doomed before the cancer struck, and she thought Jane knew too. Symbolically, Jane gave her a doll and she made clothes for it. This was to replace a lost doll that Mary had cherished from childhood. Mary saw this as Jane giving herself to her mother to be held. This holding became important throughout the illness, but it was a helpless holding. Jane had been her baby, the youngest of three. As a child, she had always turned to Mary – mother could always help. But, this time, she could not put a plaster on the wound or 'kiss it better'. In her own words:

> I had to sit helpless, and watch my beautiful daughter's body change and deteriorate. I had to observe the terrible mutilation of the operations. I had to watch her prepare for a journey I should have been making myself. I had to do nothing because there was nothing I could do. I tried to hold my baby to the end and then let her go. Her body was ravaged, but her spirit and her integrity remained. I was proud of her.

Mary feels angry with Jane's husband and angry with the doctors for not letting Jane die in peace. She says that they refused to face the truth and went on with punishing treatment, even when there was obviously no hope. She compared them with the wise vet, who was honest with her in saying her dog would die and 'she did so without pain, in complete dignity, and in my arms'. That is what she would have wished for Jane and, in due course, for herself.

Jane died in December. A week before her death the family gave a party, anticipating the Christmas she would not live to see. After that, she deteriorated quickly. It was Mary who got her into hospital and stayed with her. Jane's husband had to take the boys home. He had not wanted Jane to be given spiritual help. He hated God, even though denying his existence. As soon as Mary was alone with Jane, she asked for the chaplain to come and anoint her. Jane had been saying 'how do I go?' She 'went' peacefully, in the early morning at much the same time as she was born.

After the death Mary went on feeling that she had to 'hold' her baby. She discovered, in Coventry Cathedral, a special ministry for bereaved parents. It seemed to her that the arms of Christ on the tapestry were open to receive Jane and she began, very gradually, to let her go. She then dreamed of a transformed Jane in a new body.

Mary says that losing a child is 'all wrong' and 'it should have been me'. These feelings have not gone away. More than a year later she still has 'bad days'. She finds herself sitting and rocking, wanting to nurse the baby who is not there to hold. I suggested that she was also holding herself and that she, too, wanted to be held. She has not had much support in her life. Her husband left the home when the children were small and she has been used to coping and holding things together.

Jane's brother and sister are coping with their own mourning. They are also helping Mary. They know how much she needs to talk about Jane, and the best thing they can do for her is to listen. She, in turn, listens to them.

Mary works as a counsellor. Sometimes, it is hard to carry on. Some years ago she had a long Jungian analysis. Friends and colleagues expected her to pick it up again but she insists that she is not ready for it yet, though, at some time in the future, it may seem the right thing to do. I asked whether the past analysis was helping her now and, if so, how. 'Without it', she said, 'I wouldn't have been able to cope at all'. She explained that she had learnt how to be sad. What she was suffering now was a natural sadness, not neurotic like depression, nor was it paralysing, but could be worked through. What was important was not to run away from it. 'How could you do that?', I asked. 'By immersing myself in work', she said, 'That's what my family always do'.

She has moved to a cottage in the country and has been able to cut down on some of her work. She is busy creating a garden. She is aware of a new sense of timelessness and is beginning to find peace. Jane's two boys are coming to stay and she will have them to herself for two weeks. Of course, she will talk to them about their mother. 'Perhaps one has to be close to death to acquire the necessary freedom to talk about it' (Jung, 1967, p.330).

CHAPTER 3

A Plague Called AIDS

But Lord how empty the streets are and melancholy, so many sick people in the streets, full of sores, and so many sad stories overheard as I walk, everybody talking of this dead and that man sick... And they tell me that in Westminster there is never a physician, and but one apothecary left, all being dead – but there are great hopes of a great decrease this week. God send it.

Samuel Pepys, 16th October 1665

Dying is a ghastly business however it happens, but seeing people die of AIDS was one of the most deeply traumatising experiences that I've ever been through.

David Mellor (Minister of Health), 1986

When the doctor first told me I was HIV positive, I think she was more upset than me. It didn't sink in at first – that took weeks. I thought: this is not true, then I realised the enormity. I had been pushed into yet another corner, this time for keeps. It quickly became a way of life. When the sun shone it became unbearable. I didn't say anything. I had decided to be stoic. This was a chance to be grown-up. Though I thought I ought to be crying. I walked down Charing Cross Road in the sunlight, every-one was so blissfully unaware. The sun is still shining.

Derek Jarman, 16th September 1989

Pandemic

Until the 1980s we thought plague was something we learnt about in history. All the major infectious diseases had been conquered. Smallpox was abolished; tuberculosis, polio and meningitis were no longer lethal. We knew the causes and had discovered antibiotics. Infection could at last be controlled, or so we thought.

The Bubonic Plague that hit London in the time of Pepys was the last in a series of deadly epidemics that had ravaged Europe since the fourteenth century, when crusaders returning from the East introduced new infections. The worst resulted in The Black Death, which wiped out half the English population. 'The Plague', as it was called, continued for the next four centuries, breaking out in various places, particularly in ports, where flea-bearing rats were brought in by the ships. In 1665, when, after a period of comparative immunity, the plague struck again, Londoners were enjoying more comfort and security than ever before and were unprepared for such a catastrophe in what they considered a civilized age. Not knowing the cause, many feared that with the restoration of the monarchy and a general laxity of morals, the English people were being punished by God for disobeying his laws.

When illness cannot be contained, fears and superstitions abound. We look round for scapegoats. In the middle of Mrs Thatcher's back-to-the-family campaign the Chief Constable of Greater Manchester declared that homosexuals were 'swirling around in a cesspool of their own making' and claimed that God was speaking through him (Garfield, 1994). At the other extreme, since in orthodox medicine there is as yet no certain cure for AIDS, the door is wide open for alternative therapies. Some of these may soothe and hold out fragments of hope, though, at worst, there may be disappointment and feelings of inadequacy if positive thinking and loving oneself fails in actually getting rid of the disease. What human beings find hardest of all is living with uncertainty.

What is Aids and Where Does it Come From?

The word 'AIDS' seems to me like a sick joke. The French succeeded in coining a new word, 'SIDA', which does not mean something else. 'AID', in English, used to stand for Artificial Insemination by Donor, a process to aid mothers in bringing life, not death, into the world. But a diagnosis of 'AIDS', meaning Auto Immune Deficiency Syndrome, may amount to a death sentence.

Unlike The Plague, AIDS is a new disease, although it is thought by some researchers to have been endemic, in a non-pathogenic form, among certain breeds of African monkey. There is evidence that monkeys have been infected with retroviruses similar to HIV for thousands of years without symptoms of any disease. The virus could have been passed to humans by contact, through open sores, with an infected animal's blood. At first, the spread would have been confined to isolated communities, accelerating in recent times through enormous increases in global travel. Long before the disease of AIDS was identified, the virus could have been doing its deadly work on unsuspecting populations all over the world.

To describe the biology of AIDS as simply as possible, viruses are not classified as cells but, nevertheless, contain nucleic acid (RNA or DNA), which is the fundamental property of life. They reproduce themselves, but only as parasites inside another cell. Retroviruses are viruses that are able to reverse the normal flow of genetic information from DNA to RNA by transcribing RNA into DNA. They are fragile and not easily transmitted. The HIV retrovirus responsible for AIDS is only passed on by exchange of blood, semen or vaginal fluid through sexual intercourse, blood transfusions or the sharing of needles between intravenous drug users (IVUs) and also from mothers to babies, either in the womb or in breast feeding. After infection there is a long period of latency while DNA is being integrated into its host cell before reproducing. HIV attacks or destroys T lymphocytes, which are vital to the human immune system.

Far more insidious than highly contagious diseases (such as Bubonic Plague), HIV leaves the body disarmed against subsequent infections – chiefly pneumocystis carnii (PCP) and Kaposi Sarcoma (KS). Both are life-threatening. The shock of HIV is that those it attacks are usually young and vigorous – in their prime:

> There has never been a disease as devastating as AIDS. My basis for making this statement is less the explosive nature of its appearance and global spread than the appalling paraphysiology of the pestilence. Medical science has never before confronted a microbe that destroys the very cells of the immune system whose job it is to co-ordinate the body's resistance to it; immunity against a swarming score of secondary invaders is defeated before it has a chance to mount a defence. (Nuland, 1994, p.172)

Some, though by no means all, of those infected with HIV become ill after a few weeks and have symptoms similar to glandular fever. After this initial illness they will produce antibodies and may remain asymptomatic for as long as ten to fifteen years, although they remain infected, probably, for life and can infect others. On the way to developing what has come to be called 'full-blown AIDS', they will be prone to a number of debilitating illnesses that are AIDS-related but not fatal. In the final stages they will succumb to severe 'opportunistic' infections, so-called because the depressed immune system can no longer fight them off. The long incubation period has complicated both diagnosis and prognosis, to the extent of delaying measures to deal with an epidemic that was thought by some officials (and especially some of our politicians) to have been exaggerated.

Back in 1985, Norman Fowler, who was then Social Services Secretary, stated that 'prevention is the only vaccine we've got' (Garfield, 1994, p.108). Azidethyidine (AZT) was introduced in 1987 and was found to prolong life and alleviate symptoms, but not to cure. Despite side-effects and considerable expense, it remained until recently the only effective treatment. Now, in the 1990s, a combination of drugs has had dramatic effects and hopes are again raised, though it is still too early for any certainty. Combination Therapy is being given to patients who are already quite ill, on the basis of a last chance. A lot of drugs have to be taken at frequent intervals, with or without various mixes of food. If the routine is broken, the patients will become immune to the efficacy of the drugs. They have to be seriously committed to the treatment and need help in regulating the doses. It is not a treatment that fits with a chaotic life-style.

Health Education, Tests and Counselling

This is how matters stood in the early 1980s:

> What could you tell people who had tested positive? With no cure and no effective treatment, and with newspapers daily muddling the number of virus carriers with the number of AIDS cases, how could you convince anyone that their life wasn't as good as over? Some patients convinced themselves that optimism was all there was; this wasn't self-deception, it was what their doctors believed too. There were advantages in early diagnosis: warning signs could be heeded, new drugs tried. (Garfield, 1994, p.56)

In 1985, Charles Farthing, who was a research registrar at St. Stephen's Hospital in London, wrote some advice for people who were HIV positive. 'It was a type of written counselling, the first of its kind in Britain' (Garfield, 1994, p.56). Health education and counselling went hand in hand. People needed to be warned. They had to know what counted as 'safe sex'. But Farthing's advice had limited circulation, only reaching those already infected. The Health Education Council issued a pamphlet but shunned details of practices such as oral or anal sex. It did little to enlighten gay men, those considered most at risk: 'The timidity of the leaflet provided a significant pointer to what the Department of Health and government ministers considered to be politically acceptable when dealing with such intimate matters' (Garfield, 1994, p.58).

Mrs Thatcher supported Clause 28, which forbade the kind of health education in schools that might seem to promote an acceptance of homosexuality. As far as possible, she ignored the subject of AIDS. She made no mention of it in her memoirs. Government ministers appeared to know very little about sexual behaviour. 'Oral sex?', said Norman Fowler, 'I had no idea you could get it from talking dirty!' (Garfield, 1994, p.118). And medical science was reported to know 'more about the molecular structure of the HIV virus in a leucocyte than it knows about human sexual behaviour in the bedroom' (ibid. p.119).

In 1987, pamphlets were distributed to people's houses all over the country but the message was cautious, with a taboo on words such as 'penis', 'anus', 'back passage'. Religious leaders feared that too much specific information would encourage promiscuity. 'AIDS', said the Chief Rabbi, 'is the consequence of infidelity, premarital adventures, sexual deviation and social irresponsibility – putting pleasure before discipline' (Garfield 1994, p.121).

With the introduction of tests in the mid-1980s, health employees in STD clinics were given some training in counselling, with particular reference to how to talk to a patient before the test and how to give news of the result. In Simon Garfield's *The End of Innocence* (from which I have been quoting) there is a macabre description of how not to carry out an HIV test. The patient had rung the Gay Switchboard to find out where he could be tested anonymously without making an appointment. He was shy and embarrassed but was given a bit of what he called 'earnest and well-meaning' counselling before the test. He came back two weeks later for the result. The interview went like this:

> Doctor: Er, well, I'm really sorry, but it seems to be positive and I haven't a clue what I'm supposed to do now because it's my first day on the clinic. Just sit here while I go and find out what it is I'm supposed to do now. You're the first I've done.

> Five minutes later: I'm very sorry, I've misread your diagnosis. It's negative. (p.83)

The relief of a negative test makes some people vow never to put themselves at risk again. Others decide that perhaps they can allow themselves an occasional lapse. But there are also quite a few who enjoy playing a game of Russian Roulette with the risks.

Terry's Story

Terry was nine when he found his grandfather dead in his bed. They told him that the old man was asleep and Terry wondered when he would wake up. Not long afterwards, death struck again. This time it was his three-year-old brother, who died of cancer. Terry had known about his brother's illness but, when he died, no one said anything and it seemed that no one mourned. He was sent to school instead of to the funeral. A few years later, his parents split up. When he was 14, two Mormons came to the door and he warmed to them because they took an interest in him. He was easily converted and went to live with a Mormon family, who informally adopted him. He thought that God had called him to be a Mormon, so he went to Salt Lake City and became a missionary. For the first time in his life, he felt special.

He already knew he was gay, but he also knew that the Mormon Church considered homosexuality a sin. He had an affair with a fellow missionary and they both went and confessed to their boss in the Church. The result was excommunication and being sent home in disgrace. He was rejected by his adopted family and soon gave up being a Mormon.

He ran a hairdressing business and settled down with a gay partner, Clive. They decided to buy a house and applied for a mortgage. To their surprise, they had to be AIDS tested. Terry was not worried, he thought that AIDS was solely an American disease. He and Clive were shocked to discover that both of them turned out to be HIV positive. Clive quickly got ill and died within two years. Terry has survived eleven years and gives himself another fifteen. He has recently been tested to determine the amount of virus in his body. The result was higher than expected. A combination of drugs has brought the level down but he feels further along the road to death. He is aware now that the disease is being artificially controlled, whereas, before this test, he was proud of the fight he could manage on his own.

At first, his situation was too painful to talk about, but, having been through shock, shame and mourning, he wants to help people by sharing his own experience. He has done some work for the social services and has taken a counselling course. He now works at 'Open Door', a drop-in centre in Brighton for HIV patients. I asked whether talking about his own experience of HIV fitted with what he had learnt about counselling. He said that the course had taught him when it was relevant to share and when it was not. He has been seeing a counsellor himself for the last five years. He also has contact with her as a colleague. Her way of preserving the boundaries is to work from two different rooms. In one she sits behind a desk. The other is a counselling room with two chairs. Terry tells her which room he would like to use, according to his needs.

'Open Door' is run by the Diocesan Board of Social Responsibility. The centre provides a midday meal and its volunteers do the cooking. Counselling is free but contributions towards the meal are welcomed. Volunteers counsel relatives as well as patients and are willing to go out and visit anyone acutely ill or dying.

I asked Terry how he felt he was affected by his shortened life span. He remembered how, as children, he and his sister would play a game of 'if you were given only a short time to live, what would you do?' They had imagined all sorts of treats and spectacular voyages. But that is not what he wants now. He said he would like to discover that his life had some meaning. He has given up organised religion but believes in God. He thinks this life is probably part of 'something bigger' but says that it is no good expecting to understand what that bigger thing is and doubts if we ever will.

There was a time when being turned out of the Mormon Church and being infected with HIV seemed like a punishment. Now he thinks it is part of God's plan to prevent complacency. He encourages people to talk to their dead friends. He still talks to Clive and has no feeling of his not being there.

Both his parents have re-married. He gets on with them fairly well, except for his mother's new husband, who is not friendly. They know he is gay but not that he is HIV. His sister knows. She is a nurse and says that when he gets ill she wants to give up her job and nurse him. But he tells her that is not what he wants. When he gets really ill he will tell his parents the truth, but he would like to avoid fuss. He thinks we should all separate from our parents at 16. Then, perhaps, we can meet again later as equals.

AIDS in the Family

The 'family' may be the patient's most important social system; it may be a biological or social entity. We do not have predetermined views about relationship constellations... (Bor, Miller and Goldman, 1992, p.5)

When AIDS was first discovered as a killer disease, the chief concern of the medical establishment was an urgent need to know its etiology and prognosis and to get to work on finding a cure. The other concern was to disseminate as much information as possible and warn people against 'dying of ignorance' – this being the message of the first publicity campaign.

So, health education, as we have already seen, was a top priority. Then, with the introduction of HIV testing, patients were given supportive counselling, usually by nurses or carers with some basic training in counselling skills. No long-term psychotherapy was envisaged. But, gradually, expectations changed, both as to the patients' chances of survival and who the infected people would turn out to be. We used to think of AIDS as a gay disease. Now we became aware that any family member might be a victim.

Systems Theory

A systemic approach to group dynamics is one that emphasises the importance of context. In the case of HIV the context is the illness, which affects individuals in the family in different ways, depending on their beliefs and prejudices, and also their habitual roles, either as carers or those cared for. Inner-city families in England today may be of different cultures, black or Asian, with complicated networks, including relatives in other countries. The grandparent generation, imbued with their age-old traditions and taboos, can easily feel alienated from young descendants born and brought up in a freer society without respect for ancient lore. It is this younger age-group who may have been infected, through drugs or prostitution (just as likely as gay sex), with the AIDS virus. Reactions of one generation to the other will be strong and, perhaps, both of them will feel punished. Parents may try behaving as go-betweens but the alienation and bewilderment of grandparents to grandchildren is likely to increase. It is this painful situation that, without any 'predetermined views', a systemic therapist may hope to resolve.

In my experience, no reputable therapist would describe the task as 'doing something to someone'. It is through a reciprocal relationship that change may come about. On the other hand, those of us undertaking long-term individual therapy would expect to do more listening than talking. We wait for the patient to inform us, through free associations, dreams and fantasy, about the secrets of his inner life. He gives us the material in which we try, with his co-operation, to find sense and meaning. And, in the transference, we expect a replay of relationships from the past. Therapists vary in the importance they give to an initial assessment, which involves taking a history and asking questions about family background and past traumas. I was taught that everything we need to know would come to light in the patient's own time in the course of our regular fifty-minute sessions. But, faced with a distressed family or partnership thrown into a state of shock by a diagnosis of HIV in one or more of its members, neither the therapist nor the family group can afford such passivity. Moreover, in meeting the family rather than the individual, transference onto the therapist is bound to take a back seat. Parents and children are actually there in the room with us and the action is in the present tense.

Systemic therapists ask a lot of questions. First, they make a hypothesis, a 'calculated guess about the problem and what it may mean' (Bor, Miller and Goldman, 1992, p.13). Starting with their own view of what is going on, therapists must be prepared to revise and change their minds about the reality of the problem according to what comes up in the context of the group. 'Questions are the main catalyst for patient change and healing and provide patients with opportunities to make further choices in their lives' (Bor, Miller and Goldman, 1992, p.15). A difference is made between 'closed' and 'open' questions, also called 'linear' and 'circular'. Questions such as 'are you depressed?' can only be answered by 'yes' or 'no'. Hence they are closed and do not lead easily to further dialogue. Circular questions address future possibilities – for instance, 'how do you think your parents will cope with being told that you are HIV positive?' Circular questions do not concentrate on finding one unchanging truth but on introducing new ways of seeing that truth from different points of view.

The main theme will be how to cope with loss. There may also be anger and blame, as well as shame and fear of social stigma, all of which may get in the way of experiencing the enormous pain of losing a child or sexual partner. Components of this pain will be separation anxiety, existential aloneness, denial, sadness, disappointment, anger, resentment, guilt, exhaustion and desperation.

An issue that keeps coming up in both group and individual therapy is secrecy. Not only are the patients concerned about their HIV status but, very often, they have not 'come out', either to their families or to the world, about their homosexuality. A bisexual man may be determined not to tell his wife the results of his test. The therapist will, of course, be worried lest he infect his wife. Using the systemic approach, she asks future-oriented questions: 'what might be the worst thing that could happen if you told her?' He says that she would probably leave him when he needs her most and would cut him off from his children. She would also tell other people his secret. The therapist asks how he thinks he would cope without her. He says he has a boyfriend but fears that he, too, would leave. Then he begins worrying about one of his children; perhaps he should be tested, but then his wife would have to know. He asks the therapist: 'will you tell her?' Yes, that would be possible, but another suggestion is that she meets them together, with one of her colleagues, so that all the family may get some help (Bor, Miller and Goldman, 1992).

Another emotional issue is what to say to infected children. If they have been born with the infection or caught it through breast feeding, they will get ill during their first few years. Adolescents may have been infected through intercourse, being tattooed with unsterile equipment or through injecting drugs with shared needles. In both cases parents will have to cope with uncertainty about their child's life span. Nobody knows what new drugs may be developed to cope with HIV and AIDS in the immediate future or, for that matter, how long the present epidemic will continue. Parents want to protect their children and so may postpone telling them their future prospects. If asked in therapy, it is often found that the child already knows more than the parent suspected. Asked what he knew about AIDS, a child replied that people could die of it. He was then asked if he ever thought about dying. Yes, his mother said one could become an angel (Bor, Miller and Goldman, 1992).

HIV changes family expectations in that children, instead of growing up and leaving home, may need rather more than less looking after. Planning for the future becomes difficult, especially when both parents and children are infected and no one knows who will be first to get ill. The illness is so unpredictable that no one can offer permanent solutions. All that a therapist or counsellor can hope to do is introduce new ways of facing the problem, some of which may lighten the burden. In systemic therapy there can be continuing redefinition and the presentation of choices and modification of a family's belief system. In choosing what questions to ask it goes without saying that the therapist must continually question herself as to whether her interventions are appropriate, whether her hopes for the patient are obscuring his own and if she is pushing for possible change. The expertise in this approach must lie in knowing the right questions to ask.

Attachment Theory

Away from the big cities, there tends to be more secrecy about AIDS and the sufferers may become isolated. Chris Purnell has set up a counselling service in a rural area where there is a low prevalence of HIV infection. Those who do get infected feel particularly vulnerable, aware of a social stigma in a small community, where ignorance and prejudice are barriers to confiding their problems to family or friends. There seems, for these people, nowhere safe enough to turn for support.

Unlike the systemic therapists, with their emphasis on here and now, Purnell (1996) draws on Bowlby's Attachment Theory and stresses the importance of a 'secure base' in childhood:

> Based upon the attachment figures which we experience during childhood, we all create our own internal working models of attachment relationships which we carry with us into adult life ... Thus when the attachment system is activated we react and behave according to our internal working model. Based upon our experiences we form working models of attachment which are either secure or anxious. (p.522)

But he believes that these internal models are not unchanging and new attachment figures can, if reliable, provide security. Familiar surroundings may produce some of the same effect, as also being part of a community or culture. Partners, family and friends may all be attachment figures but the HIV diagnosis, unless kept secret, poses a threat to their willingness to keep on being supportive. Even when there is no actual threat, those whose working models are anxious will, nevertheless, feel threatened and isolated. Purnell believes that counsellors or therapists can provide the necessary base through an ongoing contact which is flexible enough for patients to feel they have some control over their lives and, despite grief and fear, are seen to be coping:

> Such an approach places less emphasis upon the need for a consulting room environment, and is distinguished from the role of befriender by the skill which the therapist is able to employ in developing an approach to the relationship which the client can use psychotherapeutically, particularly the client whose working model is anxious rather than secure. (p.523)

The therapy described is rooted in theory but is not rigid. Purnell believes there is a place for 'a problem-focused systemic approach' in cases where communication has broken down among families and friends or between partners: 'The existence of a third party can sometimes help to break the silence, by providing a place to off-load and open up communication' (p.524).

Purnell also works with AIDS patients who have become very ill and are near to death. He used to think that all he would have to do was listen to them expressing their feelings about what it was like to die, but, perhaps, this was his way of distancing himself from the process. He has come to realise that providing a secure base means being actively engaged in that person's dying. The therapist inevitably gets drawn into the drama, with all its terrors and uncertainties. He has to experience and acknowledge a helplessness that both of them share and to resist any temptation to 'rescue' either of them by a reassurance which would be a denial of the pain: 'There are times when words are inadequate and will never express whatever it is that you and the client are working through. At such times actions speak louder, and being there together sharing a silent moment is a powerfully therapeutic experience' (p.530).

Purnell ends his paper with a reference to his own grief when an AIDS patient dies. The temptation might be to share his mourning with the family of the patient, but he reminds himself that his own secure base must be elsewhere, with his family, friends and colleagues as well as with his supervisor and therapist.

A response to Chris Purnell's paper appeared in a later issue of the same journal (Brown, 1997). Jill Brown describes herself as a psychodynamic counsellor at the Harbour, a centre in Bristol for counselling those affected by HIV and other life-threatening conditions. She is also training as a psychotherapist.

She expresses the view that a secure base is essential in any kind of therapy. She herself sticks to a psychoanalytical approach and stresses the need to stay within the analytic framework without too much alteration for this special group of patients. She issues a warning about the dangers of getting too much involved in 'sharing a silent moment':

> In the grip of primitive anxieties about life and death it can be terribly dif-
> ficult to remain thoughtful about the patient who is dying. We find our-
> selves thought-less and speech-less so that actively attending to physical
> and spiritual needs can become a solution to relieve the intense anxiety
> and the feelings of helplessness. (p.559)

She says that 'the patient's struggle is eased by truth' and the therapist should strive to remain separate from the patient: 'The translation or interpretation of the anxiety, which is often expressed as fear of death, is an integral part of the containment that the therapeutic relationship can continue to offer' (p.560).

She describes her work with a dying haemophiliac who also had AIDS. She had been seeing him for five years at the counselling centre and, for the last four months of his life, in the hospital where he died. Because of his haemophilia he had spent much of his childhood in hospital and had memories of being left in physical and emotional pain. The coming and going of his parents added to his feelings of abandonment, since he never felt that they listened and contained his pain but left him after every visit to bear it alone. He now felt victimised, first by his mother for passing on the haemophilia and now by the health service for giving him contaminated blood.

While he was hospitalised and dying of AIDS, his chief wish was never to be left alone and he managed to organise a team of 'nursing staff, friends, parents, spiritual healers and various carers' to give him 24-hour cover. This team felt that it was important not to abandon him. His counsellor kept herself separate from the team. She directly tackled his fear of death, which was so intense that he was afraid of going to sleep because that would be too much like dying. She asked him to describe what he thought it would be like after death. He thought of it as 'being eternally conscious of being unconscious, or like being for ever conscious of being dead which was a state of being in pain and alone' (Brown, 1997, p.561). She pointed out that what he feared had already happened in childhood. It was the same infantile terror that he was suffering again and, every time she left him, the feelings of abandonment were revived. These interpretations had been made before, but, now that he was really dying, they became more poignant and she left the hospital wondering if she would see him again: 'I saw him once more for a short period during which he said goodbye and he told me that he had slept for 16 hours after the previous session. He died not long after' (p.561).

The London Lighthouse

A year before it closed, I visited the London Lighthouse to find out how to practise therapy with people who are going to die. I had read about the centre and the vision of its founders: 'On its completion, AIDS care would have come of age. Part hospice, part alternative treatment centre, the Lighthouse would treat people with AIDS and HIV in an environment of support and spiritual nourishment' (Garfield, 1994, p.156). I had also heard criticism of its New Age mentality, the expense of its upkeep and complaints about its luxury. Virginia Bottomley is reported to have said: 'If I see one more gay man sitting on a Heal's chair, I will scream' (Garfield, 1994, p.158).

I certainly found it comfortable and an oasis of peace after the hassle of getting across London. I had an appointment with Stephen Adams-Langley, who headed a team including a systemic family therapist, three psychodynamic and one humanistic practitioner. Langley himself is an existentialist. I asked him why he had chosen to work with HIV patients. He said that he had always been fascinated by death and this was the subject chosen for his MA thesis. He told me how he had, three times in his life, through accident and near drowning, come close to dying and managed to survive. He quoted Heidegger – 'Death is not an event but a phenomenon to be examined'.

It is not easy to avoid some examination of the phenomenon when diagnosed as HIV positive, but it might also be said that dying is the easy bit. What is much harder is having to go on living with the infection and watch friends die, all the time aware of one's capacity to infect others. When the epidemic began, people were ignorant and, therefore, innocent of the risks. With today's knowledge, there can be guilt.

We talked about some of Langley's patients, not all of them young. A man of 73 had a rich and varied life, including being a bear trainer in a circus and living in Hollywood in the 1930s. With death on the horizon, he wanted to make sense of it all. In therapy he asked himself: 'What has my life been?'

Combination Therapy, with its sometimes dramatic results, causes anxiety as well as optimism. The cure seems too good to be true. Will it be cruelly snatched away? People prepare for death in all sorts of different ways. Some of them have got caught in a 'Lazarus Syndrome'. A business man had liquidated his assets, sold insurance policies and settled for a short life on a limited income. Now he is suddenly back in the marketplace, but for how long? Amassing wealth was one of his ways of diminishing death anxiety. Now, stripped of this defence, he is left with nothing but a precarious existence, 'being' in the face of 'non-being'.

In the spring of 1998 I heard a rumour that the Lighthouse had closed. I asked why. The friend who had given me this news supposed that people had stopped dying. Unconvinced, but aware that the story of AIDS changes all the time, I wrote again to Stephen Langley, who confirmed that the building was on the market though there was some hope of relocation in a smaller house. The reason for this closure was a massive withdrawal of funding from Westminster and Chelsea councils. He had been made redundant but had done his best to provide free once-a-week therapy through student placements at Regents College, resulting in second-year trainees on an MA psychotherapy course seeing HIV and AIDS patients under supervision. He had nothing new to say about Combination Therapy. The situation is much as it was a year ago – expensive, difficult to take and with unpleasant side-effects – although, in some cases, the results have been amazing. What has been lost is the ease of having so many services accessible under one roof and the work with the families, which seems to have suffered most of all.

The Existential Approach

We all of us, all the time, have to live with uncertainty, but most of us, some of the time, manage to block it out. HIV reveals the tragedy of life. To quote Rollo May (1969):

> The confronting of genuine tragedy is a highly cathartic experience psychically, as Aristotle and others through history have reminded us. Tragedy is inseparably connected with man's dignity and grandeur and is the accompaniment, as illustrated in such dramas as Oedipus and Orestes, of the human being's moment of great insight. (p.83)

Important existentialist themes are freedom and choice, but these are limited by 'facticity', the given-ness of the human condition: 'One of the many ways of defining tragedy sees it as a clash between the aspirations of human freedom and creativity with a cosmic order that is stronger and defeats man' (Macquarrie, 1972, p.189).

We do not ask to be born, but, since we exist, it is up to us to create what we can. HIV is part of life's facticity, part of the tragedy. But the facticity of death can, paradoxically, give us vitality. We need the limitation to give meaning to the life we have had and continue to have, with its choices as well as its limits.

What gets shaken is our ontological security or, in ordinary language, a take-it-for-granted sense of being more or less in charge of our own existence. With HIV, 'the individual may experience him/her self as more unreal than real; feel partially divorced from his/her body; lose all sense of temporal continuity or inner consistency; feel precariously differentiated from the rest of the world; and consequently feel that his/her sense of identity is thrown into doubt' (Crossley, 1997, pp.72–3).

Crossley compares a feeling of 'being more dead than alive' with Laing's schizophrenics (Laing, 1965), who felt a separation between self and body and whose divided 'true' selves, although cut off both from their bodies and from other people, had to be clung to even though only existing in imagination. She presents the case of Darren, a bitter and angry young man who had lived with his HIV-positive diagnosis for 12 years. After losing two partners, he 'blanked out' his other friends, stopped working, met nobody and held fast to an imaginary ideal of getting more out of life. In fact, he was doing and getting nothing. His original sense of security had been shattered and he had tried desperately to get it back, but was bound to fail because he could not bring himself to come out of his fantasy of a good life and live in a real world with other people. He avoided non-being by avoiding being (Tillich, 1974) and was full of hatred and destructiveness, not least towards himself: 'I just get so sad and just think, please let me die...' (Crossley, 1997, p.92).

In all this sadness we need also to think about the ways in which we cope as therapists. We may find ourselves put in the position of 'Ultimate Rescuers', quite magically powerful, and this is not comfortable. We may have a passionate desire to relieve another person's suffering but this will be followed by helplessness and hopelessness because it is so impossible. Martin Milton (1996), another existential psychologist, mentions feelings of hollowness, withdrawal and difficulty in being able to listen, also awareness of our own mortality:

> People react differently to this 'given' of eventual death. It has been sug-
> gested that the differences may also be evident in the differing ways peo-
> ple react to the boundary of psychotherapy sessions, e.g. the inability to
> complete a task until the deadline is imminent, or the living of their lives in
> the future rather than the present. Death and therapy are private and in-
> tense experiences that cannot be fully explained in an emotionally or
> experientially accurate way. (p.118)

He mentions that we sometimes have to be flexible about the usual boundary issues. If someone is ill or dying, therapy may have to be conducted at the bedside. Boundaries then have to be changed, but this is quite possible without giving up professionalism.

When thinking about specialised training for counsellors and therapists working in this field, he writes:

> The anxieties that are likely to be activated when facing HIV are those
> same concerns that face us all – it would seem sensible that those providing
> therapeutic services are well trained in the facing of those fundamental

concerns. Yet, currently, an insistence on HIV training can be seen as a priority in the person specifications of those providing HIV counselling. (p.127)

So what further training is needed? I think most of us would agree that a thorough and painstaking training in psychotherapy (or counselling), including several years in analysis and ongoing supervision, should equip us to face the life-and-death problems of HIV and AIDS, just as we face a range of human tragedy in our day-to-day working lives. As a supervisor, I might suggest that a therapist does not specialise in only treating HIV and nothing else.

Although therapists with a professional training behind them come to HIV well equipped, they would obviously benefit from a thorough medical knowledge of the condition and this should be continually updated as new treatments are developed. Emotional and existential issues should, of course, be examined carefully in supervision.

Milton ends his paper on a note of warning:

If ... the HIV counselling field continues to rely on expertise in HIV, without this thorough training in psychotherapy or counselling, we run the risk of being 'experts' on an issue. Clients would then run the risk of being related to as 'HIV patients' rather than individuals with the infection. (p.127)

CHAPTER 4

Sudden Death

From battle and murder, and from sudden death, Good Lord deliver us

The Litany, *Book of Common Prayer*

Death by Proxy

Death is a mystery. We may be afraid but it has a fascination. Violent death, as so often displayed in all its gore on the media, makes us shudder, and yet few actually turn away and resist looking or reading about it. When I first learnt to read well enough to pick up a newspaper, I remember finding most of the news boring until I came upon a story of a man being tried for murder, a story that continued for many days and ended with the judge putting on his black cap and condemning the murderer to be hanged by the neck until he died. Years later, I kept a private vigil for Derek Bentley, waking myself in the early morning at the time when I knew he was to be hanged. I still felt fascination, but this time I was also overwhelmed by the unfairness of what was happening to this retarded boy who had not even been the one to pull the trigger yet was just old enough to be hanged. It seemed unfair that the law in those days allowed a person to hang at 18 but withheld his right to vote until 21. From that moment, I turned violently against capital punishment and remember my relief and feeling of celebration when, at last, the law was changed.

Reading detective stories is something I have always thought of as a game, preferring the Agatha Christie type of story with two-dimensional characters and an unwritten rule that the reader's sympathy must never be enlisted on the murderer's side, however unlikely a criminal he turns out to be. The excitement is in working out the clues or guessing the outcome. And yet, I wonder, would the game be as much fun without the murder, or, for that matter, would hunting be exciting without the fox?

I was musing on the public's appetite for sudden death, when I heard from a friend on the telephone about Princess Diana's fatal accident. I decided not to run straight to my television set. It was not my tragedy and I thought the details could wait until the evening news. A little while later, another friend telephoned for no other reason than to talk about it. He had been up watching television and 'crying his eyes out' for most of the night. He blamed the paparazzi and thought they should be punished, but 'you should have seen that mangled car', he exclaimed. Yes, I thought, it was people wanting to see such sights that created a market, not just for intimate shots of the rich and famous in life but also in death. So I kept my resolve to postpone television until later in the day.

But, looking back at my last paragraph, I was shocked to see that I had actually written the word 'published' instead of 'punished'. I felt in the grip of the Trickster Archetype, who tampers with the meaning of things and turns them upside down. Yet I also realised that I had to own this Freudian slip as part of myself. This made me feel ashamed.

The German word 'schadenfreude', meaning pleasure in someone else's pain, seems to me not quite appropriate. I would be inclined to describe the phenomenon as 'brinkmanship by proxy'. Adventurous people push themselves to the limits and get a kick out of risking their lives. How else would Everest have been climbed or space explored? The rest of us do it vicariously. I suppose writing this book is my own kind of brinkmanship, pushing myself to the edge of what it would be more comfortable to run away from. Practising therapy with disturbed, psychotic or psychopathic people is another exciting challenge, which some of us heroically – or, perhaps, rashly – are prepared to meet, despite the risks. If we are serious about this, we will not, I hope, be courting danger in order to be admired but because the task urgently needs to be done and because we feel our training and experience equips us to take up the challenge. The brinkmanship is at least our own and not vicarious. But, obviously, we need to tread carefully, and with maximum support, if we are to enter this highly specialised field.

Describing the public appetite for sensational accidents, violent crime and murder (though, of course, only by proxy), Dr Patrick Gallwey (1997), an expert on forensic psychotherapy, issues a warning:

> Social attitudes to killers are the most obviously ambivalent of all social pre-
> occupations. The juxtaposition of morbid, often eroticised fascination for
> details of horrific killing and craving for either the punishment and death
> of the killer or his elevation to heroic status is fully exploited by the enter-

tainment industry, including the press and television. The real complex cycle of events that determine such atrocities becomes more and more obscured by a cloud of outrage and perversity as pseudo-morality competes with pornography dressed up as sociology or art, so that the gratification of these collusive appetites obliterates the slender chance of getting closer to the truth. (p.474)

At the beginning of television programmes we are sometimes warned that we will be watching distressing sights. Yet, with skilful cutting, the worst of these are not lingered over for long. We are spared close contact with the stickiness of actual blood and the stench of rotting flesh. Since we are not part of the scene, perhaps thousands of miles away, it is not difficult to become inured to such a second-hand experience. The voyeur that lurks inside us all may even be disappointed. It takes a lot to shock the average television viewer.

In some cases words may have a stronger effect than pictures, for instance:

> Pieces of brain, blood and pieces of dirt covered much of the pink velvet headboard above and behind her head, with numerous bloodstains and tissue stains on the wall ... On the white ceiling above the body were bloodstains and pieces of adherent tissue resembling brain tissue ... Part of a cerebral hemisphere lay on the carpet under the bedside cabinet. (Stern, 1996, p.208)

That is how the pathologist makes his report: flat, factual and without glamour. For him, such sights are 'all in the day's work'. Violence enters the bedroom and becomes domesticated.

The pathologist has been described as a 'special kind of detective' (Stern, 1996, p.1). It is the corpse that provides most of the clues; the work involves matching blood groups – and now DNA – discovering details of the victim's last meal, fibres on the clothing, the body's position and the nature of the wounds inflicted. Forensic scientists 'are dependent on the information and evidence they receive from the scene of the crime and they cannot produce answers out of thin air' (Williams, 1991, p.10). Reading detective stories may mislead us into thinking that 'thin air' or Hercule Poirot's 'little grey cells' provide all the evidence needed for the crime's solution. The dapper little Belgian detective sips his aperitif, twirls his moustaches and, by astute questioning, magically solves the mystery that confronts him. Miss Marple does her knitting and gossips to the villagers with the same unfailing results, while forensic science seems to take a back seat.

More up to date, P.D. James' Inspector Dalgleish is at least a police officer, but she also makes him a poet with refined sensibilities. In one of the stories he is shown shrinking from the pathologist's investigations. She describes him as finding it difficult to contemplate a body that was still warm, and its sudden transition from youth and femininity to dead flesh. He could hardly bear to look at those intrusive fingers, as, with what seemed an offensive lack of modesty, they probed the girl's most private orifices. Later, on the mortuary table, there would be a systematic dismemberment, necessary to science and the cause of justice. Later still, a mortuary attendant would have the job of stitching the body up in an attempt to make it look human again, before handing it over to family or friends for burial.

We are invited to be squeamish with this lovable, though unlikely, detective, but the average reader is excited and curious. Crime fiction is becoming less of a parlour game and, inured as we are, it does sometimes succeed in shocking us.

But, always, the greatest shock is to stumble across the dark places in ourselves, those shadows which we so stubbornly refuse to admit to in the cold light of day: 'With what pleasure...', says Jung (1967), 'we read newspaper reports of crime. A true criminal becomes a popular figure because he unburdens in no small degree the consciences of his fellow men, for now they know once more where evil is to be found' (p.70). His 'once more' refers to a time when human beings believed in a convenient external devil to carry their shadows for them.

Meeting the Shadow

In introducing us to the shadow, Jung described it as the most accessible and easiest to experience of those powerful, inherited predispositions which he called archetypes: 'Over and over again he emphasises that we all have a shadow, that everything substantial casts a shadow, that the ego stands to shadow as light to shade, that it is the shadow that makes us human' (Samuels, Shorter and Plaut, 1986, p.138). He gave credit to Freud for uncovering 'the abyss of darkness in human nature that the enlightened optimism of Western Christianity and the scientific age had sought to conceal' (p.139). Jung did not necessarily equate shadow with evil but with unlived potential, neutral in itself unless actualised for good or ill. In one discussion with his colleagues he got exasperated by heavy-handed attempts at definition. 'This is all nonsense', he exclaimed, 'the shadow is simply the whole unconscious' (Von Franz, 1987, p.5). In the personal unconscious one could say that the shadow is what we disown, repress, dream about and project onto other people. It is also archetypal and pertains to the collective unconscious: 'One cannot fail to be ambivalent about this part of the human psyche because, inevitably, it inheres all that is worst and best in mankind' (Stevens, 1982, p.215).

In dreams we meet the shadow as a criminal or a monster by whom we may be chased, conned, stabbed in the back or threatened with death. Sometimes, we stand our ground and fight. More often, we run away. A 'clinically' depressed patient, whose dreams habitually menace him in these ways, makes his own attempts at interpretation. Sometimes, he is on the edge of a pit, afraid of being sucked in and overwhelmed. And yet he can observe, as though from outside, write his dreams down and think analytically about them. He had a dream of being in a car with Inspector Morse, whom he saw as the sane part of himself, and who was going to rescue him from a maniac who tried to drag him away. Morse started the car with the dreamer half in and half out of it. In and out of psychosis? The same night, he was walking along a street and saw that he had two shadows. We wondered together about these split-off aspects of his usually compliant 'good-boy' self. He used not to be afraid of death but sees it now as absolute destruction of all life, a corruption from inside life itself, with no rebirth. His waking fantasies are often worse than his dreams and he has periods when only the dreams are positive, as if to compensate for his bleak depression. In dreams, as in waking life, the shadow is projected. The villains who chase us are exterior and personified. So are the rescuers. Inspector Morse, in my patient's dream, embodies the archetype of the wise old man. But, in owning the dream, the dreamer needs to accept both the bad and the good as belonging to himself.

Our waking projections are even more difficult to take back and own. Whereas the dream seems to happen to us irrespective of our will, we like to think that we have some control over our lives when we are awake. We all have uncomfortable memories. I remember a time when I was teaching a group of disturbed children. I could be conscientious and patient with most of them but one little girl I found extraordinarily irritating. She was clumsy, dishevelled, untidy. She whined and never seemed to listen or make any attempt to learn. I felt a strong temptation to shake or hit her and I am sure my words were cruel. It was her weakness that undermined my strength. It was hard to realise that what I wanted to attack was the helpless child that once was me and whom, on achieving adulthood, I had not finally relinquished. Gradually, I managed to look with some shame at what I was doing and be a little kinder, perhaps also more humble, and able to feel empathy with those who, with dire results, have not managed to contain their anger.

An upbringing of ethical teaching, with the subsequent build-up of conscience and superego, helps us to tame our instincts, but they do not disappear. We all have criminal propensities buried in our psyches and are liable to be gripped by the shadow's archetypal force: 'Hitler knew the shadow all too well, indulged it, was obsessed by it, and strove to purge it; but he could not admit it in himself, seeing only its projected form as Jew, Slav, intellectual, foreign, weak and sick' (Hillman, 1996, p.234).

Nations and political parties get caught up in a collective shadow and terrible destruction can result. There needs to be a collective refusal to project our shadows onto some scapegoat, known as 'The Enemy', if civilisation and the planet itself are to survive. My patient's view of death as 'corruption from within' opened up a picture for me, like an apocalyptic vision, of the kind of global destruction that irresponsible humans are capable of bringing about, the deaths not only of individuals but of every living organism, without hope of renewal. The possibility of this happening is terrible and terrifying. That it actually happened in my patient's psyche was, while he experienced it, the only reality. But the mood passed and a spark of hope revived, as also my hope for him.

At worst:

> The effect of projection is to isolate the subject from his environment, since instead of a real relation to it there is now only an illusionary one. Projections change the world into a replica of one's own unknown face. In the last analysis therefore, they lead us to an autoerotic or autistic condition in which one dreams a world whose reality remains for ever unattainable. (Jung, 1977, p.9)

There are many examples in literature, some of which have an uncomfortable dream-like quality, reflecting the split in the author's mind. Dostoievsky, for instance, when he wrote *The Idiot*, laboured with at least eight trial versions of the novel before he was prepared to let it loose on the public: 'I have my own idea of reality in art', he wrote to a friend, 'and what most people will call almost fantastic and an exception sometimes constitutes for me the very essence of reality' (Magarshack, 1978, p.25). He had set out to depict a perfect man, one who is mocked by conventional society, is called an idiot and suffers, as he did himself, from epilepsy. In so far as his hero's reality comes across to the reader, it is by no means perfect. What Dostoievsky brilliantly conveys is a dangerous innocence and he shows how this can only lead to disaster. He had been much haunted by a Holbein painting of Jesus being taken down from the cross, the body already decomposing. Just as the story of Jesus is entwined with that of his betrayer, Judas, so is Dostoievsky's hero twinned, from the first to the last page, with a ruffian whom he both loves and hates and cannot be parted from. Inevitably, they fall in love with the same woman, who is murdered by the shadow figure, the man of action. The two of them come together at the end to keep an all-night vigil with the body. One is struck by the opposition of these characters, one to the other, and their mutual unconsciousness. Jung (1977) wrote of 'those rather rare cases where the positive qualities of the personality are repressed, and the ego in consequence plays an essentially negative or unfavourable role' (p.8).

Anthony Stevens (1982) says: 'to be ethical we must be conscious, and consciousness means awareness of things as they really are' (p.240). As individuals, we must each take our own share of society's guilt. Morality has opposite poles of good and evil and we cannot, much as we should like to, stay always on the side of the angels and deny the devil:

> Unfortunately there can be no doubt that man is, on the whole, less good than he imagines himself or wants to be. Everyone carries a shadow, and the less it is embodied in the individual's conscious life, the blacker and denser it is … if it is repressed and isolated from consciousness, it never gets corrected, and is liable to burst forth suddenly in a moment of un-awareness. (Jung, 1977, p.76)

He also says that 'it is quite within the bounds of possibility for a man to recognise the relative evil of his nature, but is a rare and shattering experience for him to gaze into the face of absolute evil' (p.10). I suspect that if it were possible to gaze into the face of absolute good, the experience would be just as shattering. Most of us are neither villains nor saints and our views and values can only be relative, which is, perhaps, just as well if we are to get on with each other and remain on the safe side of sanity and the law.

Salvation, in Jung's view, lies in what he called 'The Transcendent Function', through which the opposites of good/evil, life/death can be reconciled: 'awareness of the shadow means suffering the tension between good and evil in full consciousness, and through that suffering they can be *transcended*' (Stevens, 1982, p.241). But how?

Some of us, some of the time, can 'take a step back' or 'rise above' our blinkered, ego-centred attitudes. But Jung tells us that the transcendent function can only work through symbols. I am reminded of Ernest Becker, whom I quoted in my first chapter. He describes the human dilemma as conflict between our instinctual and symbolic natures or, one might say, body and soul. The only solution he can offer is to live partially – that is, to compromise. 'Men are not built to be gods'. Jung, more optimistically, insists that transcendence is possible.

We need symbols in order to move between the poles of our dual nature and open up communication between conscious and unconscious ways of being. If we attend to our dreams and also to our fantasies, symbols will arise spontaneously, as though 'invented' by the unconscious in answer to our conscious problems. They will affect us personally and yet be recognisably archetypal, as, for instance, the wholeness of the mandala or the fourfold pattern of the cross that holds and unites the polar opposites. Symbols transcend time and conflict. They belong neither to one side nor the other and cannot be pulled to either extreme.

Marie-Louise von Franz (1987), who worked closely with Jung, elucidates how symbols work in our lives. She writes about:

> that strange capacity of the unconscious psyche to transform and guide the human being, who has been blocked in a situation, into a new one. Whenever human life gets stuck and arrives at a shore from which it cannot proceed, the transcendent function brings healing dreams and fantasies which construct on the symbolic level a new way of life which suddenly takes shape and leads to a new situation. (p.224)

But a person without any capacity for symbolism may be quite dangerously impoverished, not least because human instinct is less sure than that of other animals and is not by itself a reliable guide through life.

Murder in Mind

Those who commit murder act out our shadows for us. We may be innocent but not, perhaps, totally without complicity. We find ourselves murmuring 'there but for the grace of God go I', a popular saying, almost a superstition, like touching wood to prevent catastrophe. As humans, we are able to have fantasies and perform symbolic acts but sometimes these are not enough and only concrete fact is real. It is not always true that murderers are incapable of fantasy but, for some, the impulse to act is too strong for the imagination to contain and, if the shadow is sufficiently unconscious, this hidden side of the self can become dangerously out of control.

Ruth Rendell, in her book, *The Reason Why: an Anthology of the Murderous Mind*, explores the feelings that lead people to commit murder, the passions and terrors which turn a sordid event into something compulsively fascinating. No one coming into contact with Crippen found him hateful. Even those with least reason to praise him enjoyed his company and had warm feelings towards him. His behaviour in prison, while awaiting execution, was exemplary. There have been many examples of murderers who are friendly, likeable people. The may be highly intelligent, adaptable and creative. But, often, their family backgrounds turn out to be dysfunctional, with evidence of abuse, alcoholism, drug addiction and psychiatric illness.

Some of the most repellent murders have been done out of loneliness and to prevent a chosen companion – or the companion's body, even when turning into a corpse – getting up and walking away. Denis Nilsen recorded such an experience in a piece he called *The Psychograph*. This was a fictionalised account of his first killing. He had picked up a boy for sex and spent the night in bed with him. As dawn approached, he became overcome with panic. All he could think about was that this boy of his dreams would abandon him as so many others, in the same circumstances, had already done. Threatened by an unbearable loneliness, he realised that the only way to keep him was to kill him. Somehow he mustered what seemed a super-human energy and was able to smother the boy to death, thereby making sure that he would stay passively beside him and never walk away.

In such bizarre cases as Nilsen – and many others come to mind, such as Jeffrey Dahmer who feasted on his victims' flesh – we do not easily identify with a universally shared shadow. Many other explanations for murderous actions have been produced and there is probably some truth in all of them. The nature/nurture argument is brought up regularly. Does the evil lie in the genes or in a brutal infancy? What part is played by group mores and social conditioning? Is there some lack, like a hole, in the personality, a total absence of warmth and fellow feeling? Or is there, as already mentioned, a lack of symbolic capacity and the triumph of concretism?

James Hillman (1996), a rather surprising Jungian (or post-Jungian) writer, believes the murderer has a demonic call and this is just as compelling as the vocation of the artist or mystic: 'Transgression as transcendence; lifted out of your circumstances, filled with the power or the "glamour", and in touch with the transcendent origin of the calling urge' (p.235). He disagrees with conventional ways of preventing crime. The daimon in the demon needs to be respected. Evil cannot be ousted by whatever we mean by 'good'. What we need to address is the demon's 'single track obsession', its literalism and repeat performance of the same action. The actor needs to be introduced to more meaningful rituals than those on offer from the prison service or from mind-numbing drugs. Hillman is vehemently against innocence as a virtue, describing it as 'America's mystical cloud of unknowing', and we find him coming back to shadow projections: 'We are not forgiven simply by virtue of not knowing what we do. To wrap ourselves round in the Good – that is the American dream, leaving place for the evil nightmare only in the "other", where it can be diagnosed, treated, prevented and sermonised about' (p.247). This diatribe is aimed both at the killers and those who either punish or attempt to cure them. I see it as a plea for more understanding, for less pride in innocence and for as much conscious knowledge as is humanly possible. But, says Ted Bundy, serial killer and also law and psychology graduate, 'If anybody's looking for pat answers, forget it. If there were, the psychiatrists would have cleared this up years ago' (Williams, 1991, p.85).

Forensic Psychotherapy

At a time when politicians tend to favour harsher punishments for offenders as the only effective treatment, it is heartening to discover a strong impetus on the part of psychotherapists and psychiatrists towards exploring and understanding the criminal mind.

Compassion for victims has always been encouraged and it is usual today to offer short-term counselling to survivors of rape and violent crime through the organisation called 'Victim Support'. But neither the criminal justice system nor the general public are so enthusiastic about humane treatment of the guilty. They are also slow to recognise that victims may, in their turn, become perpetrators of the same crimes that they managed to survive. Psychiatric and legal specialists incline towards different values.

Specialist training in Forensic Psychotherapy has a very recent history and is a phenomenon of the 1990s. The training is based at the Portman Clinic, whose roots go back to 1931 when a group of psychoanalysts came together 'to promote a better way of dealing with criminals than putting them in prison' (Welldon, 1997, p.14). Sixty years later, in 1991, The International Association for Forensic Psychotherapy was at last established, incorporating the clinic's original aims.

If treatment is to succeed, there needs to be a professional team, which may include psychologists, social workers, nurses, occupational therapists and administrators, as well as the psychotherapist and consultant psychiatrist responsible for the individual concerned. Instead of the therapist heroically coping alone and in private, with little or no outside support, treatment is within the health service and the team members in regular contact with each other so that ideas about aims and progress can be fruitfully shared. Rules of confidentiality may have to be more flexible than in the private sector, particularly when a member of the team might be exposed to danger. Information about non-attendance, violent acting out or possibilities of re-offending are discussed for the sake of mutual support; how much or how little is up to each team member's discretion. It is as well to tell the patient right from the beginning that some of what he says may be passed on.

Working with Murderers

> Working in forensic settings, one is soon struck by the uncanny power and primitive fascination that the murderer exerts over those around him: it is impossible to banish the sense that the killer has crossed a line that demarcates a profound, irrevocable difference. (Taylor, 1997, p.103)

In the clinical situation such fascination makes for an uneasy counter-transference. The therapist respects the line of demarcation, perhaps to the extent of wanting to exaggerate the difference, rather than recognising that the patient, in acting from his own shadow, has dared to transcend those limits which we impose and which have been imposed on us through the conventions of our various upbringings so that our murderousness explodes only in dreams and waking fantasies. The therapist may even envy the patient for having done the unthinkable, for having gone over the edge of acceptable behaviour and stayed alive – feeling enriched, perhaps, and made *more* alive by the victim's death.

But if the line has been crossed once, might it not happen again? The therapist needs to look out, in a practical way, for his or her own safety and, in doing so, make things safer for the patient. By containing our fears, we are more likely to become reliable containers for our patients, receiving and hoping to neutralise their savage projections.

Besides being impressed by the murderer's power over life and death, the therapist will be aware, even at the assessment stage, of empathic feelings towards the patient. It is the lack of essential containment as a helpless child that has led him to act on his unrestrained impulses. Invariably, there has been a history of neglect, deprivation and, probably, abuse. He (or she) is also traumatised by the crime itself, perhaps to the extent of producing a temporary psychosis. Certainly, the crime is often forgotten since the guilt, if not repressed, would be unbearable. Guilt is an important theme. The child of

SUDDEN DEATH   85

abusive parents hangs on to the illusion that they must be good and, therefore, it is he who has to be bad. The offender, later in life, can dispense with some of this guilt only if, at the trial, he gets the punishment that he thinks he deserves. He may feel uncomfortable with anything less severe.

A psychiatric diagnosis has to be made and a report prepared for the court, with recommendations about the prisoner's 'health care disposal' – which is jargon for what the judge decides should be done with the convicted person. Psychotherapy may have begun when the prisoner is on remand, but only as part of the assessment procedure and, therefore, with no promise for the future. After the trial the murderer may become a 'lifer' and, on the basis of the psychiatric report, referred, or not, for psychotherapy. Contra-indications could be the (sometimes very real) danger of a re-enactment which is not symbolic and the patient's failure to own a frightening aspect of himself without retaliation in the transference against his original abusers.

Beginning a life sentence, or any prolonged imprisonment, is obviously stressful. Family and friends are cut off, as is the freedom to move about in the world. Horizons shrink and, despite the routines of meals, work and exercise, there are stretches of time when there is not much to do other than contemplation of self and the crime committed. I have already mentioned guilt, but not the defence mechanisms of splitting and projective identification that operate with particular force to ward off these painful feelings – hence the almost universal resentment felt by prisoners towards their custodians. Kleinian theory becomes particularly meaningful when applied to the 'us' and 'them' culture of prisons. Bad parts of the self are disowned and projected onto staff members, who, in turn, are split into the really hateful and those who can perhaps be seduced into granting favours. This splitting into 'good' and 'bad' is a way of protection against loss or emotional inadequacy. As patients, these prisoners find it intensely difficult to admit to vulnerability and, knowing that their defences will be challenged, may try to avoid therapy altogether. Therapy with a murderer is risky in various ways. The therapist – who is not a custodian but someone who sits and listens without judgement – can be seduced into colluding with the patient's good/bad view of the world. Alternatively, by putting just one foot wrong, the therapist can become a persecuting parent and give rise to a re-enactment of murderous rage. It takes courage as well as skill to steer one's way between the Scylla and Charybdis of the patient's divided world and to emerge as neither persecutory nor malleable.

The therapist sets out to heal the splits by gradually revealing to the patient the poverty of his enclosed and paranoid psyche. There is a need to make linkages between extremes and, in Kleinian terminology, to reach the depressive position, thereby building a capacity to tolerate depressive anxiety and have a realistic concern for others. If this position can be sustained, without relapse, there is hope of destructive tendencies becoming integrated with altruistic concern and of part objects coming together to make whole persons. The work may be long and exhausting and can only be achieved by a careful working through in the transference of whatever childhood scenario triggered the patient's latent murderousness into action. Gradually, the holding power of the therapy sessions may foster some degree of trust, both in the therapist and, perhaps, in the institution itself as a safe and convenient container. Thus even if the patient's response to therapy is limited, he may at least be enabled to lead a more settled life within the prison environment.

Patricia Polledri (1997), writing in the *British Journal of Psychotherapy*, describes treating a prisoner in a regional secure unit on a pre-discharge ward. This was a man who had murdered his mother when he was 21. There was much discussion with her clinical team when setting up and planning the treatment but it was during his subsequent individual psychotherapy on a once-weekly basis that he was discovered to be a potential serial killer: 'In view of the index offence, my being a female therapist, and his claustrophobia having spent eight years in prison, the implications for treatment and transference were hard to predict, as it was a new experience from which to learn' (p.475).

The patient came from a broken home, his mother leaving him with a depressed father and, to his fury, returning every now and then. During adolescence he was heavily into LSD and amphetamines and admitted himself to a psychiatric hospital. He was discharged on the condition that he lived with his mother. His reaction was that he would rather kill himself. Instead, he stole a knife from her kitchen. His mother, after many rows, evicted him. He took drugs and drank in the pub till dark. He then rang the bell and decapitated his mother on the doorstep. He remembered killing chickens in the same way.

His therapist found herself making links in the transference with his childhood and with his behaviour leading up to the murder. She was uneasy. Leaving him for a three-week Christmas holiday, she identified with the mother who had evicted him in December after he had been released into her care in October. Therapy with this patient had started in October, so these were significant anniversaries. During the Christmas break he visited his mother's grave. He then dreamed of being in the coffin and inside his mother's skull. He woke screaming. This was a few hours before his first session in the new year.

He would lurk in the corridors of the unit, just as he had waited for dark to murder his mother. He would also walk past his therapist's window, as if needing to know that she was there. She wondered 'whether this behaviour was some indication of a gradual internalisation of a non-delinquent therapist who clarified his reality sense' (p.480).

The crux came when he had planned (and was allowed parole) to go on a mountaineering trip with his father and his father's fiancée, whom he knew and liked. News had come through of an accident in the Alps. The therapist had a fantasy that her patient might rig an accident and get rid of the fiancée before her marriage to his father. The expedition was to begin on a Friday, the same day of the week as his mother's murder. He came to the next session 'dressed to kill' in commando outfit, wearing a beret. He told the therapist that he had worn a beret to kill his mother. He asked if there was double-glazing (sound proofing) on the windows. The therapist thought that he had killing in mind – or was it fantasy? The expedition was called off and the patient was hurt that anyone had suspected him of wanting to harm his father's fiancée, yet he also admitted to feelings of relief.

Polledri's paper was written during the first few months of treatment, so it was not possible to do more than speculate about the outcome. Her hope would have been to enable a change in 'his primitive perception of his mother as "Satan's dog" and "the devil's jackal"' (p.437). There did seem to be a change in the way he interacted with her in the sessions. In the language of Object Relations it was as though he had begun to relate to her as a 'whole' rather than a 'part' object.

Caecilia Taylor (1997), in her contribution to a book on Forensic Psychotherapy, describes how a young man suddenly erupted into one of the classrooms of his old school, brandishing knives and threatening the teacher. He forced the children to line up against the wall and started to stab them. The teacher managed to summon help and the police were called, but he had already stabbed one girl to death. In prison, a few days later, he remembered nothing beyond sitting and drinking the night before the killing. He had to ask the police what he had done. During his first psychotherapy session he came across as calm and seemingly unconcerned.

In a drinking bout before the murder he had written a suicide note. He drank to get courage to kill himself: 'My patient knew that his ability to keep his violent impulses within the realm of the imagination was wearing thin – hence the development of an idea related to the flip-side of the coin of being victimiser: that of becoming the victim of his own suicide as a solution' (p.105). But, instead, he attacked the school children as symbols of his victim-self. There had been a re-awakening of the repressed pain of his mother abandoning him during his first year at secondary school. Coming across a school report of that date had pushed him into this violent acting-out with himself as perpetrator.

It was difficult for him to decide what to plead at his trial. How could he feel responsible for a crime that he could not remember committing? 'At the core of his being he did not feel as though he had' (p.109). He also shrank from a plea of 'diminished responsibility' because that would mean he was 'mad'. Eventually, his awareness of needing help led him to agree to psychotherapy in hospital instead of serving a conventional prison sentence.

Drinking, forgetting and intending suicide seem to be frequent accompaniments to these unpremeditated murders.

I have a first-hand account by a counsellor working in an open prison. Although 'lifers' do sometimes serve the last period of their sentence in this freer environment, it had seemed unlikely that any of them would ask for her services. She was one of a team of volunteers, with varying experiences of counselling but without any specialised forensic training, who came together under the auspices of the prison chaplaincy. They had an outside supervisor as their only support.

Steve presented himself for counselling having already served 13 years of his sentence. He seems to have opened up easily to his counsellor, describing an unhappy childhood in a family of four children whose parents left them every evening to go out clubbing and drinking. Steve was bullied by the others and described himself as the 'runt of the litter' and the family 'scapegoat'. At 18 he escaped to join the Army and was sent overseas. At first the life seemed to suit him and he enjoyed driving heavy vehicles, though he complained about the length of his duties, which often amounted to 36 hours at a stretch. One night he stopped to rest in a lay-by and was caught and punished. With his morale at a low ebb, he began to drink. He said that it was almost impossible for squaddies not to drink as it is so crucial to acceptance and conviviality. But he was not used to it. He found a girlfriend, who worked in the camp, but, because of language difficulties, she left him for a local man. So he tried to make her jealous by dating her best friend.

One night he took her friend home and she invited him in. Steve remembers the journey to her house and how she undressed and seduced him. They made love and he fell asleep. He was very drunk. He woke next morning and found that she was dead. He went back to the camp and went to bed. Later that day he was arrested.

At his court martial he was not convincingly defended and had nothing to say for himself except that he could not believe that he had killed the girl. He was discharged from the Army and sent home to England unescorted. It never occurred to him to try and escape. He went straight to the police and gave himself up. He had no help from his family, who did not want anything to do with him. The charge was murder, not, as might have been expected, commuted to manslaughter. He was convicted and given a mandatory 15 years. No memory came back of the crime and he was too honest to tell any story except that he had forgotten how or why it had happened.

By the time Steve met his counsellor he was soon due to be released. So it was a shock suddenly to find himself re-categorised as a sex-offender and sent to a secure prison in a different part of the country. This was part of a drive by the Conservative government to take a tougher line in fighting crime and to be seen as protecting the public from 'dangerous' men. Steve had to go through what seemed to him an endless series of parole boards, visitors' boards and psychiatric assessments, with piles of written reports and a succession of different people interviewing him. He was made to undergo a course of group therapy for sex-offenders, which he felt bore no relevance to his situation. He actually missed out on the useful preparation for re-entering working life after 18 years inside which would have been available to him at the open prison. Released at last, he still has to attend a course laid on for him by the probation service to prevent him re-offending and finds this pointless. During the long years in prison he took advantage of every available opportunity for further education, became a Christian and got married. He shows no sign of being a violent person.

His counsellor has maintained contact and has been able at least to be consistent in her relationship with him, to give him a sense of continuity and to support him in his transition from prison to the world outside. She maintains that murderers tend not to be habitual criminals but are often driven to one-off offences by unbearable emotional burdens.

To quote Murray Cox, who used Shakespeare to prompt the forensic psychotherapist into understanding the mind of the murderer: 'It can be stated with incontrovertible certainty that there is no single uniform intrapsychic constellation which holds true for all offender patients who kill. There is no ubiquitous psychopathology of homicide' (Cox and Theilgaard, 1994, p.389). And he gives us this passage from *Julius Caesar:*

> Between the acting of a dreadful thing
> And the first motion, all the interim is
> Like a phantasma, or a hideous dream;
> The genius and the mortal instruments
> Are there in council; and the state of man,
> Like to a little kingdom, suffers then
> The nature of an insurrection.

Julius Caesar, II, 1, 63

This is a description of Brutus' inner world before taking part in the murder of Caesar, who had believed him to be a loyal friend. It is also universal in that it gives us a glimpse of the intrapsychic disturbance which is likely to affect all killers. Whether or not there is lasting amnesia, as in Steve's case, 'Time seems to be suspended, and the contemplation of the act has an imperative force which prevails over external reality' (Cox and Theilgaard, 1994, p.390).

Murder remains the ultimate crime, but even the most virtuous of law-abiding citizens must have experienced some hint of the 'hideous dream', however forceful their capacity for repression. 'There but for the grace of God....' go all of us.

Capital Punishment – The Outcasts

In Britain the death penalty was abolished in 1965, the government of the day having at last come to the conclusion that the threat of being executed was not a deterrent. Since then a vociferous minority has clamoured for its restitution but, to most citizens, the possibility of mistakenly hanging an innocent person is enough in itself to outlaw the ultimate punishment. So it comes as a shock to learn that the penalty still exists for 'high treason, piracy and on the military penal code'. Tony Blair wants total abolition, in order to comply with the European Human Rights.

There is some evidence that executions may actually boost the murder rate. In the USA research has shown an increase of killings in those States that abolished, and later resumed, the penalty, thus validating Bernard Shaw's dictum: 'It is the deed that teaches not the name we give it. Murder and capital punishment are not opposites that cancel one another, but similars that breed their kind'.

The USA is the only NATO country that still executes its citizens. This applies particularly to the southern States, and, notoriously, to Texas, which has the highest number of prisoners held on Death Row, waiting, sometimes for years, either to be killed or reprieved. California is not far behind, using the same gas, Zyklon B, that the Nazis used at Auschwitz. Most of the other States have adopted lethal injection. But neither method ensures instantaneous death. There seems to be a general tendency to reinstate capital punishment after periods of liberality, the self-righteous 'us' distancing themselves from the terrifying 'them', who are sometimes black, and in whom is lodged the cultural shadow.

A friend of mine has let me see her correspondence with a Death Row prisoner to whom she is a 'pen friend'. Letter-writing is not necessarily second-best as a means of befriending. Three or four pages, once a month, can be re-read and mulled over, as well as being looked forward to. It is unlikely that these prisoners will have any other form of therapy. Clergy of various denominations are there to attend to spiritual needs but prisoners do not welcome their help, which may be seen as part of the Establishment, the 'us' side of the great divide, with the aim of keeping prisoners quiet through turning to Jesus and giving up the fight to get their sentences reversed. On the other hand, those who write to the prisoners do have a counsellor to contact should they find the correspondence distressing.

Reading these letters, I get some idea of the wretchedness of life on one of these Death Rows. Gary, now in his fifties, was convicted in 1990 for a murder to which he has never admitted: 'You probably think that everybody here claims to be not guilty, but that really isn't the case. I will always be honest in anything that I say to you ... If you really want to know what it is like in here, I'll try to tell you ... But it certainly isn't very nice'.

Gary spends a lot of his time engaged on 'legal work' – that is, submitting his case to the Court of Criminal Appeal, at first without a lawyer and later with one who appears not to bother over much on his behalf. At first he was hopeful but, as the years go by, he has become increasingly embittered. He seems to have a good case. The crime was armed robbery, resulting in the death of more than one person, but there was no physical evidence, such as blood or finger-prints, to implicate Gary. He claims that his conviction was obtained through the perjury of a so-called accomplice, who was given a lighter sentence as a result of testifying against him. 'While I have done a lot of wrong in my life, that wrong never included killing anyone'. Gary's most treasured possession is his typewriter. He is highly literate and a fluent letter writer, as well as keeping himself thoroughly informed on legal matters. He has now been on Death Row for a number of years, during which time many of his friends have been executed and others reprieved at the last moment. One of these had already been strapped down, with the injection ready. He was reprieved but executed at a later date. Gary cares a lot for these friends, who share with him a life lived every day on the edge of death.

A letter, written on Christmas Day, is full of rage, as he describes the killing of his friend, Charlie, 'not a dangerous man. In fact, he was a gentle man, and he would share anything he had with others'. Gary comments that the other prisoners took Charlie's death very much to heart: 'Most of the anger and bitterness is due to him being murdered by the corrupt system ... and also because of the Death Row chaplain assisting in the killing ... My opinion is the preacher was there to antagonise and torment him one last time'.

From information passed on through the sister who witnessed Charlie's execution, Gary is able to describe what happened in the death chamber. He blames the chaplain for holding Charlie down with his 'slimy hands' while he struggled to finish his final statement. Gary feels nothing but hatred and rage for the 'preachers' and refuses to believe in their ministry: 'I don't see how the ones we have in here have anything to do with Christianity, or belief in God. The ones we have are the most evil people there are'. That is Gary's opinion. Some of the chaplains care very much for the prisoners and must suffer considerable anguish when they see them die.

One of Gary's letters was written on the back of a list of forthcoming executions. It was a long list of names and dates, each entry with the letter W, B or H for white, black or Hispanic. It was chilling to realise that this was not a rota for duties or interviews but appointments with death.

Writing to his friend in England, Gary is aware of her freedom and the differences between her life and his but he has no resentment and takes an interest in her family, her travels and walks in the countryside. He often says 'thank you for your wonderful letters'. He has very little contact with his relatives and hardly ever has visitors. He writes:

> I've got to stop gazing out at the picnic table area where the population prisoners get visits on the week-ends. It makes me feel really strange,

maybe lonely, to watch them hugging their visitors hello and goodbye ... That, plus all the little kids, or some of the guys holding little babies. Not that I'm jealous of them or anything like that. I'm glad they have contact visits, but it kind of highlights the different ways those of us here on Death Row are treated ... It has quite an effect on me. It would be great just to sit at one of those picnic tables.

One can sense his longing to be touched instead of being treated as a sort of sub-human pariah. Visitors on Death Row can only be seen with a metal and glass barrier between them and the prisoner. One wonders – if Gary gets his freedom at last – how he will cope with the world after being locked away all these years and what help he will get to channel his rage in any way that can be constructive.

Gary's letters show us a warm, sentient human being. Questions of guilt or innocence seem to me to have surprisingly little relevance when it comes to how he, and others like him, get treated by other human beings. With the issue of human rights so prominent in today's politics, it hardly seems believable that such abuses can be perpetrated in the name of justice, not only in the third world but in a country so prosperous and seemingly advanced as the USA.

But I must not let myself feel smug. I know that English prisons are shockingly overcrowded, understaffed and, often, insanitary. It is probably only since we stopped killing our murderers that we have begun to concentrate not just on punishment but rehabilitation. Forensic psychotherapy is still new and there must be many lifers whom it fails to reach, but, that it happens at all, gives hope of a changing attitude. The late Murray Cox brought Shakespeare to Broadmoor and showed how, in a secure psychiatric hospital, there may be possibilities, through imaginative mingling of theatre and therapy, of tapping into the creative potential of the most violently disturbed criminals. His sensitivity and respect for individuals is worlds away from the degradation of Death Row.

There is no reason for complacency. Gitta Sereny's *Cries Unheard, The Story of Mary Bell*, gives us a serious critique of the British judicial sustem and an exploration of why and how children like Mary are driven to kill. The title, 'Cries unheard' speaks for 'the thousands of children who are in prisons in Europe and America for crimes they committed, not because of what they are, but because of what, unheard, they were made to be' (Sereny 1991, p.xx).

Mary co-operated with the author because she wanted her story told. The cathartic hours in which Sereny listened and questioned her, both about the murders and her own horrifyingly abusive childhood, seem to have been the closest Mary ever came to psychotherapeutic treatment. Sereny has no professional training in psychotherapy, but has more experience than most therapists in getting to know the criminal mind. In the case of Mary Bell, she waited many years for the chance to hear the girl's own account of what drove her to murder her two small victims. Sereny was in touch with two psychiatrists, one of whom was so concerned about the 'unrelenting intensity' of the sesions that she advised her to give them up. The other, Professor Dan Bar-On, from Israel, urged her to continue because, he said, Mary 'urgently needs to say it' (p.348).

Mary's mother, Betty, was a prostitute and, later, an alcoholic. She lived with Billy, who was not Mary's biological father, though she used to think he was and called him 'Dad'. When she was born, Betty, in front of her horrified sisters, said 'take this thing away from me'. Her attitude to Mary was always 'look what you're doing to me' and how could she bring such shame on the family, though she was forever contacting the press and offering Mary's story for money – often successfully. Billy was kind to Mary but often away from home, sometimes in prison for burglary.

During the sessions with Sereny early memories of abuse emerged bit by bit; some were so horrific that Mary was asked to repeat them several times. She spoke in a monotonous voice, through desperate sobs, often in the present tense. At an early age – she thought about four or five – she had been made to witness Betty's antics with a variety of men. Then, to an accompaniment of laughter, she was blind-folded (playing Blind Man's Buff) and tied up with something round her face to keep her mouth open for a man to insert his penis and ejaculate. Afterwards, she would be sick.

During the murder trial no enquiries were made about Mary's background.

Telling Sereny about the two boys she had killed was hardest of all: "'I don't know if I can'" (p.348). She gave eight different versions. During her imprisonment, she denied killing either of the boys although she admitted on one occasion that she was present when Martin died as the result of an accident. To Sereny, to whom she first told three versions, she finally admitted killing both boys.

> I'm not angry. It isn't a feeling … it is a void that comes … happens … opens … it's an abyss … It's like a light being switched off without your

knowing it's on ... Now I'm ... looking back, I feel an element of panic in me which wasn't there, but which, as an adult, I imagine to be there. (p.350)

Only now, grown up and with a child of her own, can she realise the enormity of what she has done and that the guilt will always be with her.

Eventually, she admitted to killing the second boy, Brian. Of the two friends, she knows that she was the stronger but Norma's weakness had spurred her on. She admitted to trying, unsuccessfully, to cut off Brian's penis with a razor blade. Then she denied it. Sereny had recorded it on tape and played it back to her. She described it now, using adult words, as 'symbolically castrating, taking away the offending organ' (p.354), which, in view of what she had suffered earlier, made sense.

In these talks Mary recalled the fantasies, shared with Norma, that led to the killings, each daring the other to do their worst. She was used to crime and lying to the police to protect 'Dad' (Billy). In her family, authority of any kind was seen as an enemy. She called herself a 'dare me' child who imagined 'being in a sort of Jesse James gang, you know, ride a horse and break someone out of prison by wrapping a rope round the bars' (p.42). This fantasy was fed by watching Westerns on TV with Billy.

Describing the murder trial in 1968, Sereny stresses how unprepared the two girls had been for the solemnity of the occasion and the crowds who attended, the ceremony provoking them to nervous laughter. As for the proceedings: 'for nine days, two incomprehensible languages would be spoken in that ancient chamber' (p.34). Norma was thirteen, Mary was just eleven, having killed Martin the day before her birthday and Brian nine weeks later. The girls were assessed as knowing the difference between right and wrong, as if that were a straightforward question in a family like Mary's. With no experience of anyone dying, except on TV, there can be difficulty, even as late as eleven, in experiencing death as a permanent state. 'Both children seemed unaware of the nature or gravity of the crime – the finality of death' (p.64), even though, talking about it years later, Mary said she had been certain they would send her to the gallows, an image that must have come from a movie or from something she had read.

When convicted, she went to a secure unit where there was no psychiatric care but an understanding headmaster, 'the first honourable adult she could respect and love' (p.xvi). Her intelligence was recognised and plans made for higher education. But, at 16, in accordance with the judicial system, Mary was removed, despite the protests of her mentor, to be punished in a prison of maximum security – where she was to fight for seven years against institutionalisation and lose most of what she had gained in a more congenial environment. She was finally released at 23, an emotionally disturbed young adult, to cope, under a new and unfamiliar name, with an unforgiving world. With the help of the probation service and, in due course, a sympathetic partner, one can hope she may be able to battle through to something like normal family life – if only the media will allow it.

Suicide

Laurence Van der Post (1982), writing about Japan, describes a favourite place for suicide much frequented by couples frustrated in love: 'It was so common indeed that at one time notices were posted in the valley below requesting "honourable suicides" to leave their names and addresses with the police … "It would greatly help the authorities in communicating with the relatives afterwards"' (p.247). The place described was a beauty spot above a waterfall, the perfect setting for a honeymoon with death. To the Japanese, it would seem that 'death not life was the ultimate romance' (p.143).

In England, too, we have favourite places for suicide but the attitude is different. At Beachy Head and the Clifton Suspension Bridge there are notices bidding any potential suicide to call the Samaritans. A public telephone box is situated nearby. Suicide, in our culture, is more shameful than honourable.

The history of Western civilisation embraces a variety of attitudes. In classical Greece the magistrates kept a supply of hemlock for those who wanted to die. Among the stoics, the question was not whether one should kill oneself but how to do it with dignity. To quote Seneca's famous exhortation:

> Foolish man, what do you bemoan, and what evil do you fear? Wherever you look, there is an end of evils. You see that yawning precipice? It leads to liberty. You see that flood, that river, that well? Liberty houses with them … Your neck, your throat, your heart are so many ways to escape from slavery … Do you enquire the road to freedom? You shall find it in every vein of your body. (Alvarez, 1972, pp.54–5)

The Romans had no concept of human life being sacred. Gladiatorial combat, fought to the death, theatre with real-life criminals as victims, Christians devoured by wild animals – all these were popular entertainment as important as football and television have become in our own culture.

The early Christians took over the Roman attitude but with the variation that death was a gateway to a better life and to seek it by martyrdom ensured eternal glory, whereas this 'vale of tears' was full of temptation to sin, which, if not resisted, barred the way to heaven: 'Why then live unredeemed when heavenly bliss is only a knife stroke away?' (Alvarez, 1972, p.59). There was no shortage of martyrs. They pursued their suicidal ends with a dedication that has been applauded in churches for two millennia. I remember being brought up on these daunting stories and shuddering secretly at my own unwillingness to join the martyr throng, should this ever be demanded. There was no way I would commit suicide for Jesus.

When Christianity was accepted by Constantine and no more martyrs were needed, suicide was condemned as a sin against nature: 'An act which, during the first flowering of Western civilisation, had been tolerated, later admired, and later still sought as the supreme mark of zealotry, became finally the object of intense moral revulsion' (Alvarez, 1972, p.63).

This attitude persisted through mediaeval times. In the sixteenth and seventeenth centuries suicide was still considered to be so shameful that the corpse was dragged through the streets, hung on a gibbet and buried at a crossroads with a stake to pin it down so that its ghost would not haunt the living. The suicide's property was confiscated and could not be inherited.

Until as late as 1961, suicide was a crime and anyone who attempted it unsuccessfully could be sent to prison. The phrase 'while the balance of the mind was disturbed' was used as protection against a law which deprived the dead person of the right to a religious burial or the bequeathing of property.

Since the Renaissance, there have been opinions voiced about the individual's right to suicide, notably by philosophers. The Church maintained its hard and fast attitude, though with decreasing confidence, and it is unlikely today that Christian burial would ever be denied. The modern attitude has shifted from sin to psychiatry. The problem is no longer moral but social. Suicide is generally regarded as something we should try and prevent. The question is how and by whom?

The Samaritans

When Chad Varah started the movement in 1953 by publicising the tele-phone number of an inner-city church, he saw himself as a professional counsellor and did not immediately realise that his untrained helpers who manned the telephone and made coffee were often just as effective in helping the callers as he was himself. Rather than becoming a suicide prevention service, the Samaritans developed a way of befriending that depended not on professional skills but on the sharing of a common humanity and, above all, an ability to listen. Fundamental to the tenets that evolved as the movement grew was respect for the rights of the individual caller. There was to be no interference of any kind if that was not what the caller wanted, no preaching of religious doctrine, no imposition of the listener's own ideas and, in fact, no actual counselling, even of a non-directive nature.

I am not the only psychotherapist who started my present career as a Samaritan, ready to 'be there' in a crisis, often with severely disturbed people. Later, as I launched into a professional training, there was nothing to *unlearn* but a sound basis on which to build.

The Psychology of Suicide

Not all suicides are pathological. Some are even heroic, as, for instance, that of Captain Oates, the explorer, who walked out to die in an Antarctic blizzard, hoping to save the lives of his companions. Others, less altruistic but wholly rational, decide, when faced with intractable pain and inevitable death, to accelerate their passing in a voluntary and, perhaps, more dignified manner. Arthur Koestler committed suicide in 1983. At the last minute, his wife, for her own reasons, joined him. When discovered, the room was described as a scene of calmness. Some months earlier, Koestler had written his explanation and left it behind him as a suicide note:

> My reasons for deciding to put an end to my life are simple and compelling: Parkinson's disease and the slow-killing variety of Leukaemia (CCL) ... After a more or less steady decline over the last years, the process has now reached an acute state with added complications which make it advisable to seek self-deliverance now before I become incapable of making the necessary arrangements. (Voluntary Euthanasia Society, 1992, pp.46–7)

No one, I think, would consider the balance of Koestler's mind to have been disturbed.

Other, seemingly rational, motives for suicide might include loss of money, loss of face, loss of safety. One remembers the suicide epidemic on Wall Street during the great depression of the 1930s. It sounds reasonable enough to hear of English Jews in the last world war keeping loaded pistols to turn against themselves in case of invasion and that some of the Nazi leaders, during the Nuremberg trials, managed to take poison as preferable to being hanged by the allies. These are extreme examples. Where the alternative is not to be killed by someone else but to find some way of living with one's loss, the fact remains that numbers of people do choose to continue, even a much diminished life, rather than opting out altogether. The suicidal option seems, therefore, to have more to do with the character of the person concerned than with external circumstances.

In the literature of psychotherapy we find references to suicidal states of mind and speculation about what might cause these states, rather than the generalised diagnostic labels that belong to psychiatry and serve to facilitate a decision in favour of drugs or ECT. It is probably true that these invasive treatments save more lives than the 'talking cure' and it would be foolish to take an aggressive 'anti-psychiatry' attitude towards them, but those of us who listen and talk are not into life-saving at all costs and we respect those patients who come to us and talk, even though suicide may still prove to be their ultimate choice. Indeed, it is of enormous importance to some people that such a choice is possible, even though they may never act on it.

Freud (1984) links suicide with narcissism and struggles with the concept:

> So immense is the ego's self-love, which we have come to recognise as the primal state from which instinctual life proceeds, and so vast is the amount of narcissistic libido which we see liberated in the fear that emerges as a threat to life, that we cannot conceive how that ego can consent to its own destruction. (p.261)

Mourning does not get classed as pathological when it is clear who or what it is that is being mourned. In melancholia (known these days as depression or depressive illness) there is the same turning away from the outer world and, in Freud's words, here too there 'may be the reaction to the loss of the loved object' (p.253), but it is hard to see exactly what has been lost. This 'object' may not be known, even to the sufferer, since it is an unconscious loss: 'In mourning it is the world which has become poor and empty; in melancholia it is the ego itself' (p.254). Thus he accounts for the sufferer's impoverished feelings – guilt, unworthiness, self-hate. Freud maintained that, in such cases, there had originally been a failed relationship with another person (object) and, instead of this other object becoming the recipient of the sufferer's hate, the 'free libido' had been withdrawn into the ego which then became identified with the abandoned object, or, as Freud poetically puts it 'the shadow of the object fell upon the ego' (p.258). With regard to suicide, the shadow must be so strong that the ego treats itself as the object that has to be killed. The ego is overwhelmed by the object, just as it is, though in an opposite way, through the intensity of being in love.

Narcissism is much written about and discussed in analytical circles, whether they be Freudian or Jungian. The simple definition, based on the Greek myth of Narcissus, is 'self-love'. Classical Freudian theory distinguishes between the *primary narcissism* of the infant and the *secondary narcissism*, meaning love of self, which results from the identification and introjection just described. If narcissism is deemed pathological, where, one wonders, do we draw the line between healthy self-esteem and neurotic self (or ego) love? Jung, attacking Freud's reductive attitude to works of art, declared, slightly mockingly, that 'every man who pursues his own goals is a narcissist' (Jung, 1979, p.68). The narcissism that pushes people towards suicide suggests self-hate rather than love, and yet Freud himself made the connection. To understand the contradiction, it is worth studying the original myth.

Narcissus

Perhaps all we remember is the yearning, beautiful boy and his metamorphosis into a narcissus flower. What we seem easily to forget is that Narcissus *commits suicide*, either by wasting away, presumably through not eating (anorexia), or, in some versions, by stabbing himself to death. On a simple level, it is a moral tale of 'pride must have a fall' and conjures up for me memories of being rebuked for vanity as a child, especially for gazing in the mirror and admiring the beauty and blueness of my eyes.

Narcissus was the son of a blue nymph, ravished by a river god. All his life he was admired by all who saw him, leaving a trail of hopeless suitors in his wake. His doting mother consulted the blind seer, Teiresias, about his future. She was told that this perfect specimen of a son would have a long life, but only if he never got to know himself.

He was pursued by Echo but he rejected her because all she could do was reflect back to him his own thoughts. It was only his reflection in a pool of water that enchanted him. The only person (seemingly a person) whom he could love was his mirror image, which, try as he might, he could not catch and hold. As soon as he became aware that he was in love with himself, he realised that he was pining for something that already belonged to him and which would never satisfy him. 'Only death', writes Mario Jacoby (1993), 'can bring redemption' (p.11). Jacoby gives the myth a Jungian interpretation with emphasis on transformation, ending his chapter on a positive note: 'It seems to me, then, that our myth deals with the human drive for self-knowledge and self-realisation, with the admonition "Become who you are!" and thus it implies the possibility of transcending the narrower forms of narcissistic problems' (p.29).

That may be so, but only after a prolonged course of analysis or psychotherapy. What I would like to emphasise is the hopelessness and empty yearning experienced by so many narcissistic people, who, like their prototype Narcissus, may be driven to suicide through their inability to relate to a world outside themselves. And, assuming the aim of psychotherapy to be self-knowledge, I find myself disturbed by the prophecy of Teiresias and its implications.

It certainly seems that some people regard suicide as their destiny which, sooner or later, they will fulfil. Years ago, when I worked in the occupational therapy unit of a psychiatric hospital, a patient confided in me that since he was to be allowed home for the week-end, he would, on Saturday night, put his head in the gas oven. When I tried to remonstrate, he said: 'but my father and my grandfather did it. Can't you see, I have to do it?'. He then wanted a promise from me that I would keep his secret. I *did* tell, though not, as far as I remember, the right person, and when I came to work on Monday morning I heard that he had carried out his threat. I was scolded for my irresponsibility and felt genuinely sad because he was someone I had liked, and yet there was also just a hint of relief that his destiny had not been impeded. I was positive that any interference would have resulted only in postponement and that he was certain, eventually, to succeed.

'Suicide is a closed world with its own irresistible logic' (Alvarez, 1972, p.105). It becomes an obsession and the mind is cut off from any other kind of logic. Alvarez tells us how it feels from the inside, admitting at the end of his book that he is a failed suicide himself. Those 'destined' to kill themselves are impervious to argument. Often, they spend a life-time preparing meticulously for the last act, planning to make it perfect – like, for instance, the man who spent a relaxed afternoon with a friend's children before driving to a vertical cliff and making a perfect swallow dive over the edge.

When he was resuscitated from his own attempt, Alvarez felt that death had let him down:

> I had looked for something overwhelming, an experience that would clarify all my confusion ... I thought death would be a synoptic vision of life, crisis by crisis, all suddenly explained, justified, redeemed, a last Judgement in the

coils and circuits of the brain. Instead, all I got was a hole in the head, a round zero, nothing. I'd been swindled. (p.236)

He never tried again.

Anna Karenina

The word narcissism would not have been used in the time of Tolstoy, but the psychoanalyst, Neville Symington (1993), chooses one of Tolstoy's most famous characters to illustrate, among other things, the connection between narcissism and suicide. Symington does not believe that patients become narcissistic solely on account of severe trauma in childhood but because of their emotional response to the trauma. He bravely departs from the usual psychoanalytic language, especially that of drives and instincts, and concentrates 'unscientifically' on his own concept of what he calls the *'lifegiver'*, by which he means 'a mental object that the mind can opt for or refuse at a very deep level' (p.3). If, in Freudian terminology, narcissism develops when the libido takes itself as a love-object, there must be an alternative object which *could* have been taken. This object:

> is the mother, but it is also not the mother. Instead one has to posit the existence of an emotional object that is associated with the breast, associated with the mother, or in later life associated with the other person; it is *in* the other – an object that a person seeks as an alternative to seeking himself ... there has to be a turning to this object and this object has to be taken in. (p.35)

That is how he describes the *lifegiver,* that through which one initiates creative action and relationship with one's fellow human beings: 'The *lifegiver* is real and is essential to our mental life, in the same way that friendship is an essential ingredient of human happiness' (p.37).

Symington gives examples of refusing the *lifegiver.* The refusal starts in infancy but there is always a split. In order to survive at all, the *lifegiver* is necessary, but part of the infant repudiates it, resulting later in manipulative, instead of creative, behaviour. Symington shows us how Anna Karenina and her lover, Vronsky, can neither of them find their own creativity. Vronsky takes up painting but can only imitate other painters' styles and is envious, though outwardly disparaging, of a dedicated artist who paints with genuine inspiration. The narcissistic person denies envy but manages to get others to envy *him.* He thus avoids knowing himself with all his hating and destructive feelings. Such knowledge is always a risk. When Narcissus knew himself, he died.

Right through Anna's story, Tolstoy gives us glimpses of hope. But Anna wanted too much – respectability, a glamorous lover's lasting adoration and her beautiful child, in whom she saw nothing of her husband but only herself and for whom she was prepared to sacrifice nothing. I find, thanks to the author's skill, that Anna is manipulative. She invites our sympathy and makes us love her better than his other more deserving characters.

Before finally deciding on suicide, Anna went to see her best friend, Dolly, but only to talk about herself. 'Yes, I will tell Dolly everything ... It will be painful and humiliating but I'll tell her everything. She is fond of me and I will follow her advice' (Tolstoy, 1975, p.803). But she arrived to find Dolly and her sister, Kitty, occupied with Kitty's new baby. Anna took no interest in their conversation and did not stay long. '"How beautiful she is!" Kitty said when Anna had gone. "But there's something pitiful about her, terribly pitiful"' (p.806).

Anna was obsessed with one question: did Vronsky really love her? In the middle of her obsession she almost began to hate him. That might have been a turning point. Instead, she found herself on the railway platform, dazed at first but then knowing what she *had* to do. When it was too late there was a moment of regret, 'and for an instant life glowed before her with all its past joys'. But still she jumped and the train went over her. A bright light 'illuminating everything that before had been shrouded in darkness, flickered, grew dim, and went out for ever' (p.814).

Wendy

Wendy came to see me off and on over a period of three to four years. I say 'off and on' because, as well as breaking off therapy for several months in the middle, she frequently failed to turn up at the time expected. This would happen after suicide threats and she liked me to worry about her but could not always believe that I cared. She had turned away from life and felt she might as well kill herself. Talking to me was an effort. She hid behind her hair and started sentences which she could not finish, having forgotten what she wanted to say. Whenever she felt that I expected something, even that she should speak instead of being silent, she withdrew, determined to disappoint me. Any hints of my approval meant to her that I had expectations which she would find it impossible to fulfil. She was without hope, though she allowed me to do some hoping for her. I might hope but I must not expect.

Her favourite suicide fantasy was taking a box of pills to a quiet spot under trees. The branches were like protective arms. Trees were safe. They would not get up and walk away.

Her story was given to me in fragments but with recurring themes. Everything was blamed on her parents' divorce when she was nine. She described it as a great cut across her life, which had been on a downward slope ever since. Her favourite person was her grandmother, who poured out kindness and was like a fountain that never dried up. Other people's fountains always dried or else she sucked them dry, which was what she imagined doing to me. Her mother left her father and she used to cry and cry for him but could get no comfort from her mother as she had been the cause of the split. Then she changed the story and said that crying for father was an excuse and she only cried for herself. Mother married again and, from that time on, hatred of stepfather dominated Wendy's life. He married her mother for money, which he soon got through, sucking her dry.

Wendy saw her life as full of lost chances. There had been a moment when she should have screamed at her stepfather. It was too late now and her lack of action made her feel responsible for everything that had happened afterwards. If she was mad – and she knew that she had been labelled 'borderline' – her mother was madder. More children had been born, whom she thought she should have rescued but it was too late now. Sometimes, she had a grandiose confidence in her power over people's lives but usually she felt helpless and hopeless.

Her father lived alone and all he did was go to work, go to the pub, go to bed. She told him that his life was useless and he might as well commit suicide. How could she get up and live unless he showed some sign of life? She also had an older brother who was a bit more alive, but all three of them were withdrawn from each other, non-relating. Both families survived by each member propping the other up. If one prop were to be removed, the structure would collapse. Wendy felt locked into the propping situation and responsible for everyone. She cared about none of them except her grandmother, who was getting old and needed looking after. As well as sucking each other dry, she said that her mother had left her high and dry – complete freedom but no boundaries. No one had taught her how to live – she was stuck in a pre-birth stage.

After leaving me and coming back again, she at last managed a bit of hope in that when she first came into the room she thought something might be about to happen – a miracle, or a birth perhaps. But there was no magic and she went away disappointed. She said it was her fault that she was unable to live. Any attempt of mine at interpretation was powerfully resisted. She would just tell me I was wrong or missing the point.

I wondered about this so-called 'good time' before her parents divorced. She described her father tucking her up in bed. She anticipated my saying that this was a good memory and told me that he did it wrong, he tucked her up too tight. She said that even if life had been all wrong before the divorce, she might have made a better job of it by screaming at her stepfather. Then she tried to scream now, in the session with me, as if that was the miracle she wanted. But she never managed more than a whisper.

She missed a session but turned up on time for her next appointment and, at first, carried on without any explanation. Then she decided to tell me what had happened. She had taken a train and a paracetamol bottle. She had found a wood and decided to lie down and die under the trees. But she discovered that she had left her bag on the train with her name and address, and this meant she might be traced. She gave this as a reason for not committing suicide. I commented that she took the train at the time she was due to see me. She told me that she came home and burnt all her papers and bank card. Was that an aggressive act? I said that she was being aggressive towards me, to which she answered that she wasn't relating to me. 'Why d'you always think you're so important?' But she paid for the missed session and said she had enjoyed the freedom of paying for her time and using it to do something quite different. After all, it was her own time and why shouldn't she spend it how she liked. She thought she might also give up her job. She telephoned me the following week-end to thank me for both stopping her from suicide and from giving in her notice.

Externally, her life seemed to improve, though, even when she finally left me, I was aware and so was she of inner chaos and an inability to use either her talents or qualifications. With me, she went through a period of regression and being quite infantile, yet was able to survive the adult world outside my room. It was important to her that I too was a survivor, especially when she attacked me verbally and – just once – threatened physical violence, although this was done self-consciously and without spontaneity so that I was not really as afraid as she would have liked. She alternated right to the end between angry disappointment and affection, but communication had very much improved and there seemed to be more life in her. My feeling was that she would only kill herself if she already felt dead inside, in which case suicide would seem like a tidy way of completing the job.

Wendy suddenly turned up on my doorstep two or three years after our last session. We had a cup of tea together and communicated easily. There had been a suicide in the family and she thought that was enough and perhaps she needed to stay alive for the sake of the rest of them. She really seemed quite strong.

Looking back over the years, I wonder if my more mature experience would have added anything to the quality of our relating. My approach might have been based on a lot more theory and I might have done more interpreting, but I doubt if it would have made any difference to whether Wendy lived or died.

As it is, I hope she has managed to stay with the *lifegiver.*

Suicide, Psychotherapy and the Saving of Souls

Theology has its own language. Our bodies belong to God and are not ours to kill. Medicine is concerned with saving the body from death. James Hillman (1997), always provocative, explores suicide not only 'as an exit from life but also as an entrance to death' (p.11). He sees the practice of psychotherapy as a meeting of souls in which the body takes second place and argues the case for *non*-medical analysis, whose practitioners, unlike doctors, do not necessarily regard death as failure. An analyst is concerned with the individual meaning of a suicide. It is not his job to prevent it. He needs to speak to the soul in its own language and share the other person's inner mythology as it shows itself in dreams and fantasies. Hillman asserts that 'entering death releases the most profound fantasies of the human soul' (p.51). Because the meaning of death is largely unconscious to the person who is dying or deciding to die, the analyst can act as a mirror to understand and articulate what is happening without getting caught up in a mutually unconscious process with no reflections.

Psychology, says Hillman, has not paid enough attention to death. The natural sciences, including medicine, have seen death as an end-state, an entropy and decay. We can only look at human death from *outside* the experience, so cannot judge with any certainty what is natural or appropriate: 'We do not know at what point in a longevity curve each life is statistically supposed to enter death. We do not know what bearing time has on death. We do not know whether the soul dies at all' (p.58). He reminds us that we are dying right through life, each of us building our own deaths day by day. Death is the only human *a priori*. We live in order to die.

Suicide can be considered natural because it is an ever-present possibility, a choice open to us all. It is one way of entering death consciously, and this can be seen as a major human achievement. 'Until we can say no to life, we have not really said yes to it, but have only been carried along by its collective stream' (p.64). To be an individual, one needs to separate enough from the stream to make one's own choices about how to live and how to die.

Hillman refuses to see growth just as 'an additive process requiring neither sacrifice nor death' (p.68). There must be a death experience for life to change: 'Suicide is the attempt to move from one realm to another by force through death' (p.68). When there seems no other way for the soul to experience anything new, the choice may be for a hasty, if desperate, transformation. The soul already seems to have left the body behind to move about in the world 'like painted cardboard', indifferent and apathetic. To kill the body may seem the only way to set the soul free.

An experience of death may be necessary for the life of the soul but is *actual* suicide also necessary? And how should a psychotherapist react? Hillman sees the suicide threat as a confusion between inner and outer, between concrete and symbolic modes of being. By non-interference, the therapist allows the death experience. In doing this he is doing 'the most that can be done to prevent the actual death' (p.92). It is out of despair that transformation will most probably come about.

Non-interference is something that the Samaritans manage instinctively. Those too active, too eager to save life (of the body though not necessarily the soul), are discouraged from joining. Hillman's challenge is not *just* provocative but a guide in how to do one's utmost through apparently doing nothing at all.

Jung did a lot of 'simply listening to the soul' (p.65). He found that death has many guises (and disguises). As the body's life comes near to its end, the soul's images often show continuity. I will leave these musings of Jung to explore in my final chapter.

Euthanasia

There is in most people an inclination towards wanting to control the future and, sometimes, this amounts almost to a duty. Life – and also death – must be tidy. The trouble is that we are all of us thrown into this world without choice and with never more than a limited freedom to create the kind of lives we want to live. We can only operate within a framework of what the existentialists call facticity, the limiting factor in existence. Today's rapidly advancing technology results, perhaps, in dangerous flights of hubris, but 'facticity and finitude are in principle not able to be overcome and will remain permanent characteristics of the human condition' (Macquarrie, 1972, p.193).

Confronted with our inevitable deaths, there is bound to be enormous anxiety as well as a strong element of defence against that anxiety. When death cannot be avoided, we can at least decide its time and setting, either through suicide or euthanasia. Those who argue in favour of the latter being legalised, usually stress the importance of dying with dignity as a human right. The arguments are persuasive, but so are some of the arguments against. As a psychotherapist, I am aware over and over again, in listening to my patients, of a quite desperate tension between chaos and control. Those who advocate euthanasia often deny fear of death as a fear of non-being. Their focus is on fear of the process of dying, either in pain or in an uncontrollable demented state. I mean to discuss these two fears in a later chapter.

An elderly patient in therapy wrote to the Voluntary Euthanasia Society for advice on how to commit suicide and was disappointed when this was not forthcoming. She had never been enthusiastic about life, having been an anxious, shy child without many friends. In adult life she had enjoyed outdoor activities, which she had to relinquish as she got older. She thought of death as rest, an end to anxiety. She would bequeath what money she had to a younger relative who might be able to enjoy it more than she did herself, and she thought how much better it would be for him to have it now before it got used up in supporting her own unwanted life. She did not seek help to overcome her depression as she preferred to think of it as a terminal illness from which she would soon die. But she was not depressed enough to interest the doctor. If she could not die, she hoped she would reach the stage of having to be looked after in a rest home, but first she would have to sell her house, which no one seemed to want to buy. Suicide, unless professionally assisted, was not an option for her as she felt unable to take the responsibility of carrying it out. I am describing someone who had given up on life and who lacked the energy either to live or die. She decided there was nothing I could do for her therapeutically but thanked me for trying.

My patient was not typical of those seeking euthanasia, many of whom do take it on themselves to commit suicide before becoming too ill to do on their own what doctors are forbidden by law to do for them. 'I am sure that I have passed my watershed', runs an old lady's suicide note, 'and I'm sure that my decision to wait no longer is the right one ... But how much easier it would have been for everyone if I could have asked my doctor to call on her rounds, and how happy I should have been to see her pleasant face looking down at me as she gave me the injection and said goodbye' (Voluntary Euthanasia Society, 1992, p.47).

One of her sons sent her letter to the Voluntary Euthanasia Society with the comment: 'I feel that if she could have relied on help to die when she was ready to go, we'd have had her with us now. She wasn't ill' (p.47). The argument is that people are killing themselves too soon because no one is going to do it for them when they become powerless to do the deed themselves.

Ludovic Kennedy writes:

> In most countries in the Western world there is now a growing realisation that modern medicine, in increasing our span of living, has increased our span of dying too: and we all know of those who feel that because of cardiac resuscitators, antibiotics and so on, they are now being obliged to linger beyond their natural term. (Voluntary Euthanasia Society, 1992, p.24)

Like so many other euthanasia supporters, Kennedy had watched the long-drawn-out death of his mother and wished 'she could have summoned her nearest and dearest round her bedside, opened a bottle of champagne, and in an atmosphere of total love, taken a suitable pill from the doctor and bidden us farewell' (Voluntary Euthanasia Society, 1992, p.24).

Some doctors are such fervent believers in the patient's right to die that they behave like martyrs. Jack Kevorkian, from Detroit, practised secretly with his home-made suicide machine. He lost his medical licence in 1993. Since then he has been threatened, arrested, tried and jailed, but, after being acquitted, he has continued what he believes to be a crusade (Channel 4 TV, 22.4.97).

In Holland, doctors who practise euthanasia are not prosecuted as long as they observe strict guidelines. These include responding only to repeated requests from the patient to end severe suffering from incurable disease, when there is no other hope of relief and when all alternatives have been exhausted. The Dutch Reformed Church has given guarded support to this policy. Euthanasia is usually carried out by the family doctor in a patient's home. The request must be made in writing in front of witnesses and a second doctor consulted who is not known to the usual practitioner. Next of kin are informed but with the understanding that they must neither authorise nor veto the act. The majority of requests are refused because they fail to meet the criteria.

Even in Holland, the practice seems to be carried out in secrecy. Bert Keizer (1996) gives us the doctor's point of view. A patient asks: 'You're not letting me down, are you?' The doctor reassures him: 'Of course not'. Enter the granddaughter: 'How long will you keep going round in circles trying to avoid the issue? Don't you really see, Doctor, what he wants from you? He wants to die and he wants you to give him a shot' (p.36).

Keizer goes on to describe the doctor's doubts and nervousness and lack of support from his colleagues, but he does not let his patient down and arranges a time when the eldest son can be present at his father's death. They lock the door. He gets out his syringe and asks the patient if he is ready. The patient thanks him and tells him not to be scared. He dies peacefully three-quarters of an hour later with doctor and son watching. The doctor pronounces the death to the hospital staff and feels immensely relieved that his ordeal is over. As he leaves the building, a nurse asks if he has heard about his patient's death and how amazing it was that his family knew he was going to die that night. But always, afterwards, 'I am visited by the usual migraine' (p.281). It seems that patients expect too much of their doctors.

Freud, who suffered for years from a painful cancer in his jaw, was able at the end to have an almost telepathic understanding with his doctor, who had treated him for a long time in Vienna and now attended his death-bed in London. Ernest Jones (1964) records for us Freud's last plea:

> 'My dear Schur, you remember our first talk. You promised me then you would help me when I could no longer carry on. It is only torture now and it has no longer any sense.' Schur pressed his hand and promised he would give him adequate sedation. 'Tell Anna about our talk.' There was no emotionalism or self-pity, only reality. (p.657)

Freud had never wanted drugs, preferring to be clear-headed, even when in pain. Towards the end he consented to an occasional aspirin. So Doctor Schur had only to give him a small dose of morphia to induce a deep sleep. He died the next day. 'Freud died as he had lived – a realist' (p.657).

Whatever we may feel about euthanasia or assisted suicide, I think most people would agree with the idea of an 'Advance Directive', or, as it is sometimes called, 'A Living Will', made at a time when the person is still 'of a sound mind'. Doctors probably welcome such a directive, which removes from them some of the decision making and responsibility. The conditions listed in the document are as follows:

- advanced disseminated malignant disease
- severe immune deficiency
- advanced degenerative disease of the nervous system
- severe and lasting brain damage due to injury, stroke, or any other cause
- senile or pre-senile dementia, whether Alzheimer's, multi-infarct or other
- any other condition of comparable gravity.

The directive is that the patient, in these circumstances, should not be subjected to any mechanical intervention or treatment aimed at prolonging life and that distressing symptoms (including any caused by lack of food or fluid) should be controlled by appropriate analgesics, even when such treatment may shorten the patient's life. The document is signed and witnessed in the same way as any legal will bequeathing money and possessions. Such a directive exactly fits with that much-quoted verse: 'Thou shalt not kill; but need'st not strive/Officiously to keep alive' (Clough, *The Latest Decalogue*, 1862). In such cases what is being demanded is *not* euthanasia.

The chief argument against doctors being allowed to kill their patients comes from the Church, with its belief in the sanctity of human life. The counter-argument would be that our society is mostly secular. It is a society that expects to avoid pain, and modern technology makes a lot of avoidance possible. So the question arises: is avoiding pain a human right? I remember someone, whom I much respected, coming out with what I thought a very wise statement: 'Only when we realise that we have no rights at all will we appreciate how many privileges we have been given'. Perhaps that is rather sweeping, but at least it makes room for a certain gratitude (whether to God or chance) for the *privilege* of life itself, without seeking to control its end. If euthanasia were legalised and choosing death accepted as one's right, I can only hope that this right would not turn into a duty and that people coming to the end of their lives would not begin feeling guilty at having outstayed their welcome by becoming nuisances who should get out of the way of the young and busy. Undoubtedly, the best reason for governments to hesitate over changing the law is the ease with which that law might come to be abused.

I had the privilege recently of witnessing a slow death in a convent. There happened to be five sisters dying in the course of one week. Watching by the death-bed of the oldest, who had already drifted beyond human communication, one of the watching sisters talked to me of her conviction that, all the time, there was 'something going on' in the old lady's mind and that she would die when she was ready. This, the sister declared, was an argument against euthanasia.

I will have more to say about that convent, but 'slow-death' belongs to another chapter.

War

Attitudes and Illusions

The twentieth century has seen the end of any illusion about war as a 'chivalrous passage of arms' (Freud, 1915, p.54). Looking at the English poets of the First World War, we are struck by how attitudes changed in the space of two or three years. In 1914 Rupert Brooke thanked God, 'who has matched us for His hour/And caught our youth and wakened us from sleeping...' (Brooke, 1915, p.11). As for death, 'our last friend and enemy', he romanticised that honour and nobleness had come back to earth and commanded the bugles to blow 'over the rich Dead' (p.13). He never knew the strain and terror of trench warfare but joined the Navy and died of fever on an Aegean island in 1915. He was 27. Wilfrid Owen weathered nearly two years in mud, squalor and freezing winter, facing barrages of shells and machine guns, often with dead soldiers close enough to soak him with their blood. He had trench fever and, with supposedly shattered nerves, was sent to a war hospital in Scotland, where he made friends with a fellow poet, Siegfried Sassoon. Sassoon had thrown away his MC, which he had been awarded for 'conspicuous gallantry'. He had also sent an anti-war declaration to be read in the House of Commons, thereby risking either a court martial or being labelled as mentally ill and shut away for the duration. As things turned out, Sassoon went back to the front and survived. Owen also went back, won the MC and was killed one week before the armistice. He wrote, not of the glory but the 'pity' of war, of mental cases for whom 'dawn breaks open like a wound that bleeds afresh' (Owen, 1933) and, most poignantly, in a poem called *Futility*, of trying to revive a young man's corpse by moving him into the sun. 'Was it for this the clay grew tall?/Oh what made fatuous sunbeams toil/To break earth's sleep at all?' (p.73). Owen was 25.

Freud, whose country fought on the other side, was disillusioned as early as 1915. He had persuaded himself that the civilised 'white' races of the world should by now have found less savage ways of settling their disputes and no longer needed to kill each other. He wrote nostalgically of the wider fatherland, 'in which he could move about without hindrance or suspicion', (Freud, 1915, p.62) and was lyrical about:

> the beauty of snow-covered mountains and of green meadowlands; the magic of northern forests and the splendour of southern vegetation; the mood evoked by landscapes that recall great historical events, and the silence of untouched nature. This new fatherland was a museum for him, too, filled with the treasures which the artists of civilised humanity had, in the successive centuries created and left behind. (p.63)

Europe he had thought of as a gentlemen's playground in which any struggle for superiority could be carried out according to the rules of fair play, with 'utmost consideration' for non-combatants, immunity for the wounded and for the medical staff who attended them, and that 'the international undertakings and institutions in which the common civilisation of peace-time had been embodied would be maintained' (pp.64–5).

Then came 'the war in which we refused to believe' and these precepts were largely ignored:

> It (war) tramples in blind fury on all that comes in its way, as though there were to be no future and no peace among men after it is over. It cuts all the common bonds between contending peoples, and threatens to leave a legacy of embitterment that will make any renewal of those bonds impossible for a long time to come. (p.65)

But he went on to argue that we were not justified in our disappointment since what was happening was the destruction of an illusion. Humans were not born moral and psychoanalysis had shown that our deepest essence consisted of instinctual impulses which aimed at the satisfaction of primal needs. Although the impulses could be inhibited or sublimated through our desire to be loved and to be seen by society as good citizens, we were usually misled into regarding our fellow men as 'better' than they were. Anyone 'compelled to act continually in accordance with precepts which are not the expression of his instinctual inclinations is living, psychologically speaking, beyond his means' (p.72). This results in hypocrisy, a certain amount of which, said Freud, the cynic, might be necessary for maintaining civilisation. The illusion was that we had suddenly sunk from a previously high standard. In fact, we had never risen as high as we thought. Freud maintained that in the development of the human mind every earlier stage persisted alongside the later stage that had arisen from it. Nothing got left behind. 'The primitive mind is in the fullest meaning of the word imperishable' (p.73). He ends his essay, however, on a tentative note of hope:

> It is just as though when it becomes a question of a number of people, not to say millions, all individual moral acquisitions are obliterated, and only the most primitive, the oldest, the crudest mental attitudes are left. It may be that only later stages in development will be able to make some change in this regrettable state of affairs. But a little more truthfulness and honesty on all sides – in the relations of men to one another and between them and their rulers – should also smooth the way to transformation. (p.76)

Perhaps the greatest illusion after 1918 was that of having fought 'a war to end war'.

In the Second World War an older and sadder Freud, as a Jew in Vienna, came close to becoming a victim of Hitler's 'final solution'. His books had been destroyed before him, having been thrown on a bonfire soon after the Nazis came to power. In 1938 Austria had been invaded and taken over. Freud was ill with cancer, in no mood for a major upheaval. He resisted exile until Ernest Jones persuaded him to come to England and, through influential friends, obtained the necessary permission. He settled in Hampstead with his immediate family but had to leave his four elderly sisters. He gave them money for their welfare and saw no special reason for anxiety. He never knew of their fate, some years later, in Nazi death camps. Like his books, they were incinerated. Freud was welcomed in London, which flourished as a centre for psychoanalysis. He died in the first month of the war.

Jung, in neutral Switzerland, was in a different position. He broke away from Freud in 1913 and this was a shattering experience for both of them. Jung went through a personal crisis, a war within himself, that coincided with the war outside him (and actually outside, though surrounding, his own country) between 1914 and 1918. A series of apocalyptic dreams and visions threatened him with psychosis and yet also reflected the menace of war. When someone asked him what he thought was about to happen in the political world, 'I replied that I had no thoughts on the matter, but that I saw rivers of blood' (Jung, 1967, p.199).

At the beginning of the Second World War, Jung laid himself open to criticism by Germany's opponents, and especially by the Jews, for having accepted the presidency of the German Society for Psychotherapy, which 'had come under Nazi control and masqueraded under the aegis of an "International General Medical Society for Psychotherapy"' (Jones, 1964, p.619). This was after Jews had been banned from serving on scientific councils. The society set out to discriminate between Aryan and Jewish psychology. Perhaps, at first, Jung felt more at home among the Aryans than he had among the Jews. Although he clearly did not support the Nazi attitude towards Jews, and must have been as ignorant as most outsiders about plans for their total liquidation, it seems that he had wanted to wrest psychoanalysis from its purely Jewish roots and, perhaps, to push his own variant of analytical psychology into pride of place. But disillusionment followed. In a letter to Mrs Mellon in 1945 he declared that 'on account of my critique of German tyranny, I was on the black list of the Gestapo' (Samuels, 1993, p.469). The letter continues: 'I tell you these things, because you have probably heard the absurd rumour that I am a Nazi. This rumour has been started by Freudian Jews in America'.

This is not the place for arguing the extent of Jung's anti-semitism, but, in writing about war and death in war, one cannot be unaware of the political, and sometimes dangerously racist, currents in organisations as well as in nations and the inter-connectedness of outer and inner worlds, where death can be psychic as well as physical.

Victims and Survivors

We need, of course, to take back our projections and mourn our enemy's victims as well as our own. The Second World War has by now become history. Looking back over half a century, compassion comes more easily than when we were in the thick of it and intent on victory. When, early in 1945, Bishop Bell, speaking in the House of Lords, condemned the saturation bombing of German towns, he provoked passionate criticism and anonymous telephone calls from the mothers of fighting soldiers. The bombing continued. Finally, after the European war was over, the first two atom bombs were dropped on the Japanese, causing unimaginable damage and after-effects that continue to haunt us. This should have been a bombing to end all bombing but the build-up of nuclear weapons in the years that followed has given human beings the means of bringing about such total devastation that we stand now always on the brink of apocalypse, with no hope of a return to the taken-for-granted stability enjoyed by our forebears:

The present world situation is unprecedented, in that for the first time the human race can destroy itself in reality, and for the first time most of us know it. Hitherto we could all have private versions of the unthinkable catastrophe; now we have one we can all use. We can all displace our personal fears onto one realistic possibility. (Redfearn, 1992, p.9)

In mythology there are a variety of stories describing titanic struggles between good and evil. The earth is destroyed and the forces of good prevail, a new world rising from the ashes of the old. But:

The present danger of concrete historical enactment of the apocalyptic fantasy is different in an important respect from this black/white moral/military conflict between the forces of good and evil. Perhaps nowadays the most sane people foresee a cold and empty world of no triumph and no survival. (Redfearn, 1992, p.11)

This is a world that I have already described in my depressed patient's fantasies.

So we are all victims. But how many of us are sane enough to realise it? Fanatics, convinced of their own righteousness and their mission to destroy the wicked, still attract massive followings and, in building up their arsenals, they nowadays have increasingly dangerous toys for their games of destruction.

The psychotherapist may wish that experience of group dynamics could influence negotiators and foster more awareness of self and other among nations. Meanwhile, we are up against vested interests and power politics, the latter no longer regarded as the 'art of the possible' (Bismarck, 1867) but, more likely perhaps, as 'choosing between the disastrous and unpalatable' (Galbraith, 1969). Our business, therefore, is with the individual victims of war, who can, and often do, benefit from psychotherapy.

Bomber pilots, whatever they may have felt during their raids, did not always have quiet consciences after the excitement and danger finished. An ageing man, who bombed Dresden, found himself troubled long afterwards with images of death. He sought catharsis forty years later by discharging his anguish in a therapeutic group. Later still, an old man came into counselling because of loneliness and emptiness. It was as though he was still mourning his 'finest hour' when he had flown night after night over Germany, dropping his weapons of mass destruction. He had clung to his status of gallant young hero rather than moving on and ageing appropriately. Both pilots, in their opposite ways, were casualties of war.

On the losing side, those who fought for the Nazis became victims of their country's mistakes, and this was an almost impossible burden. What could they pass on to the next generation? Honesty was rare. A German psychoanalyst, at an International Congress in Hamburg in 1985, reported that they did not come to analysis but that their children did: 'They (the children) do not know what their parents thought or did at the time. Yet their reactions to these fathers and mothers have played an integral part in the overall process of identification' (Eckstaedt, 1986, p.317).

She describes two male patients who were born during the war, at a time when their fathers still adhered to Nazi ideology. Both came into analysis in their forties and she learnt about the fathers through their sons. In one case the father was quite unable to accept the collapse of the 'Third Reich'. He stopped working and refused welfare support from 'Adenaur's state':

> The father had refused to speak about his total reliance on Hitler and the ensuing disappointment. His obstinacy had developed into a false state of self-sufficiency, allowing him to deny that he was now dependent on his wife who was expected to meet his every need. (p.319)

His son also denied dependency. He was ambitious and successful in his 'own lonely way'. The father was stuck in his loyalty to the past and 'the collapse of his omnipotent fantasies, which Hitler had incited in him and which he in turn made his own' (p.322). His life was as empty as that of his 'enemy', the bomber pilot, just mentioned, whom I might describe as stuck in the hero archetype.

The other patient's father would never answer his son's questions. He refused to acknowledge shame or guilt but held his son in contempt. The son, in turn, blamed and persecuted anyone who seemed to stand in his way. Both these patients combined the role of perpetrator with that of victim. Neither father had been able to hand on a clear sense of reality or any values with which their sons could live.

All those associated with the Nazi movement, even those who 'have returned to the historically normal way of thinking since its collapse, face a similar need to account for the discontinuity in their mental life and to make some sense of the bizarre, unnatural, and in fact delusional views that they espoused and promulgated – or at least tolerated – during this episode' (Ostow, 1986, p.277).

There were a lot of delusions. Nazis and Jews shared apocalyptic visions. Each was a member of a chosen race, destined to survive the violence that would usher in a Messianic age. Both believed themselves special, but, without a land of their own, the Jews lived through centuries of exile and persecution, and, even now in Israel, are not safe from 'enemies' in the states that surround them. Six million were killed. Those who escaped were bound, in some way, to be scarred, but so are the defeated Germans. Only gradually can younger generations manage to live with the disillusionment and shame that accompany their forebears' defeat and failure. Patriotism is a doubtful virtue in that it tends towards self-righteousness and extreme projections and it may be all to the good that, at least in the West, patriotism is no longer fashionable.

The Holocaust

That it could happen at all – in a country which produced great art, philosophy and all the attributes generally considered necessary to civilisation – is the greatest disgrace of the twentieth century. Whether through disbelief, indifference or silence, none of us can be altogether exempt from responsibility. This was brought home to me by an English Jew, who, because our island, though threatened, was never invaded and over-run, took on himself some of the shame of all those who distanced themselves, in their various ways, from the horror. In fact, all thinking people, who have been able to get on with their lives in safety, deserve to share some modicum of survivor guilt.

After fifty years, when we celebrated the end of this destruction, publicity was again given to its worst excesses and even if we want now to close this painful chapter of history, as many people do, we are not being allowed to forget. While endeavouring to bring more recent perpetrators of genocide to courts of international justice, we continue to pursue relentlessly those few old Nazis who, though harmless now, have succeeded for half a century in evading the law. That the victims want vengeance is understandable, but 'sweet revenge grows harsh', says Shakespeare (*Othello,* Act 5, scene 2), and I doubt if it has much to do with healing.

It is well known that Hitler's 'final solution' was principally aimed at the Jews: 'It was the Jews alone who were marked out to be destroyed in their entirety: every Jewish man, woman and child, so that there would be no future Jewish life in Europe' (Gilbert, 1987, p.824).

We know that the Nazis set about doing the job thoroughly. Once the Jews from the ghettos were herded into cattle trains travelling towards Auschwitz and other death camps, there was little chance of survival. Yet, survive some of them did, and their witness became a 'historic impediment'.

A poet from Warsaw, before he was transported to his death, stressed the
need to recall any acts of resistance that there were: 'Sing a hymn to the hero
of the remote hamlet! Sing loud his praise, see his radiant figure!' (Gilbert,
1987, p.825).

But we should not overlook the gypsies, homosexuals and 'mental
defectives' who were also systematically put to death, along with unarmed
civilians, men, women and children, Soviet prisoners-of-war, Spanish
republicans, Greeks, Poles, Yugoslavs and Czechs who were either murdered
or worked to death as slaves of the 'New Order'.

It so happened that the first concentration camp survivor I met was not a
Jew but a Pole. Maria and her husband had, as far as I remember, taken part in
a resistance movement when their country was invaded in 1939. They had
both been arrested and sent to different camps. Maria's determination to
survive was animated by the hope of eventually being re-united with her
husband when the war was over. When we first met in the early 1950s,
through being students together, I knew nothing about her experiences
except that she was older than the rest of us, had been married and was
obviously a refugee finding it hard to adapt to a new life in a strange country.
She struck me as depressed but with a dignity and reserve that seemed to
keep her at a distance from those who would like to have known her better. I
respected her silence and made no effort to probe: '"The pact of shameful
silence" between the survivors and the world stemmed from the need of the
survivors to forget and the world's need to deny' (Klein and Kogan, 1986,
p.47). It was only when I invited her to my home, together with a South
African student who knew nothing about the war, that Maria was stirred into
telling her story. I never wrote it down and have to rely on the fragments that
stayed in my memory, leaving a lasting impression.

In the camp Maria befriended another Polish woman, a bit younger and
more delicate than herself. Together, they shared Polish memories and hopes
for the future. Each knew that if they were to escape death, they must force
themselves to work and prove their usefulness to the authorities, who would
reward them by not gassing them – or not until all their energies were
exhausted. Maria insisted that they resist all temptation to look out for
themselves individually at other inmates' expense. This meant never
descending to a purely animal level by stealing food or clothing. Only thus
could they keep their self-respect. They must neither openly defy their
guards nor must they give up all hope, either by suicide or by entering that
limbo state that later came to be called 'mussulman' – an identification more

with the dead than the living. One could call it 'psychic death'. In this way they managed each day with the single aim of keeping going till the end, and they were both still alive when the tide of the war turned and allied forces approached. They probably had no detailed news of what was happening but when, at last, they found themselves on the move, marching out of the camp with armed escorts each side of the road, they were sure that they were heading towards death in some isolated place. Maria's will to live – and, perhaps, see her husband again – had never been stronger and kept her alerted to any possibility of escape. Her friend was on the outside of the line of prisoners that was spread across the road. She moved like a Zombie, with Maria close beside her, willing her not to stumble. Those who stopped or fell were immediately shot by the guards. They marched for miles. Just as darkness came on, the road took them through dense forest. Maria saw her chance. With one eye on the guard, whose concentration was, for a moment, on the ranks just ahead, she gave her friend a big push and together they tumbled into the darkness of the forest. They were saved.

After so many years, my memory of the rest of Maria's narrative is less clear. I think they found their way back to the evacuated camp and waited for the Americans, but it was some time before they could taste real freedom. They were moved to various camps for displaced persons and went through a lot of formalities before eventually coming to England and I no longer remember how that was arranged, nor do I know how long it was before Maria had certain proof that her husband had not survived.

Between Maria and her friend there seems to have been something of a reversal of roles. Maria, with her one hope taken away, became the weaker of the two. Whereas her friend settled easily among the Polish population of London, Maria had a lot of mourning to do. During the short time that I knew her I would say that the mourning had barely begun. She seemed in a frozen state. Perhaps she did not dare experience her disappointment and allow herself to be sad. My memory of her is almost totally confined to that evening when she told her story, though a year or so later I visited the hospital where she was working with Polish soldiers. She showed me their paintings and I particularly remember some agonising stations of the cross in stark black and white. She told me that her friend from the camp was happily married to a Pole. I have not seen Maria since 1954 but I seem to remember hearing that she too had married a Pole. Perhaps she found some happiness at last.

It was difficult to survive at all, but impossible to do so undamaged. I know nothing of the after-effects on Maria and her friend but I often wonder about them when reading case studies of survivors who sought therapy or analysis during the post-war years. Survivors of both sexes wanted to restore normality by creating a new family. Women longed for pregnancy and feared infertility as further loss. Children became replacements for those who had died and that has been a heavy weight for them to bear. We are now faced with a second, and even a third, generation of those affected.

Dinora Pines (1986) describes the difficulty of the survivor living through her children's adolescence, letting go of what these children stand for and allowing them to develop as individuals: 'It was as if their adaptation to life after the war had collapsed with their children's separation from them and the parting of the secure world of mother and child' (p.295). This was a time 'to face the destruction of their previous world, attempt to come to terms with the violent deaths of important figures in that world, to mourn them and to face the guilt of their own survival' (p.295).

Most observers of these patients report on their concrete thinking, inability to use metaphor and somatisation of psychic pain. I have witnessed some of this myself when working with the victims of child abuse. Devastating trauma impairs imagination, emotion is denied and dreaming avoided. Doctor Pines found herself having to be flexible in her normal structuring of the analytical sessions. She describes a patient who could not lie on the couch because she needed to face her analyst and watch her reactions. This had to be allowed rather than interpreted as resistance. The patient needed to test the analyst's ability to bear what she was hearing and accept its reality. Without dreams and fantasies, countertransference became the main vehicle through which painful re-experiencing could be expressed. The patient told her story calmly as if it had happened to someone else. It was the analyst who had to take on the 'horror and anger at the senseless destruction of her [the patient's] world and the dehumanisation and humiliation of the camp' (p.301). In a maternal countertransference the analyst had to receive and contain the patient's distress and strive to give it meaning without becoming totally overwhelmed.

One of the women described discovered both an ability to mourn her murdered family and a new creativity. She wrote about her life and about the camp experience, and it was as if mourning the dead brought them to life in her book. In the case of another survivor success was more limited: 'I helped her exist but not to live again, and we shared a feeling of resignation' (p.304).

Ilany Kogan is a psychoanalyst working in Israel, where, inevitably, she encounters survivors and their descendants. She has written about her clinical experiences with sons and daughters and explores the transmission of trauma from parent to child up to the third generation. Not only does she describe the concrete ideas (concretism) already mentioned but also the phenomenon of 'concretisation', whereby 'the children's impaired capacity to deal on a fantasy level with the traumatic experiences of their parents leads to their acting out in the present reality' (Kogan, 1995, p.154).

'Acting out', instead of remembering, is a well-known unconscious activity. The special term 'concretisation' is used when 'These children, in their endless efforts to understand and help their traumatised parents, try to experience what the parents went through by re-creating their parents' experiences and accompanying affects in their own life' (p.87).

In one case a boy acted out a despair that belonged to his grandmother's and father's lives rather than his own and had been transmitted through stories told him by his grandmother, who used him as an outlet for her terrible, though denied, anxiety. The boy shot and wounded his father, thereby, it seems, acting out different roles in his father's past, both as victim and aggressor. It was when, in the course of his analysis, it was suggested that his attack on his father could have been an attempt to kill the father inside himself that he expressed a wish to learn the details of his father's past, which he now knew were somehow connected with his grandmother's stories. So he questioned his father, who answered as if he had been waiting a long time for the right moment to tell his secrets. The boy felt as if this was a story he had always known because he had lived through it himself. He realised at last that he needed to separate from his father and from an earlier generation's tragedy. He also needed to work through various attempts to kill his analysis and to learn neither to destroy nor blur the boundaries between self and other.

In cases such as this it is not so much a question of 'visiting the children unto the third and fourth generation' (Exodus, ch.20, v.1) as the iniquity of those who persecuted those fathers and blighted the lives of their descendants. How long, one wonders, will this bitter legacy continue to haunt future generations of innocent survivors. (I think, however, that we should also bear in mind that it must be just as hard for all those German children and grandchildren whose families contributed, or turned a blind eye, to the final solution).

In Israel today there are real threats from external enemies, as well as the terrifying dangers experienced more than fifty years ago and which live on, as concretised fantasy, in the minds of subsequent generations. A new dictator, Saddam Hussein, declares his intention of cleansing the Holy Land of 'American Zionist Jews' and the racial fanaticism of the Nazis rears up again in Islam. During the Gulf War, Israel was attacked by Scud missiles and people had to wear gas masks. To the children of survivors, the attacks seemed to herald another Holocaust, which they were powerless to avoid: 'The present terror was the frightening realisation of fantasies of a traumatic past' (Kogan, 1995, p.145). Patients in analysis could no longer safely assume that their emotional home in the transference would not be destroyed. They had to realise that, in a very real sense, analyst and patient were each as helpless as the other in the face of possible destruction and death. The analyst had to admit to a shared fear of what might actually happen in the present while, at the same time, separating it from the trauma of the parents' past which the offspring had not actually lived through. During this period the 'real relationship' of analyst and patient came to the fore. A common fear was acknowledged and the patient's ego supported until it felt safe enough to differentiate fact from fantasy. When the war was over, the analytic work was, in many cases, found to improve.

A common threat is always likely to bring people together and, while the danger lasts, accentuate what is mutually shared, rather than what alienates. In our own country the London blitz united disparate people in such a way that a sense of community made individual fears easier to bear. This holds true in adversities such as hurricanes or floods.

So how did my friend Maria and all those other survivors cope with the horrifying reality which confronted them? With family and homes wiped out, there was nothing left for them to value but their memories and the presence of their fellow sufferers. Inevitably, new bonds were made. I am sure Maria took on the nurture of her younger friend as lovingly as she would have cared for her husband or the children that were denied to her; and I am equally sure that her friend found a new mother in Maria: 'Denial of chaotic, demonic reality sustained by cognitive processes of memory, fantasy and words as well as by acts, was one of the adaptive defences in the day-to-day fight for survival' (Klein and Kogan, 1986, p.46).

They sang songs and told each other stories. Many of them prayed. Above all, they identified with each other and, out of this, identification came: 'fantasies projected on the future, using relevant interpersonal experiences, from the past and present, denying other fragments of reality which could be devastating' (p.46).

'Denial sustained by fantasy' was a way of surviving and sustaining each other with some faint glimmering of hope.

The Manner of our Dying

The litany, quoted at the beginning of this section, beseeches God, perhaps surprisingly, to save us from sudden death. This is because it was addressed to people of a bygone age to whom dying without repentance meant damnation. Shakespeare, writing earlier in the same century, made Hamlet reluctant to creep up behind his uncle while at prayer, when killing him would have been easy. His hesitation was not out of respect for the Church, nor was it because such a deed would be lacking in chivalry, but that 'to take him in the purging of his soul' was to punish him less than he deserved. So Hamlet sheathed his sword and preferred to wait until his victim was engaged in some sinful pleasure:

> that has no relish of salvation in it;
> Then trip him, that his heels may kick at heaven
> And that his soul may be as damned and black
> As hell, whereto it goes. (*Hamlet*, Act III, sc.3)

Now that belief in hell has diminished, sudden death, provided it is painless, seems to be most people's preferred option. To die unexpectedly of stroke or heart attack is considered hard on the relatives but merciful (except in youth) for the person concerned. People worry a lot about the manner of their dying, hence the drawing up of living wills and demands for legalised euthanasia. What they fear most is continued existence with impaired faculties and being a nuisance to their children and friends.

There are still some of us, not necessarily religious, who would like time to prepare for death, not so much through fear of judgement as to have a chance, willingly, to let go of attachment to the world, to say goodbye and to leave our affairs in some sort of order. This will mean facing whatever fears we have, whereas those who want to make their exit without knowing anything about it may manage to avoid all fear through unconsciousness. In a materialistic age it is the known fears of life that are acknowledged. The vast unknown, to which we are all of us heading, cannot be thought about. Belief in life after death is becoming weaker, even among Christians.

Here is an account of sudden death from a friend working in an Intensive Care Unit:

I was talking with a middle-aged patient about his life as a cook on the wing, when he suddenly stopped in mid-sentence, due to a fatal coronary. He was looking me straight in the eye as he died, and, for a second or two, I was aware of being on the edge of another dimension into which he was disappearing. It all happened so fast that, although I summoned the Registrar at once, I knew the patient was gone for good. Within seconds, the crash trolley arrived and the ensuing efforts of half a dozen people round the bed to bring him back to life seemed rather sad. A similar group was round the bed when I watched my son being born. I felt a brief awareness of another dimension as he appeared, but then suddenly it was as if he had always been there and the other dimension hadn't. (Reeves, 1998)

Sometimes, dying happens slowly after long labour, but, whether sudden or slow, the moment of disappearance is one of radical change, a birth not into life but into death. This is a birth we cannot attend and there is nothing we can say or hear about it, except – and only up to a certain point – in cases of successful resuscitation. The actual moment is described as going into nothing:

The only thing I can recall is just – not hurting, but just collapsing. And then the lights went out, as if you're in a little room and you flip the switch. The only thing different from that was that it was in slow motion … The change from light to dark was very evident, but the speed with which it happened was – well gradual. I was aware that I'd collapsed. I felt like somebody took the life out of me. (Nuland, 1994, p.16)

The light went out for him because the circulation to his brain was suddenly cut off: 'sight and consciousness were turned down as though by the gradual twist of a dial rather than the suddenness of a switch. That was [his] slow-motion spiral into oblivion and almost death' (p.16).

Some of those who almost die report stranger happenings, which I will describe later on. But for those who are not revived, perhaps the best we can do is to echo Hamlet's dying words: 'The rest is silence' (*Hamlet*, Act V, sc.2).

CHAPTER 5

Slow Death

An illness in stages, a very long flight of steps that led assuredly to death, but whose every step represented a unique apprenticeship. It was a disease that gave death time to live and its victim time to die, time to discover time, and in the end to discover life.

(Guibert, 1991, p.319)

O Rose thou art sick!
The invisible worm
That flies through the night
In the howling storm,
Has found out thy bed
Of crimson joy,
And his dark secret love
Does thy life destroy.

(Blake, 1977, p.107)

Terminal Illness – The Invisible Worm

When Sherwin Nuland (1994) wrote his best-selling book, *How we Die*, he described processes that had certain features in common. These were 'the stoppage of circulation, the inadequate transport of oxygen to tissues, the flickering out of brain function, the failure of organs, the destruction of vital centres' (p.xviii) These are the universal experiences of dying. Yet in his first chapter he also stressed the uniqueness of each person's death: 'Every one of death's diverse appearances is as distinctive as that singular face we each show the world during the days of our life' (p.3).

I am not writing a medical book so I will stay with what I know about being with people when they die. I found myself reading Blake's poem to the sick rose during the hours that I spent at my sister's bedside when she was slowly dying of cancer. Although the word 'cancer' means 'crab', with its associations of grabbing and pinching, there was something about the invisible worm's secret destruction that struck me as particularly relevant. 'What a long time it takes to die', she had said to me a week earlier. Nothing showed but the worm was in her bones and vital organs and could no longer be stopped. Only morphine and oxygen mitigated her distress.

My sister was a member of an Anglican religious community and hers was one of the deaths (five in one week) in the convent that I mentioned earlier. The infirmary wing was run like a hospice with dedicated lay experts in charge of the nursing, as well as the sisters who would quietly come and go, intuitively aware of when the patient needed comfort and when she preferred to be left alone. The sisters were the dying person's family, who were as much affected as blood relations would be by any member's death. But we all realised that I had a special role as the only one left of our original family and sometimes I felt more like a mother than her younger sister.

She had known for some time that she was going to die and, when the dreaded chemotherapy only gave very short remission, she chose (and was allowed) to have no more. Nearly a year earlier, when particularly worn down by the treatment, she had said to me that all creativity had left her. I remembered that at various times in her life she had written poems, so I said 'why not try poetry?' This had a magic effect and she produced poems in short bursts, that reflected her childhood, the war, memories of working in Africa and her present illness. Death still felt unreal:

> So I'm going to die?
> Head, not gut knowledge.
> Life here is sweet,
> Beyond beckons.
> God is to be trusted.

> Our sisters in death
> Look happily surprised.
> No telling us in words
> But they are still close,
> And the veil is thin.

She also wrote of 'a final stripping'. She had no worries about not being able to control things or of an undignified ending. Being 'religious' did not mean she had no fear. She was whimpering like a child on that last night. When it was all over, one of the sisters who had stayed close to her turned to me and said: 'It's a mystery'. I was grateful that she did not pretend to know what death was all about and only voiced what I was thinking myself, without any 'religious' consolation.

During the time leading up to death we can only observe, without sharing the experience that the dying person goes through. That person's awareness comes and goes, as if too much of it would be overwhelming. John Hinton (1990) describes this fluctuating knowledge:

> She did not always want to admit that she was dying. In subsequent conversations, in spite of her earlier awareness of the true nature of her illness, she would often speak in a light wondering fashion about her symptoms, as if she could not begin to guess what caused them. There were times when she wanted to maintain this pretence with others and not refer to her real state. (p.12)

Another way of protection is to confine all thought to everyday happenings in the relative safety of the sick room, where life is monotonously peaceful and punctuated by routines of meals, medicaments, visitors and the changing shifts of nurses. People send cards, bring flowers and relay items of news from a wider world. Sometimes, they make jokes. My sister asked me to read Lewis Carroll's *The Hunting of the Snark* and joined in with the verses she knew by heart. This was the day before she died, when coherent speech had become an effort, but she had already managed to say important personal things to me which had been difficult to put into words before that time.

Sometimes, doctors try to console the relatives, and also, perhaps, themselves, by saying that the dying person's suffering is not as bad as it looks. Cheyne-Stokes breathing, which heralds death and sounds agonising, the strange gurgling of the death rattle, especially in a familiar and loved person, is deeply distressing to the helpless onlookers. I remember the doctor's reassurance just before my grandfather died. He said that it was worse for us than for the patient. I believed him. Years later, and after four more death-bed experiences, a little voice inside me seemed to murmur 'how did he know?'

It is obviously difficult to measure the degree of a person's awareness. Unconsciousness at the end is probably the best protection and I think the doctor who reassured me about my grandfather was undoubtedly right when he said that the pain was worse for us than for his unconscious patient. But some doctors are more sceptical than others about what the patient knows. Hinton (1990) gives us two discrepant views. First, Lord Horder:

> As for the dying man himself, we rarely find him 'looking death in the face' and knowing it is death. He is either very dubious that death is coming to him, or his apperception is so dimmed, that the end of life is a dream-state rather than a true awareness.

In contrast, an American doctor:

> Most dying patients have the feeling that death is near. Some know it well enough and yet want nothing said about it; or perhaps, while they like to talk of it with doctors and nurses, they cannot bear to speak of it to their families. (p.94)

Hinton chose those two views as showing divergence between 'two thoughtful, experienced physicians, whose opinions should not be readily dismissed' (p.94). I think Horder was concentrating on a person's last moments rather than those weeks or days of gradual awareness before the actual end. I also think that such divergence of opinion may have a lot to do with the attitude of the doctors concerned. Some, even if unconsciously, wish to avoid talking to a patient about death. Their job is to save lives and every death stands for a failure. The patient may be more aware than his doctor believes but keeps silent to avoid embarrassment. Or it may be that the doctor treats the illness in such a matter-of-fact way that the patient has no suspicion of any particular danger. One would have thought that such aggressive treatments as chemo or radiotherapy might give clues and yet it is extraordinary what a curtain descends on people's minds to shut out unwelcome knowledge.

In one case a patient talked airily of having electric shocks applied to his brain when, in fact, he was having radiotherapy for a tumour. He was bored with medical details, though ready to face death as not particularly unwelcome.

Thirty years ago, before the advent of body scans, a patient had a radical mastectomy. This was an extensive operation so that all the tissue removed could be examined to see if the malignancy had spread. One cannot have a breast removed without hearing the truth, so there was no question of hiding the fact of cancer. But she had her own unconscious protection. While waiting to hear if further treatment would be necessary, all her concentration went into worrying about the unpleasantness of radiotherapy and wondering if she would be able to keep up the effort of being brave. Her only fear was that she would behave badly and this minor anxiety shielded her from the greater dread of more cancer and possible death. Even when she was given the 'all-clear' she still failed to see the significance of being cleared of cancer and it was only when she recognised her husband's relief that she at last became aware of the danger that had receded. She is still alive.

It has been said that awareness comes in stages and the patient goes through denial, rage and struggle, followed by acceptance. This seems to me an attempt at simplifying a complex experience. Stages, if there are any, shift and overlap. Acceptance, even serenity, is hoped for but by no means always achieved. A lot, of course, will depend on the age of the dying person. The young (especially young mothers) will put up a greater struggle and probably suffer more than the old, possibly widowed, whose children have long since grown up.

To Tell or Not To Tell

Traditionally, doctors have tended not to be the bearers of bad news. We have been inclined to assume that they are omniscient and the patient knows nothing, but this gap between their exalted profession and an ignorant public is getting thinner as people become more educated, more trusting of their own intuitions and better able to withdraw projections on doctors as saviour figures. Eventually, death defeats us all and there are no saviours, only technicians to make the body last a bit longer than formerly and to ease the process of dying. In the face of unrealistic expectations it has been harder for these technicians to admit defeat and show that they are fallible mortals like the rest of us. Patients often know without being told. They pick up clues when the medical profession, and also, perhaps, their nearest relatives, band together to keep up a 'conspiracy of silence', thus leaving them isolated at the time when they most need to talk and be listened to.

Things are changing. Conversations about dying are often encouraged so that patients may feel freer to ask questions. But, if the patient never asks, does that mean he does not want to know? Some health workers are cautious and think it right to deny knowledge. Others feel they have a duty to tell. Doctors still tell lies if they assess that the patient is not strong enough to hear the truth. But what right have they so to infantalise a mature person simply because he or she is fatally ill?

Some of the changes, occurring gradually over the last thirty years, are reflected in my own experiences of dying and bereavement. In the late 1960s, when my father was near to death, both doctor and priest, and, because of them, my mother, decided that he was too agitated to hear the truth. I remember how, a few years earlier, when he had a sudden operation for appendicitis, he expressly asked to be told if anything malignant should be found. This was agreed, but there was no malignancy so nothing to tell. Now that he had become weaker and more worried, the agreement was no longer maintained. 'I've never felt worse in my life', he said, 'and nobody's doing anything. Nobody's helping'. If I had been alone with him at that moment I am sure I would have told him that nothing could be done, but who was I to go against priest, doctor and wife? Unconsciousness at the end eased his agitation and his death was relatively peaceful, but I would like there to have been more honesty.

Fifteen years later, my husband was diagnosed with brain cancer. This was a shock because his symptoms had been to do with heart failure. A friendly heart specialist, who had taken the trouble to talk to him, noticed a disorientation and vagueness which was worrying me too, and seemed to be getting worse, so he told me that he proposed giving him a brain scan. He also said that there was nothing to worry about – perhaps a mild stroke. When I telephoned, he told me the truth but lied to my husband because (like my father) he was so 'agitated'. I said that I wanted those lies overturned. The doctor said that he would do what ever I wanted and that, in the short term, the cancer could be treated and I would notice an improvement. What happened was that my husband became clearer in his thinking but paralysed in his movements. He came home to die and we had nurses from a local agency. He was well looked after and the heart specialist, who liked him, continued to treat him while liaising with the hospital oncology department.

There was much more honesty than there had been with my father. What to say to him was left to me and I took advice from a colleague who was both therapist and doctor. 'Don't tell lies', he suggested, but 'don't answer questions before they are asked'. It seemed excellent advice at the time but, perhaps, I stuck to it too rigidly. As it was, the question about cancer was never asked. But he knew he was going to die and faced it calmly. If I had followed my intuition, I think we would have talked more freely about his death, and that might have made things easier for me but not necessarily for him. As the illness progressed, I got caught up in the day-to-day mechanics of nursing and keeping him comfortable, as well as arranging visits of friends and family.

Another fifteen years have passed and my sister has died of cancer. This time the illness was openly talked about and each stage of treatment discussed with the patient, including, eventually, the decision to opt for no more than palliative care.

We have a more open society and a younger generation not brought up with the 'stiff upper lip' of a previous age. Feelings can be shared and crying is not taboo. Or so we like to think. But married couples can still be inarticulate with each other and misunderstandings abound in all relationships.

A family friend, whom I knew a long time ago, talked about her cancer to everyone except her husband. He both knew about it and knew that she knew. She knew that he knew, and yet nothing was said. They could not face it together. However enlightened we may think we are today, this sad lack of communication can still happen.

Not so long ago, a friend had leukaemia. He was in his early forties. He knew about his illness and the likely outcome but never lost hope that perhaps a cure would be found before his time was up. His close friends knew but he insisted that his mother should not be told. He could hang on to his own fortitude but felt unable to cope with the anguish his mother would feel if she knew. His wishes were obeyed but when he died and his mother learnt the truth that had been withheld for five years, her pain, fuelled by bitterness and anger, was all the worse in that she, coming from a medical family, had not been considered strong enough to bear her son's suffering. Yet while he still lived, how could one not respect a dying person's decision?

Telling the family can be as hard as telling the patient and the manner of giving information may matter as much as the information itself:

> As with the patient, the families receiving these tidings often need more than just a bulletin of bad news. Many cannot take in the shattering information at first. Time and much troubled thought is needed before people can accept that someone they love is about to die. They may need help.
> (Hinton, 1990, p.156)

Hinton was writing more than thirty years ago and his book has gone through a series of reprints, but the message is still the same. Help, in these days of hospices, Macmillan nurses, a proliferation of books, news items, talks and workshops about death, is certainly more available but one needs to know where to look.

Natural Death

Now that natural childbirth is well established as a means of de-medicalising birth, there is a growing movement seeking to do the same for death. In 1991 The Natural Death Centre was founded by three psychotherapists: Nicholas Albery, Josefine Speyer and Christiane Heal. An important aim is to make it possible for people to die in a place of their own choosing, preferably at home among family and friends.

The Centre is best known for its advice and information service on choice of funeral after a person's death. There is also a befriending network, which is now a separate charity, aiming to become nation-wide. At present, the network operates in London and Oxford. Diana Senior runs the Oxford network and Josefine Speyer works from the London headquarters of the Natural Death Centre. Her husband, Nicholas Albery, is the expert on funerals, whereas Josefine concentrates on helping people to die.

The befriending network recruits volunteers to visit and support dying individuals. Training involves seven intensive evening sessions exploring the meaning of death for society, for the dying person and for the befriender. Students need to review their own lives and face the inevitability of eventually dying themselves. There are discussions dealing with stress and a talk on palliative care for the dying. After this initial training the volunteers will be put in touch with a person who is terminally ill – usually only one at a time – in order to make regular visits, so that they can help in every possible way to improve the quality of life both for patient and carer. Befriending may include some practical tasks, such as writing letters, running errands or acting as advocate, but most important is the emotional help given by listening and being there with that person as death approaches. The volunteers are well supervised and their own stresses understood and supported within the befriending network. I talked to Josefine about psychotherapy for the dying but her opinion is that befriending is more appropriate. She has her own therapy practice in which she finds it important to explore the many endings we all have to make when moving through life, and this, of course, includes the ending of intimate relationship with the therapist. Therapy, like life, is full of losses and transitions, or, to put it more dramatically, death and rebirth.

To quote from *The Natural Death Handbook*:

The Centre wants to make death and dying an unexceptional topic for daily meditation and conversation and to that end has hosted a series of tea 'salons' and large dinner discussions with candlelit tables and gourmet food and wine on subjects ranging from Near Death Experiences to care for those who are dying. (Albery and Elliot, 1997, p.7)

Throughout the year the Centre gives workshops on topics such as 'Enriching the Quality of Living and Dying', 'Exploring our own Death', 'Life Review', 'Living with Dying'. These are open to anyone but advance booking is needed. Every spring there is a 'National Day of the Dead'. This brings an opportunity to look at woodland burial grounds and hear about green funerals, as well as talks and group exercises and a memorial dinner with contributions of food and drink and the lighting of candles for dead friends.

The Centre has found itself at the forefront of a movement for do-it-yourself and green funerals. I will say more about these in a later chapter.

Where to Die

If asked where we would like to end our days, I am fairly sure that most of us would choose our own homes. When families were bigger and women tended not to go out to work, death at home could often be achieved. In today's mobile society, with smaller and widely dispersed families, more than half the population dies in hospital.

The hospice movement has taken a great step forward in providing expertise, both in residential care and home visits. The only snag is that hospices are supported by the major cancer charities and patients who are not dying of cancer (75%) are unlikely to be admitted, though some also cater for motor neurone disease.

Cicely Saunders, first as nurse, then as social worker and, eventually, doctor, devoted her life to the care of the dying and was instrumental in the founding of St Christopher's in 1967. I have an account of its beginning and development from Dr Thomas West, who worked with Dame Cicely and whose father was the first patient with terminal cancer to die under her care. This was in his own home before the hospice was built.

Dr West would agree that provided everyone is able to cope, home is the best place to die, but not, he says, the only place. Most of those cared for in hospices today do, in fact, die in their own homes supported by visiting nurses who are trained in palliative care, can advise on pain-control, listen to problems and give support to patient and family. The patient may spend time in the hospice for relief of intractable symptoms and also to give family carers a rest. In-patient treatment may prove the most comfortable and comforting way of being cared for during the last few days and, for some, though not all, the hospice may prove the easiest place to die, with next-of-kin encouraged to be there at the end.

The opening of St Christopher's was the beginning of a medical, pharmacological, psychological and social experiment. By the 1990s there were, in the UK and Ireland, nearly 200 hospice in-patient units, averaging 15 beds each, '400 home-care teams, 216 hospital support teams or support nurses, and 200 day hospices' (Walter, 1994, p.88). The hospice movement soon spread to the USA and since 1982 has been supported financially by Medicare.

Where I live, in a smallish cathedral town, our hospice is ten years old and planning to add a day centre for respite care. Such centres may give assisted baths, physiotherapy, aroma therapy and massage, as well as providing some social activities. Locally, we have 240 volunteers to link hospice and community through visiting people at home, helping to organise groups for the bereaved, sending cards for anniversaries or, perhaps most important of all, just sitting with the dying and listening:

> Hospices generally have an atmosphere that is Christian, middle-class and feminine. On entering one hospice near London, I felt as I was ushered to a reproduction armchair in the peach wall-papered and thickly carpeted waiting area, that I was walking into a Laura Ashley showroom – soft, feminine, traditional and almost aristocratic, and unlike any hospital I knew of. (Walter, 1994, p.89)

I recognise this description, having welcomed the peaceful (and yes, I suppose, feminine) ambience of the hospice I visited. I felt the same at the London Lighthouse, even though that was full of men. I thought there was something womb-like about the place where people come to die. Perhaps it is a mother's care that brings most relief at the end, just as it did at the beginning of our lives. Tony Walter describes contradictory feelings. 'Some have observed', he writes, 'that hospices are also stereotypically feminine, in allowing tears but no anger' (p.89). In theory the hospice is committed to allowing people 'to do their own thing' and 'die their own way'. In practice it seems that they may persuade their patients that the hospice way is best. A social worker is reported to have said: 'Hospice staff are missionaries who see their mission as enabling people to die a certain version of the good death' (p.131).

On my visit I asked about specialist training of professional staff and how the Hospice Support Sisters (the equivalent of Macmillan nurses) are chosen. After general training they have either worked as hospice nurses or had experience of district nursing – the team is usually a mixture of these two – and have done courses on palliative care. These courses are open to all health care professionals with a minimum of one year's experience as a qualified practitioner. They look at issues of care in a social context and at the impact of facing death and progressive illness on families, as well as on themselves, how to enhance self-awareness and empathy. They explore pain and the 'multi-dimensions' of pain control, how to anticipate and assess pain and the management of symptoms. Another unit explores bereavement and how to use 'grief theory' in nursing practice. There is a course on body-image, self-esteem, sexuality and the role of supportive therapies – massage, reflexology, visualisation, to name but a few. They are also taught communication and counselling skills, all in the context of palliative care. Together with nursing techniques, there is a professionalisation of the ordinary human attributes of kindness, understanding and compassion. I find myself hoping that a 'politically correct' way of dying will not evolve out of this labelling of acceptable reactions.

Throughout the hospice movement emphasis is on team work and treatment of the whole person. As well as listening empathically to the patient, it is of vital importance that team members learn to listen to each other. Only through such listening between doctor, nurse, chaplain, social worker and volunteer will the one and only *right* model of care be avoided.

The Natural Death Handbook prints a variety of letters from carers and spouses of those who have come home to die and the various ways in which they were helped by services in the community as well as neighbours and friends. One of these letters comes under the heading 'Dying amidst Family Chaos'. This was from a wife who brought her husband home for Christmas. No transport was organised so she 'managed to get him into the car somehow. And home to his own bed, with intrusive cats, kids' music reverberating and cobwebs that threaten to garrotte the unwary' (Albery and Elliot, 1997, p.77) The Macmillan nurse was on holiday but a doctor friend was with her when he died:

> Mary and I washed him and laid him out, to the disapproval of the funeral director. It was very real, very loving, and I was able to keep literally in touch with Peter. Then I kept him at home, in our bed, until ten minutes before the funeral. (p.77)

When my husband died I was not so successful at standing up to the funeral directors and they insisted on taking him away earlier than I would have

wished. But the 'chaos' she describes resonates with some of my own memories. An occasion when he fell over while I was ineptly trying to lift him made
us both laugh. He was not hurt so I gave him a pillow and went out to look
for help. The dog thought we were having a game and joined in with enthusiastic barks. I came back with the milkman, who lifted him easily and shared
the joke. This, despite the sadness of the situation, was more like normal life
than the technical but impersonal efficiency of hospital, or even the quiet
orderliness of a hospice. Five years later, my mother also died at home, with
the neighbour's cat purring comfortably on her bed.

Fear

There are two different fears that human beings may suffer in the face of
death. One of these is probably universal. The other, a fear of death as
non-being, is individual and harder to define; 'anxiety' or 'dread' might more
aptly describe it.

Fear of Dying

This fear is quite specific. When a person knows he is dying from a long,
wasting disease, which he anticipates as giving more pain and more discomfort while the body gradually disintegrates and dies, all stratagems of denial
that may, for a time, have worked to mask this painful reality must eventually
fall apart and there comes a point where, it seems to me, it is virtually impossible not to be afraid. When my sister said, wearily, 'it takes a long time to
die', it was not being dead that frightened her but the painfully prolonged
process she would have to go through before reaching that state. It is this pro-
longation of dying which those who clamour for euthanasia seek to avoid.
Others may see the process as a necessary stripping of a lot of inessential trap-
pings that have been accessory to our human condition. In dying, there can
be no more vanity in the way we look. We have humbly to hand over our
bodies for the ordinarily private rituals of being filled, emptied and cleaned
that we have coped with ourselves since infancy. All our weaknesses are
exposed and pretences abandoned. This is a slow dying, bit by bit, a letting
go of everything familiar, of people, both loved and hated, and of all ambitions for future achievement. But, if we have the strength, it can be a time for
being honest with our friends and leaving them some sort of legacy, not just
of material things but memories, ideas and our hopes for their future.

   Not everything will go smoothly and, inevitably, both for the dying and
those left to mourn them, some of what we wanted and tried to do will be left

undone. No one dies easily if doctors and nurses behave as though death is not happening. No one is honest if others go on pretending.

Yet, until comparatively recently, a nurse caring for the dying could be told:

> I was never to mention the subject even if the patient asked, nor was I to speak about it to any relatives, no matter what the situation. I witnessed some appalling deaths. We were allowed to lay out their bodies but we were not allowed to talk about it. (from a letter to the Natural Death Centre – Albery and Elliot, 1987, p.23)

No wonder that both sides of the patient/medical divide, when faced with such unrelenting silence, experience fear. If forbidden ordinary communication, the person who is dying will cease to be an individual who is afraid and becomes a body that is already almost a corpse, an object to be handled according to regulations that have to be learnt. One can only rejoice each time the rules are disobeyed and a bit of human kindness breaks through.

But medical training is changing at last and death perceived less as the doctors' failure and more as a natural end that the patient can be helped to accept. Doctors and nurses need to come to terms with their own fears, repressions and denials, and for this to be highlighted in their training.

I also think that we need to change our perception of death as a purely medical event and give it back to the families, friends and social milieu of the person who has died. This can be done by surrendering the body to earth or fire, as a 'debt to nature', and keeping the soul alive in the memories of friends. There may also be a restoring of the soul to whatever god they and their dead friend have given their allegiance.

Fear of Death

> When one is alone and it is night and so dark and still that one hears nothing and sees nothing but the thoughts which add and subtract the years, and the long row of those disagreeable facts which remorselessly indicate how far the hand of the clock has moved forward, and the slow irresistible approach of the wall of darkness which will eventually engulf everything I love, possess, wish for, hope for, then all our profundities about life slink off to some undiscoverable hiding place, and fear envelops the sleepless one like a smothering blanket. (Jung, 1977, p.405)

Jung described a fear that many people will recognise, but some only occasionally. It is not the same as the much more universal fear of the pain of dying. Those who habitually look into the nothingness of death and shudder may think that it is only they who are sane and that those who go through life without this awareness are neurotically repressing a truth they dare not face. Yet, strangely, they may find themselves being judged as morbid, whereas not to fear death is the way to be healthy-minded. Some seem to regard happiness as a duty. William James (1974) describes these deliberately happy people as saying to the rest of us: 'Stuff and nonsense, get out into the open air!' or 'Cheer up, old fellow, you'll be alright erelong, if you will only drop your morbidness!' (p.148). But James is clearly of the opinion that:

> healthy-mindedness is inadequate as a philosophical doctrine, because the evil facts which it refuses positively to account for are a genuine portion of reality; and they may after all be the best key to life's significance, and possibly the only openers of our eyes to the deepest levels of truth. (p.169)

I am inclined to regard healthy-mindedness as a manic defence against the darker side of reality. Those of us who are undefended need to learn how we can live, psychologically, religiously and existentially, with that 'wall of darkness' that Jung described and which it is impossible for us not to fear.

Laura

One might describe this patient as chronically afraid of death, a fear that she remembered from the age of six when she had her first serious religious teaching 'at her mother's knee'. There was nothing joyless about that teaching. She was not threatened with hell fire. On the contrary, she only had to be 'a good girl' and she would go to heaven and live for ever and ever. What would heaven be like, she asked. The reply must have been vague because she has forgotten it, though she was left with an impression of always being in church. In heaven she would be expected to worship God non-stop for ever. What a strict father God must be to demand such tiring activity from his children! Heaven sounded an infinitely boring place.

So Laura began crying in the night and could not be comforted, 'because', she said, 'I'm afraid of living for ever'. Asked if she would rather just stop, she cried all the more. To stop being herself, to be snuffed out like a candle flame – that was even more frightening. So she was caught between two impossibilities.

The fear never went away. She repressed it but also managed quite a lot of deliberate forgetting so that she could get on with her life. Her consolation was that she was young and death usually happened to the old so she had time to get used to being afraid. Then came the war, and even the young could be killed. With more repression, she got through, but her defences often broke down and then she felt as though she were shut in a box from which there was no way out. She would like to have found someone with the same sort of fear but everyone else seemed to be thoroughly 'healthy-minded' and wondered what was the matter with her. 'You'll grow out of it', her mother said, 'there will be so many other things to think about'. More helpfully, she was told that there was a difference between time and eternity. There were no clocks or calendars in heaven, no endless years to be endured and counted. This thought was interesting, even exciting, but impossible to grasp. She became more than ever obsessed with time. She would have to achieve something in her life, *while there was still time*, something tangible that could be left behind when she died, or children to live after her. But none of this happened. Her fear of death extended to fear of life and she could not bring herself to take risks:

> Many young people have at bottom a panic fear of life (though at the same time they intensely desire it) … Youthful longings for the world and for life, for the attainment of high hopes and distant goals, is life's obvious teleological urge which at once changes into fear of life, neurotic resistances, depressions and phobias, if at some time it gets caught in the past, or shrinks from risks without which the unseen goal cannot be attained. (Jung, 1977, p.405)

When Laura became old enough to realise that her parents were not infallible, her religious faith began to crumble; yet she clung to a desperate hope that everything she had been told about God was true. Even living for ever (or in eternity) would be better than being left in the end with nothing. To think about such ultimate matters was like switching off a light and plunging the whole meaning of life into darkness. In trying to find a solution she found herself clinging to a series of saviour figures, some of whom, sensing her desperation, shook themselves free. She thought being in love would shut out the fear but her enormous neediness put boy-friends off:

> A person who is trying to find his salvation only in a loving relationship but who is being defeated by this too narrow focus is neurotic. He can become overly passive and dependent, fearful of venturing out on his own, of making his life without his partner, no matter how that partner treats him.

The object has become his 'All', his whole world; and he is reduced to the status of a simple reflex of another human being. (Becker, 1973, p.179)

Substitute 'her' and 'she' for 'his', 'he' and 'him' and we have quite a true picture of Laura in her twenties. Even as an adult she was afraid of the dark and of sleeping alone. When she married, she thought she had found the ultimate saviour. She and her husband were happy together and he did not mind her dependence. Then he died. Laura was well into the second half of her life when at last she came into therapy.

At first she found interpretations irrelevant. She insisted that her childhood had been perfectly happy, that her parents loved her and that it was entirely her own fault if she had felt insecure. Yes, there had been upheavals and she was sent to boarding school rather young. She had forgotten her mother's face when absent for some months but her grandparents had taken good care of her. (Later, she forgot her therapist's face and panicked). Through the transference relationship she re-lived the uncertain pre-war years shadowed by her father's anxiety about the impending cataclysm and the country's blindness – which paralleled her own isolating fear of death which nobody shared – and then the war, with its pressures to behave well and be patriotic, to be brave when the bombs fell and not to think about herself when others were suffering. In therapy she began at last to sense that her fear could be shared, or at least understood, by her therapist, who had no solutions and was not a saviour yet seemed immensely strong. Laura was able to work through anxieties which had earlier been denied in order to make life liveable. She began to admit to a few flaws in her wonderfully loving parents and a certain casualness, sometimes, in the way they treated her, times when their own concerns crowded out any worries of her own. Her archetypal heroes, who had made her inferior, became merely human and ordinary. Disillusion was not a disaster but, sometimes, a relief. She could reach the depressive position and survive the clash of opposing forces – even if never finally – and face an imperfect future with less of her former dread. She opened her eyes one night and looked at the dark. It had become a comfortable, rather than 'smothering', blanket. It was as though there was more of herself and less that could be smothered. She was able to live alone and welcome freedom as well as loneliness, to accept sadness and even depression, without falling into despair.

She is no longer afraid of life but acknowledges that a chronic fear of death will always be with her. She is no longer ashamed, nor does she feel so alone with it. She has not entirely lost her faith in God, but, if he exists, he must be beyond imagining or else he is not worth knowing.

According to Ernest Becker (1973), consciousness of death is more strongly repressed than sexuality: '*This* is what is creaturely about man, *this* is the repression on which culture is based, a repression unique to the self-conscious animal' (p.96). Becker maintains that Freud was obsessed by death and kept thinking he was going to die. By turning his death fear into a death instinct, it became less threatening. Man's fear was not of death but castration by the father. That there was any higher power than a human father he would never admit. When he broke with Jung, his psychoanalytic 'son and heir', the son's rivalry was like the Oedipal murder of the father. When Jung disagreed, he accused him of having death wishes towards him and, on two occasions when Jung argued and produced theories of his own, Freud fainted. His immortality was the psychoanalytic movement. He could never be passive enough to yield to a God, which would have been to renounce his all-important fatherhood. Yet, as we have already seen, Freud faced his own death stoically when the time came.

Daniel

This was a patient whose problems seemed all to do with castration, both symbolically by parents who preferred his younger brother and physically in that he had to have a diseased testicle removed. Later, he had a vasectomy to please his wife. Later still, he tried to get the vasectomy reversed to please his second wife. He described his genitals as 'a devastated area, a bomb site'. Daniel had a great fear of life. He described sex, when it worked, as a blissful kind of dying. When he talked about death he would sometimes say: 'it's just letting go – really quite easy', or else the thought of nothingness frightened him. He had to fill the emptiness with some sort of noise, preferably music. In everything he did he was conscious of avoiding something else. Listening to music or walking in the country, he would sometimes think of the ease of dying. Then he said to himself: 'life is precious. Why do I waste it?' He put the blame on his parents and on some of the strong women in his life who wanted him to be different. Sometimes, it seemed that I was included in this list. Yet his own passivity tormented him. He could neither live fully nor could he die. He said he was looking for a great passion, which, like that of Tristan and Isolde, could only end in death. His own passions tended to peter out in disillusion.

In our work together we explored castration more than we explored death, although themes of mutilation and murder kept cropping up in his dreams and in masochistic fantasies. The emphasis was on finding a way to live rather than a way to die, though if he had been twenty years older that might have been different.

Becker (1973) sums it up: 'Psychoanalysis has to be broadened to take in fear of death rather than fears of punishment from the parents. It is not the parents who are the "castrators" but nature herself' (p.231).

It is the existential philosophers and psychologists who concentrate most on fear of death as fundamental to human experience. Castration fear, separation anxiety, loss of a love object – all these are secondary to the ontological dread of the self's annihilation: 'Death is something that happens to each of us. Even before its actual arrival it is an absent presence ... the notion of the uniqueness and individuality of each one of us gathers full meaning only in realising that we must die' (Feifel, 1969, p.59).

The precariousness of twentieth-century living has, with two world wars and the nuclear threat, brought death both closer and further from individual consciousness; closer because the means of destruction have so enormously increased and further because the possibilities of wiping out all life on this planet are too terrifying for thought. It is in this threatening situation that the existentialist movement has developed:

> It has accented death as a constitutive part rather than the mere end of life, and high-pointed the idea that only by integrating the concept of death into the self does an authentic and genuine existence become possible. The price for denying death is undefined anxiety, self-alienation. To completely understand himself, man must confront death, become aware of personal death. (Feifel, 1969, p.62)

In terms of facticity, death is the ultimate human 'given'. From the moment of birth, we are old enough to die. So death is always with us and life is unimaginable without it. To Sartre, death was an absurdity. In Camus it produced angry rebellion. But Heidegger claimed that, if honestly confronted, death could become 'an integrating factor in an authentic existence' (Macquarrie, 1972, p.198). Tillich (1974) believed in a 'courage to be' as self-affirmation despite the constant threat of non-being and the need to try and transcend ourselves through participating in 'being-itself', which 'means that every courage to be has, openly or covertly, a religious root' (p.152).

If we think existentially, we will take Laura's fears of non-being seriously without trying to turn them into something else, however insecure we may feel her to be in terms of human relationships and her need for love. For Daniel, his castration fear may be seen as secondary to his struggle for any 'courage to be' in what seems to him a persecutory, and often meaningless, world. In Western civilization we have become increasingly individualistic. If we could think corporatively, we might feel less alone and the continuing life of the community become more valuable than one person's death. 'No man is an island entire of itself; every man is a piece of the continent...' (Donne, 1624).

CHAPTER 6

Partly Living

Yet we have gone on living,
Living and partly living.

T.S. Eliot, *Murder in the Cathedral*, p.19

O wretched man that I am:
Who shall deliver me
from the body of this death?

St Paul, Romans

To Eat or Not To Eat?

> She hadn't really meant to die. She just wanted to see what would happen. Wanted to see how far she could go. And then couldn't quite bring herself to break the fall. (Hornbacher, 1998, p.245)

No one can be fully alive while she is trying to turn herself into someone else. By changing her body, she assumes she is changing her self, or, by a gradual killing of that body, imagines she is actually saving her self. She exists, not in her body but in a place apart, a superior plane. Anorexia protects her from society's impingement. She is in a realm where she feels no difference between fullness and hunger or between heat and cold, even though she shivers and slowly grows weak. In her determination to survive as a self-defined individual, she chooses starvation. She is not committing suicide but finding a way to go on living, a way that is all her own and not imposed by family expectations and other people's patterns. She needs an indomitable will and, despite increasing weakness, battles with extraordinary energy to achieve her goal.

Meeting such a person in therapy, all I can do is to warn her that she is playing a dangerous game and that if she pushes it too far, I am not prepared to take her on without referring her to a medical specialist to whom she may have to surrender her body for the sort of treatment that she is likely to find highly abusive. Within safe limits, I am prepared to allow her to be anorexic but not to argue nor yet to collude with her triumphant thinness. Too much interpretation is likely to be seen as an attack: 'Like the body, the unconscious is private property' (McCleod, 1981, p.137). She will fight any attempt at invasion. My hope is that by my staying *with* her and learning what it is like to *be* her she will feel safe enough to make the necessary interpretations herself and recover – or not – in her own time and in her own way. Hospital tactics may succeed in getting her to eat and gain weight so that, in the short term at least, the physical symptoms are cured. But to overturn a lifetime's anorexic thinking is unlikely to be managed in a few weeks. Sheila McCleod (1981), writing as a partially cured anorectic, quotes Sartre: 'you can get rid of a neurosis, but you are never cured of yourself' (p.145).

Fasting has a long history. I looked it up in the *Encyclopaedia Brittanica*:

> (Fasting) originated in the desire of the primitive man to bring on at will certain abnormal conditions favourable to the seeing of those visions and the dreaming of those dreams which are supposed to give the soul direct access to the objective realities of the spiritual world. (Vol. 10, 1911, p.194)

Primitive man no doubt used drugs, as many do today, to enhance these experiences. The modern anorectic may not be looking for an objective spiritual world but she is quite likely trying to find her soul, and, in Jung's terminology, individuation. The encyclopaedia quotes 'the axiom of Amazulu, "the continually stuffed body cannot do secret things"'. The anorectic starves herself in secret, or, if she eats and becomes bulimic, secretly purges herself. However disgusted we may be at her vomit and her faeces, getting rid of them is her means of purification. Being clean, emptied of 'poisonous' food, brings something like mystical experience: 'Had we a god, it might have been Dionysus. We, his followers, imagined ourselves maenads, half-believing in divine possession, half mocking it' (Hornbacher, 1998, p.104).

There is a joy in disappearing:

> A disappearing act, the act of becoming invisible, is, in fact, a visible act and rarely goes unnoticed. There is a strange sort of logic to this. We ex-

pect, in this world, that human beings will bear a human weight and force – there is a fascination with all human rebellions against materials limits, with that small step into the supernatural. I am not saying that the erasing of the body *is* magic, but it *feels* magical. Houdini, barefoot, walks across the coals, and the gathered crowd sucks in its breath. Houdini disappears into thin air; the gathered crowd murmurs and looks round wildly. (Hornbacher, 1998, p.129)

One of my anorexic patients had this dream:

In a bare white room, there was a figure, neither male nor female, very slim and dressed in black. The face was covered so that it too was black and featureless. The figure began to dance, first round the outside, then moving to the middle and covering every inch of space. When this was done, the figure knelt, bowed its head and disappeared, dying and leaving no trace.

This, the dreamer said, was ideal – the figure, the dance and the death. I made a positive interpretation, which was not accepted. This is the only piece of anorexic case material I am prepared to give, since I find these patients particularly sensitive about their secrets and even to ask permission would seem like an intrusion and betrayal of trust.

Viewed from the outside, anorexia has been called 'The Slimmers' Disease' and is said to start with teenage puppy-fat, teasing, which leads to dieting and the dieting getting out of control. In so far as this is true, anorexia – and its twin, bulimia – is influenced by a society whose taste, ever since Twiggy in the 1960s, has been governed by unnaturally thin fashion models. It is interesting to look back to a similar period in the 1920s when the First World War and the suffragette movement produced liberated women in short skirts with bobbed hair and flattened chests. I had an aunt who put on weight in her teens, starved herself later to accord with the fashion and restricted herself, for the rest of her life, to a diet all her own, which failed to nourish her. In an exceptionally long-living family she achieved a mere 61, dying of no specified disease, anorexia being outside most people's vocabulary. She was said to have been beautiful but she never married, having been engaged to a war hero who was killed in action. Later, she was engaged again but, as the date drew near, she took fright and needed her father's help to call off the wedding.

Since the typical anorectic is a teenage girl verging on puberty, a notable result of not eating is a delayed maturity, involving stopping – or, perhaps, never even starting – menstruation. Having such power to switch off normal female development through sheer strength of will is a remarkable achievement. A girl, feeling helpless and, perhaps, frightened in an adult world, finds one thing at least that she can control – her body. She discovers an alternative to having to grow up. She can regress. And, round this regression, the observer can weave Oedipal themes. The girl has a fantasy of being Daddy's little girl for ever, without guilt. Anorexia can also be a means of postponing sexuality, perhaps indefinitely. Many anorectics turn out to have been sexually abused as children.

If a person's will-power is not strong enough for anorexia, there is always bulimia. One can stuff oneself with goodies and then get rid of them. Not surprisingly, bingeing and starving can alternate. As methods of coping, the two may seem contradictory, but both are means of control. More contradictory are the family messages. I remember having tea with my husband and his aunt, who was famous for her cooking and liked this to be appreciated. On greeting us she commented that her nephew had put on weight and recommended going on a diet. But, when we sat down to tea, she exclaimed: 'What's the matter? Don't you like my cake? I made it specially for you!'

Michael Eigen (1996) said to his bulimic patient: 'You are starving to death' (p.176). She got angry. She wanted him to stop her eating. But he went on telling her she was starving:

> Her fat winds like insulation around unendurable pain. Inside she is starving, wasting away … I look at her enormous body and am lacerated by *seeing* a skin and bones concentration camp self. I *see* a starving self … Her body gets more and more bloated as her inner self reaches vanishing point. (p.174)

There had been madness and violence in his patient's family and she could not bear the emotional starvation that this caused. She converted the emotion into physical hunger, hence the bingeing. Her therapist's wish was that she should gorge herself on what he had to offer, but, for a long time, he found it impossible to get through to her: 'After a year I began to get the idea that her wish for control is a vestige of her wish to have a full psychic life' (p.175). Very gradually, she found herself able to use the therapy for emotional nourishment and a widening of experience that had been so much reduced by her addiction to filling up with food.

I am aware, in this chapter, of writing only about women, even though an increasing number of men are suffering from eating disorders. I have already mentioned Jonathan, who had a period of anorexia at puberty. But he is the only example that has come my way and I shall not try and generalise from his particular case.

In an attempt to view anorexia from the *inside*, I have come across two vivid accounts written by two women, a generation apart, one in England, the other in America, and, in these two very different settings, both in time and place, have found myself looking for a common experience. Both are well versed in psychological theory but have tried to work out their own explanations:

> I am not going to repeat at length, how eating disorders are 'about control', because we've all heard it. It's a buzzword, reductive, categorical, a tidy way of herding people into a mental quarantine and saying *There*. That's that. Eating disorders are 'about' yes, control, and history, philosophy, society, personal strangeness, family fuck-ups, autoerotics, myths, mirrors, love and death and S & M magazines and religion, the individual's blindfolded stumble-walk through an ever stranger world. (Hornbacher, 1998, p.4)

Marya Hornbacher, a 23-year-old American, sees her eating disorder (bulimia/anorexia) as an addiction. It is also 'a response, albeit a rather twisted one, to a culture, a family, a self' (p.5).

Sheila MacLeod (1981), English and now middle-aged, describes her anorexia:

> like most other psychoneurotic syndromes, a positive strategy aimed at establishing autonomy and resolving what would otherwise be unbearable conflicts in the life of the sufferer. These conflicts are partially related to and arising from the anorexic's [*sic*] related history and personality structure – that is they are intrapsychic. But they are also existential, that is related to being-in-the-world, which for human beings necessarily means being-in-a-body. (p.11)

Both writers recognise the family and cultural context which drives them to such extremes. Disordered eating is an attempted solution in the midst of confusion, a bid for identity and refusal to be swallowed up in conformity, even when this entails a life-and-death struggle in which death, all too often, proves to be the winner.

Sheila, in the 1950s, went to a girls-only English boarding school, where she felt herself to be a misfit. She came from a less privileged background than that of her peers and had to rely on intelligence and an appetite for work, which only partly made up for her lack of social ease. Even without her anorexia, she was trying to turn herself into someone she was not, losing her identity in an ever widening gap between home and school, belonging nowhere. There were no boys and her sex education had been flimsy. As for menstruation, it disgusted her. It was as though she were being punished for a crime that her body, not her self, had committed, and she hated her body. When she looked in the mirror and saw what puberty was doing to it, her reaction was 'This can't be me!' The clothes she had to wear (school uniform) and the food she was given to eat were, all of them, someone else's choice: 'I had nothing: I was nothing ... I was being given what I did not want ... so my body was my ultimate weapon in my bid for autonomy. It was the only thing I owned, the only thing which could not be taken away from me' (MacLeod, 1981, p.66).

In choosing to live in her self, her body had to die. But that was a denial of biology, a denial of reality. She wanted to regress to the 'idealised world of childhood' where she did not have to be a woman and where there was no sexuality and no death, these being aspects of the adult world which she was so determined to reject. But:

> as the disease progressed, all the anxieties became more difficult to ignore – necessarily because I was growing older and, in my regressive pre-pubertal state, more of an anomaly than ever among my peers. It was, in other words, becoming more and more difficult to postpone the future. (p.105)

Marya went to boarding school in America in the 1980s. She was already bulimic and had been so almost as long as she could remember. She tried telling her parents about her vomiting and her mother just said: 'I used to do that'. Afterwards, both parents avoided the subject for as long as they could, before getting really concerned, and Marya became expert at deceiving them. When she was 13 she began 'inching' her way towards anorexia. 'Anorexia was my Big Idea, my bid for independence' (Hornbacher, 1998, p.68). She was obsessed with food. All her conversation was about weight and diet. When she achieved anorexia she would perform surgery on her plate, obsessively cutting the food into bite-sized pieces to spin out the time she spent in eating it. She was 15 when, at her own request, she went to her Michigan boarding school. The position was idyllic, buildings dotted about in a wood, boys and girls mixed. She shared a room with one other girl across the road from the boys' 'dorms'. Puberty had begun early and, unlike Sheila, she had been sleeping around from an early age, though without enjoyment, beyond the power of being able to do it. The school was full of thin girls. Many of them were dancers. All of them seem to have been hyperactive: 'The obsession with weight seemed nearly universal. We sat at our cafeteria tables, passionately discussing the calories of lettuce, celery, a dinner roll, rice' (p.102).

It seems astonishing how long it takes for such conversations to become boring!

There was no question of not fitting in. Unlike Sheila, Marya uses the pronoun 'we' rather than 'I' when describing school life. Activity was intense. There were classes, workshops, practices, rehearsals. Marya loved it and devoured art and learning, everything except food. She got a kick out of the adrenalin that comes with starvation: 'high as a kite, sleepless, full of a frenetic, unstable energy' (p.105). As in all addictions, there is a desire for more and more – or, paradoxically, less and less. Eventually, Marya collapsed. Many hospitalisations followed. She went on collapsing, until at last she *did* get bored, then curious: 'If I could get that sick, then (I figured) I could bloody well get unsick' (p.277).

> There is never a sudden revelation, a complete and tidy explanation for why it happens or why it ends, or why you are who you are ... It comes in bits and pieces, and you stitch them together, wherever they fit, and when you are done, you hold yourself up, and still there are holes and you are a rag doll, invented, imperfect. And yet you are all that you have, so you must be enough. There is no other way. (p.279–80)

Both Marya and Sheila got married. Marya's illness went on longer and her health is now precarious. She does not know how to end her story and says there are many loose ends. The experience is still raw. Death still fascinates. But she has a husband and a new sense of responsibility.

Sheila, looking back over the years, tells us:

> There is a point of despair at which one is forced to choose between life and death, however unconscious that choice may be. Without the aid of any sort of therapy, and certainly without the sympathy and understanding which should attend it, I managed to opt for life. (MacLeod, 1981, p.109)

The Dying Brain

I would like to compare two very different quotations:

> My main premise is that dementia reflects the deterioration and decay of the person or self. (Gilleard, 1984, p.10)

I often find that with the confused you can chat heart to heart. You can touch people where we really come together. (Butler and Orbach, 1993, p.153)

It depends on one's definition of self. Gilleard bases his views on those of Guntrip (1971), echoed by Foulds (1976). Dementia separates people from personal relationships. With loss of memory, selfhood is seen (by observers) as fading to vanishing point. Without 'ability to continue to interpret the present within the structure of personal experience in the past, and the ability to extend this continuity to one's future intentions' (Gilleard, 1986, p.20) there can be no self. Gilleard seems to assume that there can be no self without object-relations. Others might argue that although the early mother/child relationship is vital for the infant's mental health, the adult individual also has a need for solitude, especially if engaged in creative work (Storr, 1989). Old age, even without dementia, brings tiredness. The brain slows down and memory fades. Not surprisingly, there may be a certain withdrawal from the immediacy of family interactions and a wish to be left in peace without intrusion.

How dementia is experienced by the dementing person, apart from fear of it in the early stages, is something we can try to imagine or guess, but, in the absence of communication, never know for certain. My inclination is to respect the still existing self struggling within a dying brain, even though I have no proof that any entity one can call 'self' exists apart from the brain.

Defining self, soul, mind, psyche can lead to philosophical arguments far beyond anything I am qualified to write about. I can only acknowledge the two views illustrated in my opening quotations. Either mind and brain are two words for the same bodily organ, which stops existing on the body's death, or mind and brain are two separate entities, the self being associated with a particular body yet able to exist without it. This dualism is intrinsic to Descartes' separation of mind and matter. The only thing he could not doubt was that he existed:

This was revealed by the very act of doubting. And, besides assuming that every thought must have a thinker, Descartes argued that a thinker must be a Pure Ego, or spiritual substance. A Cartesian Pure Ego is the clearest case of a separately existing ego, distinct from the brain and body. (Parfit, 1986, p.224)

Derek Parfit, who takes a reductionist view, dismisses this separate entity as something which we have no reason to believe, any more than in the existence of 'water-nymphs or unicorns' (p.224). He calls the Cartesian Ego a 'further fact' from which, like the Buddha, he feels liberated. Instead of being the owner of my consciousness, the subject of my experiences, I am essentially my brain. When the brain dies that is the end of me.

At this point I find myself asking: what would Jung have to say about dementia? He was not a philosopher but a profound thinker and analyst of his own, as well as other people's, experience. His concept of self was both individual and more than individual, and certainly not confined to the physical brain: 'With increasing age, contemplation and reflection, the inner images naturally play an even greater part in man's life. "Your old men shall dream dreams"' (Jung, 1967, pp.351–2). But only, he adds, if 'the psyches of old men have not become wooden or entirely petrified'. No dreams in dementia?

The inner world of the unconscious would not, for Jung and his followers, be contained in the convolutions of our brains but would arise in each one of us from the accumulated wisdom of the race:

> The unconscious is the mother of consciousness ... Just as a human mother can only produce a human child, whose deepest nature lay hidden during its potential existence within her, so we are practically compelled to believe that the unconscious cannot be an entirely chaotic accumulation of instincts and images. There must be something to hold it together and give expression to the whole. (Jung, 1975, p.281)

This 'something' is not the ego, which is what was born out of unconsciousness and 'has for ever a new beginning and an early end' (p.281), but *self* – that self which, I suggest, does *not* die with the dying brain.

'Your old men shall dream dreams' (Acts 2:17; Joel 2:28). Jung's 'inner images' make their appearances both in the dreams of sleep and in waking reverie. I wonder how much brain needs to have gone before dreaming disappears. The demented are sometimes described as being imprisoned in their failing bodies. Jung (1967) writes of old people being imprisoned in their memories, getting too involved in their reconstructions of past events, in the detail of their personal (egocentric) lives. Writing in old age, he tells us: 'I try to see the line which leads through my life into the world, and out of the world again' (p.352).

At the end of life we sink into unconsciousness, which, in Jung's terms, is a return to the mother. No wonder the demented become child-like – but this time they are not growing up, *they are growing down*. At first, they are bewildered and frustrated, often angry, usually quietening down as more and more brain gets eaten away. If we are to 'chat heart to heart' and touch them 'where we really come together', we may have to rid ourselves of preconceptions, comparisons with the past or hopes for the future, and meet that person as someone living only in today, freed from the preoccupations of memory or anticipation. But that was easier for the priest who said those words after a hospital visit to a confused old lady, unknown to him in any other setting, than it could ever be for the close relative who had to witness the steady downward drift of her illness. To care for a husband, wife or parent without reward or recognition is probably only possible on the basis of having very much loved the earlier version of that person's self.

A speaker from our local branch of the Alzheimer's Disease Society uses the following piece of dialogue to show something of what a caring relative may have to face:

Narrator: This is the home on the Sussex coast of Mr and Mrs Perkins. Tom and Winnie, an elderly couple. Scene 1, one evening.

Tom: It's getting late. Aren't you going home?

Winnie: Oh, don't start that again, Tom! I live here. This is my home, just as much as yours.

Tom: How dare you say that! This is my wife's home.

Winnie: But I am your wife.

Tom: How could you be my wife? My wife is young and has lovely fair hair. You're an old woman, all wrinkled and your hair is white. I wouldn't marry you!

Winnie: Tom! We've been married 57 years.

Tom: Don't be silly, woman. I'm not even 40 yet.

Winnie: I can't stand this. I'll make a pot of tea.

Narrator: Tom watches Winnie go out of the room, quietly sneaks to the door and shuts it, then goes to the phone.

Tom: 916890 Is that the police station? I've got a woman in this house that I can't get rid of. Please come and turn her out.

Policeman: Ah – is that Mr Perkins?

Tom: Yes, but how do you know?

Policeman: I did come round to see you Sir, the first time you rang
            us.

Tom: Not to me you didn't. I've never rung you before.

Policeman: Oh dear! I think you must have forgotten. I did come
            and I established that the lady you were complaining of
            is, in fact, your wife, Mrs Perkins.

Tom: Couldn't be. I haven't seen my wife for a long time. She
            won't come back while this other woman is here.

Policeman: I really don't know what to say about that Mr Perkins.

Tom: So, you won't come?

Policeman: I don't see how I could help Sir.

Winnie: Open the door Tom. I need both hands for the tray.
            Whatever did you shut the door for? Oh, have you been
            ringing the police again? I wish you wouldn't, I get so
            embarrassed!

Narrator: Scene 2. Next afternoon.

Winnie: That's Jack's car now. He said he and Jenny would be
            early.

Jenny: Hullo Mum. Hullo Dad. Lovely to see you both. How's
            things?

Tom: Well may you ask. Why haven't you been for so long?

Jack: A week's not long.

Tom: A week! You haven't been for months. Years even. I can't
            remember when I last saw you. I call it a scandal. You've
            only got to walk round the corner.

Jack: It's ten years since we lived round the corner! Before you
            moved.

Jenny: When you retired. Mum and me are going to live by the
            sea, you said.

Tom: Are you going to tell me this isn't London?

Jack: 'Course it's not London Dad! Honestly, your memory!

Jenny: We do come every Saturday. Jack, you keep Dad com-
            pany while I help Mum in the kitchen. It's almost time
            for the match on the telly. I expect Dad would like to
            watch that too.

Narrator: In the kitchen Jenny catches up on her father's latest odd
            doings.

Winnie: I never know where anything is. I couldn't find the milk
            jug one day – and it turned up behind the television.
            Still had milk in it – nasty and sour by then. Then I had
            to buy a new bath plug. He'd taken the old one off and
            lost it. Said the chap next door needed it for his bike.

Jenny: Oh Mum! Honestly! What rubbish!

Winnie: He put two £20 notes in the waste paper basket – I
            couldn't believe my eyes.

Jenny: Why ever did he do that?

Winnie: We'd gone to buy him some new shoes, but they hadn't
            the sort he wanted in his size, so the shop ordered them
            for him. I said 'Why did you throw these away?' and he
            said 'They're no good now. We couldn't buy any shoes
            with them'. The latest is he keeps saying he wants to go
            and see his mother.

Jenny: Gran? But she's been dead for years and years!

Winnie: He keeps putting his coat on and going out to catch a
            train.

Jenny: Oh poor old Mum! Poor old Dad! And there isn't a sta-
            tion for miles and miles!

This dialogue shows a relationship sadly out of kilter, two people locked into
a situation from which neither can escape – the husband from his confusion
and the wife from a guilt-tinged sense of responsibility. Both need help, but
of what kind?

Dementia comes in many forms, not all of them to do with advanced ageing. We hear a lot today about Alzheimer's, which has been the subject of considerable research and hopes for a breakthrough in discovering possible means of prevention. Less talked about are Pick's Disease, Lewy Body Disease and multiple infarct dementias, as well as age-related dementias in those of us living to 80, 90 and beyond:

> Not only does the brain, like any other bodily organ, become vulnerable to failures in self-maintenance, but it does so from an inherently more vulnerable status than most bodily organs. To use a popular computer analogy, it cannot renew its hardware: once lost or dysfunctional, nerve cells are not replaced. (Gilleard, 1984, p.107)

The changes, common to all dementias, are memory loss, mood change and behavioural disturbance. The term 'global' is used to describe the extent of the impairment:

> The confusion that surrounds the dementing person is a confusion over reference points, both current and historical, which dislocates actions, misperceives experience and loses the thread that gives meaning and intentionality to behaviour, which taken globally reflects a fundamental loss of relatedness, to both the physical and social environment. (Gilleard, 1984, p.20)

Sources of Help

The Alzheimer's Disease Society has grown from small beginnings in 1979 in response to a recognised need for supporting the relatives of people with dementia – of all forms, not of Alzheimer's alone. There are now many branches running major services, with a Care Consortium to monitor their work. Others settle for the basic 'Core Services': listening to and providing information for relatives; making sure that the people with dementia and their close relatives are linked into the statutory services and to such bodies as the Crossroads charity, which sends trained workers regularly into the homes; running groups where the relatives can meet and support each other; campaigning and giving educational talks. Again and again relatives say: 'If only we had found the Society earlier. It has been an enormous help'.

Further help has come in the 1990s through the 'Care in the Community' concept. As our population gets older, with an enormous increase of people over 65, there has been a movement towards keeping people with dementia in their own homes, with services laid on to relieve the carers. Ideally, the clients receive 'packages of care' selected to suit individual needs. Sadly, the scheme is still limited, chiefly by finance, and the great improvements have not, at this stage, reached the levels that were hoped for.

The removal of hospital beds has resulted in a huge increase of rest/nursing homes. Because these are not officially hospitals, they are counted as part of community care. They vary, as we all know, in the quality of what they are able, or willing, to give. Although nursing homes are no longer only for the rich, they have to be paid for somehow and this often takes the whole of a person's life savings.

Most carers want to keep their dementing relatives at home in familiar surroundings. Community care holds out hope that they may be able to do so, but more – much more – is needed.

Counselling or Befriending

One Alzheimer's worker tells me she is 'itchy' about counselling, describing it as the 'in' word and the 'in' thing to be doing. She protests at the professionalism of the counsellors who refuse cups of tea from their clients. She protests also at the idea of dementia carers having to pay to have someone listen to them, even though she recognises that counsellors must have training and back-up systems which need funding. In this area there is a new venture called SAGE, a mobile service especially for elderly people who can be visited in their homes. And, for bereaved people, there is a branch of CRUSE. But she is sure that what works best for dementia carers is the support of people who have 'been there' themselves. However, some Alzheimer's Disease Society branches are now offering trained counsellors as part of their services.

On my part I can see that, when people are immersed in the overwhelming experience of looking after a spouse or parent suffering in this way they are hardly likely to spend their short 'time off' in the serious study of themselves that counselling may require. What they welcome is simple befriending from sympathetic people who know how to listen well, to hug when needed and to share cups of tea often. I would say this also applies to those caring for relatives who are terminally ill with diseases such as cancer or motor neurone. My own experience, when my husband died, was that of being too engrossed in what was happening to him to want anything extra for myself. It is after the person has actually died – in my case a long time after – when bereavement really hits, that one may think about getting counselling or other psychotherapeutic help. I stress the phrase 'think about', since there is, of course, no universal *must* about what to do or where to turn.

From Inside Out

Is there anything one can say? Even the scientists who do brain scans to demonstrate the decaying brain tissue cannot tell us how it feels to live – or partly live – with such enormous handicap. When the process begins, neither the sufferer nor the relatives get seriously alarmed. Some memory loss, they tell themselves, is expected as we get older. One may laugh at oneself and not mind very much if others do a little gentle teasing. Perhaps, one was always the 'absent-minded professor'. It might even seem like a compliment. On the other hand, if one was renowned for being practical or for having a particularly accurate memory, what is happening will, to say the least, be puzzling. Now that dementia, particularly Alzheimer's, is so much talked and written about, with programmes on television showing some of these lost and wandering sufferers, one may, when the illness is just beginning, identify with what one sees, and that must be very frightening.

One friend, whose husband had Alzheimer's, told me that in the early stages the realisation came and went. Sometimes, she would find him in tears. There was a lot of wandering about, trying to get somewhere but not knowing where, wanting to escape but always taking the illness with him. He had always had a sweet nature and perfect manners, which did not desert him. His wife and sons gave him, and each other, wonderful support and behaved to him as normally as possible. He was a much respected musician and composer with a wide circle of friends. I remember arriving one evening and he politely took my coat but let it fall to the floor. We went through the gestures of having a conversation, though with sentences that did not connect. It was better than ignoring him, which nobody did. He attended a day centre where he was still able to play the piano for the others to listen. He had forgotten his own compositions but remembered the classics.

Dementia is now a major area of research and the knowledge is increasing all the time, not least about how to communicate with the sufferers. We are learning that we should show respect for these adults for being who they *were* and for the selves, which I believe they retain, even when they have lost, or *nearly* lost, their egos.

The writer and poet John Killick, who has worked on a one-to-one basis with people suffering from dementia, asserts: 'You must listen as though your life depended on it'. Communicating with these people is like learning a new language. He recalls how a man with severe dementia said to him:

'Have you an opening? Have you a guide? Could you come along and turn the key in a lock for me? You will not find mÿ room. I've only got nothing' (Alzheimer's Disease Society Newsletter, July 1998). What the man *really* meant was that he had lost his way mentally and this was his manner of asking for help: 'Once we realize that people with dementia may sometimes use a symbolic or poetic language to describe memories or feelings, some of the puzzling things they say begin to make some sort of sense' (Alzheimer's Disease Society Newsletter, July 1998). There may be a mixture of clear and incomprehensible sentences. He suggests that the carer records some of the person's speech so that it can be read later and given some thought. Then, perhaps, the meaning may become clearer.

At a later stage, when words have almost entirely gone, there is always music – I am reminded of my musician friend, just mentioned, who went on playing the piano. There are also ways of showing affection by one's tone of voice or by physical touching, such as holding hands or giving hugs. And a lot can be communicated to the carer by a person's body language – awkward posture or twisting hands. Therapy is not *only* the 'talking cure', there is a lot to be said for a 'companionable silence'.

For John Bayley, whose account of his marriage to Alzheimer's sufferer Iris Murdoch is to be published soon, the illness has not brought despair. In many ways, amazing as this may sound, it has actually strengthened their marriage:

> Every day we are physically closer; and Iris' little 'mouse cry', as I think of it, signifying loneliness in the next room, the wish to be back beside me, seems less forlorn. She is not sailing into the dark; the voyage is over, and under the dark escort of Alzheimer's she has arrived somewhere. So have I. (*The Week*, 7.8.98)

The Death of Meaning

We all want to find some meaning in our lives. Children (unless really badly treated) find it in imaginative play, through which they may rehearse their hopes for the future. Young adults search for it through love and work. In middle age they may lose their way, find themselves stagnated and forget what they were looking for. We talk of a mid-life crisis. Sometimes, this turns out to be an incubation period before a burst of creativity, but there are also people who seem irretrievably stuck.

A striking example of a stuck or stagnated person is Edward Casaubon in George Eliot's *Middlemarch*. Here we have a scholar immersed in research for what he hopes will be a ground-breaking publication, an impressively huge volume – or volumes – to bring him the fame and recognition he longs for. In embarking on 'The Key to All the Mythologies', he sets himself an impossible task, something like the alchemists' quest for gold. What key could he possibly find to unlock *all* the myths of *all* time? He is doomed to failure by his own inflation, bogged down in so much detail that he loses sight of the whole.

When the novel opens, Casaubon has decided that it is his duty to find a wife and leave behind him a copy of himself. He meets Dorothea, who feeds his narcissism by hanging on to his every word. She is captivated by his erudition and the great task he has undertaken – 'something beyond the shallows of ladies' school literature' (Eliot, 1986, p.47). He is gratified by her ardent desire to help him. He does not think a young lady capable of learning Greek and Latin, but she might, perhaps, be able to copy the letters of the Greek alphabet. He treats her as a student – 'he has no two styles of speaking' (p.47). He proposes and she accepts. What an honour to be the wife of such a learned man! She sees it as her vocation to serve him, though we already get glimpses of her not being content with a wise husband and wanting also to be wise herself.

Having decided to 'adorn his life with the graces of female companionship', he tries to abandon himself to 'the stream of feeling' and is surprised to find it an 'exceedingly shallow rill' (p.87). Courtship, he finds, gets in the way of 'The Mythologies'. Before they marry, he expresses disappointment that Dorothea will not be bringing her sister as a companion on their honeymoon in Rome, so that he might be more at liberty to pursue his researches. This is the first occasion on which she finds his words grating on her. He is quite unaware of hurting her and she accuses herself of being weak and selfish.

In Rome Casaubon spends most of his time in dusty libraries, where he clearly does not want female company, though he dutifully lays aside some time to take his bride sight-seeing:

> 'Should you like to go to the Farnesina, Dorothea? It contains celebrated frescoes designed or painted by Raphael, which most persons think it worthwhile to visit.'

> 'But do you care about them?'

'They are, I believe, highly esteemed.' (p.229)

She finds her mind 'continually sliding into inward fits of anger or repulsion, or else into forlorn weariness' (p.228). Her disillusion has begun while still on honeymoon: 'There is hardly any contact more depressing to a young ardent creature than that of a mind in which years full of knowledge seem to have issued in a blank absence of interest and sympathy' (p.229).

The reader is told nothing about Casaubon's early life, so we can only speculate on its influence. I imagine him an only child, brought up by nurses and servants, with a father only interested – to quote his son's words – in a 'copy of himself' and a mother who doted on him, but from a distance. They were gratified by his cleverness but there was no intimacy and he probably felt unloved. He was instructed in the importance of honour and duty but was too delicate to go to school and was educated by tutors, without any competition from his peers. He was shy and made no friends. The only family detail that emerges from the novel is that his Aunt Julia made an 'unfortunate' marriage to a penniless Pole, who had to give lessons to earn his bread. She was disinherited, and probably never mentioned. But Dorothea is much taken by her miniature, which she finds in her boudoir, and learns that Casaubon has felt himself duty-bound to give financial support to her grandson, even though disapproving of his life style. He and Dorothea meet this young man by chance in Rome and he features prominently in their story.

Back in England, neither of them makes the other happy. Dorothea is still determined to devote herself to her husband's service. He says that she can sort out his notes under his direction: 'All those volumes – will you not make up your mind what part of them you will use, and begin to write the book which will make your vast knowledge useful to the world?' (p.232).

Casaubon finds her interest intrusive. His young bride seems not content with 'observing his abundant pen scratches with the uncritical awe of an elegant-minded canary-bird' but is spying on him. He rebukes her with a pompous speech. It is no business of hers to decide 'the times and seasons adapted to the different stages of a work which is not to be measured by the facile conjectures of ignorant onlookers' (p.233). He wants to be soothed, not criticised. She becomes to him 'a personification of that shallow world which surrounds the ill-appreciated or desponding author' (p.234). Dorothea is beginning to see through him and he knows it. There is nothing stagnated about *her* but a 'reaching forward of the whole consciousness towards the fullest truth, the least partial good' (p.235). The tragedy is that she is capable of genuine love but he dares not show her that his great erudition is, in any way, false. He shrinks from a pity which he could never be humble enough to accept. And there is no wise person who can be objective and show them how wretched they are making each other.

The author makes some excuses for Casaubon. He is not physically strong and his soul is 'sensitive without being enthusiastic' (p.312). He is 'spiritually a-hungered like the rest of us'. She goes on to describe his soul as 'fluttering on swampy ground where it was hatched, thinking of its wings but never flying'.

Casaubon is full of paranoia. Has the Archdeacon bothered to read those pamphlets which he brings out from time to time to test his reading public? He has painful doubts about their acceptance by Oxford professors and suspects an acquaintance of his, called Carp, of a deprecating review, which he keeps locked away in a small drawer of his desk and also in a 'dark closet of his verbal memory' (p.314). He becomes increasingly bitter and depressed, his religious faith wavering with 'his wavering trust in his own authorship' and the Christian hope in immortality seeming 'to lean on the immortality of the still unwritten Key to all Mythologies'.

He has a heart attack and is warned that he should work less and relax more, but work is the only activity he cares about. He decides that he may have another 20 years of life to prove 'Carp & Co.' wrong, as if that has suddenly become his sole ambition. He cannot altogether hide his failure from himself but wishes he had a companion who would never find him out. He questions his doctor, who admits to the possibility of his sudden death. He then tests Dorothea's loyalty. Will she, when he dies, carry out his wishes – 'whether you will avoid doing what I should deprecate and apply yourself to doing what I shall desire' (p.518). She does not refuse but asks what these wishes are that she is expected so blindly to follow. His answer: 'But you would use your own judgement. I ask you to obey mine' (p.519). She asks for time to think and says that she will give her answer in the morning. Not surprisingly, she has a sleepless night. She imagines that he wants her to continue his work. To do so would be 'as on a treadmill fruitlessly'. But compassion wins and she determines to promise whatever he wishes. Next morning she follows him into the garden and finds him sitting on a bench, suddenly dead. So she is mercifully spared from saying 'yes'. Afterwards, she learns about a codicil to his will. She will be disinherited if she marries his young cousin, Aunt Julia's grandson. With this, her disillusion is complete and, eventually, after many pages, her story has a happy ending.

This is a case of weakness turning into vindictiveness and a wish, as his power lessens, to control his victim in the only way he can. Just as Dorothea projected onto him her love of truth and wisdom, he now attributes to her his own unadmitted shortcomings and makes her an enemy to be punished. But, in the end, he fails, even in this. He has never learnt to love and, seeking only admiration, does not recognise love when he says it. As a patient in today's world of psychotherapy, it would have been difficult to get through his defences and the intensely negative transference which, I imagine, would have developed. I think I have treated at least one Casaubon in my time, but with no great success.

Long before his body died of heart disease, Casaubon could be said to have been 'psychically dead', or, in Winnicott's language, to have lived from a 'False Self'. This condition is not easy to detect. The falsity is so plausible, compliant and seemingly reasonable that we mistake deadness for aliveness and are slow to perceive that such people are living second-hand lives, contributing nothing of their own to what has been handed to them by their families and early teaching.

A daughter may find she is the one who is left looking after her mother after a family break-up. She tries, holding things together without fully knowing what these *things* are nor who she herself is. She develops a range of false selves for display to different people. She is restless, moving from one relationship to another, depressed because no one gives her what she wants, without realising that this is impossible since she has not the least idea of what it is that would bring her happiness. She works hard but achievement brings no satisfaction. She has mastered the art of using and re-arranging other people's ideas and she fills the void in herself with distractions. If abused, as well as rejected, in childhood, she may have developed no imagination or ability to play. I am purposely generalising because I have come across all sorts of variations on this theme. Winnicott (1976) writes of:

> a poor capacity for using symbols, and a poverty of cultural living. Instead of cultural pursuits one observes in such persons extreme restlessness, an inability to concentrate, and a need to collect impingements from external reality so that the living-time of the individual can be filled by reactions to these impingements. (p.150)

Celia, who knew nothing of Winnicott, talked to me about her 'Show Self', which she used in order to hide a terrifying sense of emptiness. Married at 16, she had spent nearly a decade having babies and, with each birth, she felt she

lost a bit of self. Her first-born had convulsions and subsequent brain damage. Looking into this child's vacant eyes, Celia met her gaze – or *lack* of
gaze – with the same vacancy. Afterwards, she complained of not being able
to see and was afraid that what she thought she saw was different from what
was seen by others. This, she said, meant that she was alone in an expanse of
nothingness. She was afraid of 'falling off the edge of the planet' and became
agoraphobic. Her Show Self was efficient at concentrating on jobs she could
do at home, such as dressmaking and icing cakes. Sometimes, she painted
and was pleased with her ability to make exact copies of other people's pictures. Just once, during a psychotic episode, she painted a wild seascape of
waves and rocks. She said it was rubbish and ought to be burnt but I rescued
it and kept it. Her Show Self took care of her babies and, to outward appearances, she was a 'good enough mother'. Luckily, there was also a father to
take the children out. Celia never left the house.

Sarah was well brought up by parents whom everyone admired, in an
extended family who continuously telephoned or wrote letters to each other
so that everyone knew everyone else's business. An aunt, by marriage, was
criticised for distancing herself just a little from this enveloping mob. Sarah
was compliant and allowed her parents to decide what she should do with
her life. If she disagreed, she kept her opinions hidden. All her feelings were
hidden; so was her creativity. She could never risk showing her poems and
other writings to the family for fear that they would be, as she put it,
'trampled on'. Either criticism or praise would have seemed to her equally
destructive. It took years of therapy for her to drop the secrecy and show her
True Self to the world.

Winnicott (1976) describes how patients can subject themselves to
analysis for long periods of time without showing anything but their False
Selves: 'The False Self has one positive and very important function: to hide
the True Self, which it does by compliance with environmental demands'
(pp.146–7). He stresses the need for recognising a compliant patient's
non-existence. He describes a man whose previous analysis 'had been done on
the basis that he existed, whereas he had only existed falsely' (p.151).
Another (or perhaps the same) patient said to him: 'the only time I felt hope
was when you told me there was no hope, and you continued with the
analysis' (p.152).

Conformity may be necessary for children who have to adapt to their
peers and live up to their school's conventions and expectations. Being a
member of a team has its own importance for future relationships, as also,

perhaps, an early experience of competition, but not, one hopes, at the expense of individual talent or idiosyncrasy. One child, who was a boarder at an over-structured girls' boarding school, was afraid that she would 'stop being a person'. Another broke down and had to be taken away.

When Tolstoy wrote *The Death of Ivan Ilyich*, he described the life of this character as 'the simplest, most ordinary and therefore most terrible' (Tolstoy, 1960, p.109). Ivan had a career and marriage of which everyone in his circle approved. As he rose in the social world, he and his wife shook off their shabbier friends and relatives and entertained only the 'very best' people. It took a severe illness and great pain for him to recognise, first, the falsity, both of the doctors' skill and his wife's affection, and then, only gradually, the meaninglessness of the life he had constructed for himself. All round him, he realised, people were concentrating on 'how soon he would vacate his place and at last release the living from the constraint of his presence' (p.140). The only exceptions were his schoolboy son, who did not hide the distress caused him by his father's suffering, and a peasant servant, who, without disgust or embarrassment, washed his master's wasted body, emptied his commode and gave genuine comfort. The others kept up a pretence that he was ill but not dying.

As the pain got worse, he felt as though he were being pushed into a deep black sack, further and further down but never reaching the bottom. He cursed God and wondered what he could have done to merit such torture:

> Then he was still and not only ceased weeping but even held his breath and became attentive: he listened, as it were, not to an audible voice but to the voice of his soul, to the tide of his thoughts that rose up within him. (p.152)

He had a dialogue with himself about his past life, with which, except for early childhood memories, he found himself disenchanted. But, surely, he was guilty of nothing, so why all this horror? And yet every time a suspicion entered his mind that there might have been something not quite right about the way he lived, 'he at once recalled the orderliness of his life and dismissed so strange an idea' (p.154).

He screamed and tried to fight his illness, as if battling with an executioner. 'He felt that his agony was due both to his being thrust into that black hole and, still more, to his not being able to get right into it' (p.159). What was getting in the way was his insistence that life had been good, not bad.

Then, with a sudden shock, after a moment of extreme suffocation, he sank right through the hole and saw light at the bottom. In that moment he was able to look again at his life and say: 'No, it was all wrong'. His son was holding his hand, covering it with his tears. He felt sorry for his son and also for his weeping wife. He tried to say 'forgive me' but he was too weak. Both illness and pain ceased to matter. He searched for his fear of death and that too had gone: 'In place of death, there was light' (p.160). He heard someone saying 'It's over' and he died, telling himself: 'Death is over. It is no more'.

Jung warns us of 'loss of soul', a diminishment of the personality. In what he calls 'primitive' societies people's souls are thought sometimes to run away in the night, just as a dog might run from his master, and it is the job of the shaman, or medicine man, to fetch the fugitive back. Without a soul, a person suffers malaise and loses the will to live. Complicated rituals have to be performed for returning the soul to where it belongs. It is a case of disassociation, consciousness separating from instinct.

In a legend of Moses, with Joshua as his servant/shadow, they set out together on a quest and arrive at a place where two seas meet but are unaware of its significance. They have brought fish to eat for their dinner but, through their negligence, it comes alive, leaps out of the basket and back to the sea: 'Moses realizes that he has consciously found the source of life and then lost it again ... The fish they had intended to eat is a content of the unconscious by which the connection with the origin is re-established' (Jung, 1975, p.139).

We can all of us, says Jung, recognise ourselves in the 'questing Moses and forgetful Joshua', who miss the point of what their pilgrimage was for and are left tired and hungry for the meaning they have lost with the forgotten fish.

Jung claims that we have control of our will in a way that the 'primitive' has not and that our consciousness is safer and more dependable. Living in a different era, he is a man of his time in making assumptions of superiority on behalf of Western civilisation. If we in the West suffer diminishment, it seems we do not lose our souls but experience an '*abaissement du niveau mental*', which was the French psychologist Janet's term for a 'slackening of the tenacity of consciousness, which might be compared to a low barometric reading, presaging bad weather' (Jung, 1975, p.119).

Here is an up-to-date definition of this state:

> an unnatural, neurotic and pathological condition that has threatened man from the beginning of time; the severance of relationship with one's individual psychic life ... The condition is accompanied by lack of energy, loss

of a sense of meaning and purpose. (Samuels, Shorter and Plaut, 1986, p.88)

Jung (1975) tells us that 'the listlessness and paralysis of will can go so far that the whole personality falls apart, so to speak, and consciousness loses its unity' (pp.119–20). How often have we heard patients describe themselves as 'falling apart', and how helpless we feel, lacking the shaman's magic, in holding them together!

Since 'primitive' societies tend to be collectivist, the shaman's task would seem to be that of integrating the individual into the group or tribe to which he belongs in order to partake of a communal identity, rather than attempting to go it alone. It is the group that gives meaning to the individual's existence and, in Tillich's (1974) words, 'the courage to be as a part' (p.95). In our society it is the individual who counts and the affirmation of self through ever-increasing consciousness. To lose one's souls would mean dissolution of the personality in the collective psyche. The Jungian aim is individuation.

CHAPTER 7

In Fullness of Time

...even the will to endure grows meditative
Turning from the fire to slower gentler embers
As we recollect our once uncollected childhood,
A going with it, some ease of live and let live;
In the culmulative weight of what a heart remembers,
Things tipped in a scale of yearning and understood.

Michael O'Siadhail
'Ageing' from *Our Double Time*

Being Old

Being old brings a mixture of contradictory feelings. Sometimes, there is amazement at the length of time lived and we wonder what happened to all those years that we allowed to slide away, almost without noticing. Childhood occupies a lot of space in our memories, as though time moved more slowly then with its long-drawn-out school terms and measureless summer holidays. Patterns form and dissolve. New friends appear as the old ones vanish. Eventually, more and more deaths make holes in the pattern. There is mourning and loneliness, but also freedom. Living alone, even if dreaded, liberates us from adapting to other people's whims. We are like children let out of school, without obligatory meals or bed to intrude on our leisure. We can play as long as we like with no one to insist we clear up the mess, which is, after all, our own mess to be attended to in our own time – that is, if years of over-active super ego can be adequately defied. We can revel in a long-sought autonomy, unhindered at last by other people's opinions.

There is, of course, a downside. We may be hampered by lack of money, or, even more, by our flagging energy. Freedom may have come too late to enjoy it. Few of us are immune to all the ills that beset the body and, even if tolerably healthy ourselves, there is often the pain of friends' decline. We (and they) are faded, grey, wrinkled. Our backs are bent, our joints ache. We fall over, grow fat, get deaf, forget names or words, fumble with technology and feel inadequate in a world of increasing change and complication. Sometimes, we laugh at ourselves and each other and it may be a relief to compare notes. Our futures are so uncertain that we tend to look forward only to modest treats in weeks not far ahead. Children and animals are often a comfort and may satisfy longings to touch and be touched. We cherish our memories and try to make sense of life stories. However aware we are of declining faculties, there may be a certain wistfulness as we wonder about that small amount of wisdom we spent a life-time accumulating, not much of which will be listened to or passed on to others when we die. Inevitably, we must sometimes question – what is the point of it all?

Eliot was aware of more folly than wisdom in the old. In *Little Gidding* he wrote of the 'gifts' reserved for age:

> The cold friction of expiring sense
> Without enchantment, offering no promise
> But bitter tastelessness of shadow fruit
> As body and soul begin to fall asunder.

He peels away any layers of consolation that we may have used to cover our weakness and gives a merciless 'life review':

> ...the rending pain of re-enactment
> Of all that you have done, and been; the shame
> Of motives late revealed, and the awareness
> Of things ill done and done to others' harm
> Which once you took for exercise of virtue.

There is no escape from pain, but – as long as we do not 'cease from exploration' – some glimpses of redemption. Even despair has its opposite.

Dying of Old Age

Old age is not a cause of death to be registered on death certificates. Officially, we all have to die of *something*. I watched both my parents as they gradually wore themselves out. In my mother's case she was 97 when at last her vital organs began to fail. In filling out the certificate her doctor made some sort of list but I no longer remember exactly what illness or illnesses were cited as the official cause. My mother never had illnesses, only this slow running down to unconsciousness and a final letting go of all signs of vitality. The process seemed natural rather than pathological. Sherwin Nuland (1994) quotes Thomas Jefferson as saying:

> Our machines have now been running seventy or eighty years, and we must expect that, worn as they are, here a pivot, there a wheel, now a pinion, next a spring, will be giving way; and however we may tinker them up for a while, all will at length surcease motion. (p.44)

With or without illness, the body cannot last indefinitely and, in so much as it is dependent on the body, nor can the mind. Those who insist on continuing to tinker – and the patients who want this tinkering – are defying and denying nature. Though many, in these days of medical breakthroughs, far outlast the traditional three score years and ten, there are still limits to the wear and tear that body cells can take. Some scientists are saying that our life spans are genetically pre-determined, as though set by a clock at the moment of conception to grow and then diminish over a given length of time. Other theories have to do with the accumulation of pollution from the environment – both the immediate surroundings of the ageing cells and the outside atmosphere, which will include all sorts of toxins, irradiation and microbes. Whatever theory we choose to embrace, we seem to be faced with 'the inevitability of ageing, and therefore of life's finiteness' (Nuland, 1994, p.78).

And yet some of us will push Jefferson's 'tinkering up' to extraordinary extremes. The future may be filled with experiments in genetic engineering. There is also the 'science' of cryonics. At its most modest, the cryonic aim is to freeze organs for transplant – and even this is beset with difficulties – but the more ambitious prediction is that it will eventually become possible to freeze a whole body and resurrect it at some future date.

Alcor UK is an organisation geared towards the future. Its members do not talk about death or mention corpses 'Alcor is playing the long game. What it offers is the chance of life after death and, as a possible bonus, immortality' (Andrew Anthony, *The Observer Review*, 5 January 1997). The 'patient', once the death certificate has been signed, will have his (or her) blood pumped out and replaced with glycerine. The body will then be frozen in dry ice and flown to Arizona for 'cryonic suspension' at a temperature of minus 196 degrees centrigade until such time as 'science is able to reanimate what most of us still narrowly refer to as the dead' (ibid). Whether this will ever happen remains in doubt, but, for terminal patients, it may be a desperate last hope. Cryonicists claim immortality as a right: 'Why *shouldn't* I live for ever?'

These are young people speaking. In their eagerness to avoid death, they also avoid ageing and, in their search for eternal youth, cut themselves off from a whole range of human experience. It seems to me that, being so set on a future that depends on keeping the body enough intact to be suitable for freezing, they may miss the spirit of adventure, with its attendant risks, which is so essential to getting the most out of a one and only life. How, for instance, will they allow themselves to take part in rough sports, drive fast cars or trust themselves to the air? Cryonics will cost money. Immortality may emotionally cost much more, these extended lives being filled with anxiety and heightened fear of a sudden violent and mutilating death.

Old age is not always serene but, if its onset is gradual, may lead to some acceptance of our 'debt to nature', so that eventually we may be ready to let go of our lives and allow a new generation to take our place. Or, as Shakespeare more succinctly puts it: 'Men must endure their going hence, even as their coming hither: ripeness is all' (*King Lear*, Act 5, sc.2).

Life Review

Looking back as far as one can reach to early childhood scenes is not an activity exclusive to age. From the dawning of self-consciousness, children are old enough to have memories and even two or three years of past time can seem like 'ages ago' to their rapidly developing selves. To a child of six, being two years old feels almost like a previous incarnation. Some children let the memories drop away and concentrate on being more grown-up in the present day. Others cherish and hang on to a kaleidoscope of pictures which they try to see in sequence. A habit of remembering, if cultivated early, will probably persist even though the pictures may lose some of their brilliance and fade like old photographs. In old age the pictures may be even more precious but bring pain as well as pleasure. So much has been lost that it is hard to realise how much may also have been gained.

I have heard of counselling courses that give students, whatever their age, the exercise of drawing a lifeline, beginning with birth and recording important happenings along its route. On the way to where? The other end of the line records nothing, but it would be hard to escape such a reminder of life's finitude. The Natural Death Centre gives Life Review workshops and sends preparatory homework, one of the tasks being to draw one's lifeline. I arranged to attend and take a friend with me but she dropped out when faced with so much painful remembering.

In America Life Review has been used for some time as a therapeutic technique when working with older people. It was first advocated in the 1960s by Robert Butler (1963), psychiatrist and gerontologist, 'as a normative, universal process triggered by the sense of approaching dissolution and death' (p.65). Practitioners encourage what, in many cases, happens spontaneously. Old age is a time for story-telling, making sense of individual experience and establishing continuity between past and present. There have been fears about reminiscence contributing to depression and despair but Butler believes 'it also promotes positive attributes such as candour, serenity and wisdom' (p.131). Doctors and therapists must not dismiss what they hear as senseless rambling. It is only through listening intently to all the repetitions and variations that they will gain any understanding of what the approach of death means to those who are near the end of their lives: 'The aged particularly need a participant observer, professionally or otherwise, and the alleged danger of psychotherapy should be evaluated ... Probably at no other time in life is there as potent a force towards self-awareness operating as in old age' (pp.302–3).

By constant reminiscing, individuals will maintain a sense of self through all their bodily changes and feel less diminished as their faculties fail. The repetitious nature of their stories has been compared to the remembering and working-through that features in psychoanalysis. Repetition also facilitates mourning for the many losses they have inevitably had to suffer.

A range of methods has been used for deliberate evocation of people's memories.

Autobiography

If a person feels unable to write, there is always the alternative of speaking into a tape recorder. This has the advantage of spontaneity, without later editing, and the listener can take note both of what is included and what is omitted. (Incidentally, this was something I tried with my mother in her nineties but she refused, preferring to live in the present).

Letters, Photographs, Diaries, Scrapbooks

These provide useful openings for discussion of the past, as well as pleasure, laughter and ways of establishing rapport with the listener.

Reunions

'An individual can look at himself in the context of other meaningful people and take a measure of where he stands in the course of the life cycle' (Butler and Lewis, 1974, p.167).

Pilgrimages

Visiting places where one has lived through a range of emotions is a powerful way of recapturing the past. The picture retained in memory often proves inaccurate when compared with the real thing – perhaps this is due to forgetting the details and filling up the space from imagination. There may be a longing, if the house still stands, to get back inside the family home and wander round familiar rooms. (My grandfather's house has been converted to flats and I often try to work out in my mind how this was done, an exercise that usually sends me to sleep).

Family Trees

Studying the ancestors helps establish one's place in history: 'One of the ways the old seem to resolve fears of death is to gain a sense of other family members having died before them' (Butler and Lewis, 1974, p.167).

Making a Life Review encourages exploration of all one's memories and opens up a chance to see the past in a new light: 'The success of the Life Review depends on the struggle to resolve old issues of resentment, guilt, bitterness, mistrust, dependence and nihilism. All the really significant emotional options remain available until the moment of death – love, hate, reconciliation, self-assertion and self-esteem' (Butler and Lewis, 1974, p.169).

An Irish writer describes ageing as a time of harvest:

> The beauty and invitation of old age offers a time of silence and solitude for a visit to the house of memory. You can visit all your past. Your soul is the place where memory lives ... As things happen in your yesterdays, todays and tomorrows, and fall away with transience, they are caught in the eternal net of your soul ... Old age is a time of coming home to your deeper nature, of entering into the temple of your memory where all your vanished days are secretly gathered awaiting you. (O'Donahue, 1997, pp.214–5)

Counselling, Psychotherapy, Psychoanalysis

'Near or above the fifties', wrote Freud (1953), 'the elasticity of mental processes on which treatment depends, is as a rule lacking ... old people are no longer educable' (p.264). Until recently, this dictum seems to have been believed and it has taken a long time for prejudice to die. But now that people are living longer, with an increasing proportion of the population past retirement age, society is becoming aware both of the general and specific problems that belong to an older age group, whose members are becoming bolder in voicing their needs. No one wants to be accused of ageism or political incorrectness so we are at last beginning to pay attention and respond to the old as readily as we do to the young.

In offering therapeutic help there has been caution and considerable difference of opinion as to how much is advisable and of what kind, and there has been a tendency to concentrate on short-term, focused therapy rather than intensive exploration of the entire life-span. I have already shown some disagreement (Orbach, 1996) and given a few illustrations of how I work with elderly patients. Here I would like to describe some of what is currently on offer across the broad spectrum of counselling, therapy and analysis.

With a proliferation of counselling courses all over the country, there tend to be more counsellors around than clients for them to work with. Colleges, schools and doctors' surgeries now employ resident counsellors. There are also voluntary outlets, sometimes based on churches or centres serving local communities. Some of these are specialised, such as CRUSE for bereavement, OFF THE RECORD for young people, OPEN DOOR for AIDS and HIV. A recent innovation is a service for the elderly. In some parts of the country AGE CONCERN have introduced mobile services for visiting clients in their homes. Sometimes, these counsellors are specially trained. Other districts rely on networks of befrienders. My own involvement is with a comparatively new venture called SAGE, which operates in parts of West Sussex and East Hampshire. My position is supervisor and co-ordinator. The counsellors have gained their diplomas elsewhere and are not specifically trained to work with old people. We all learn from each other as the service evolves. The general feeling is that we treat our clients like 'everybody else', but with more flexibility in that we visit them in their homes and sometimes make arrangements through a third party rather than insisting at all times that clients make the first contact themselves. Our publicity outlines some of the problems that older people may be wanting to resolve, namely adjusting to retirement, coping with bereavement, moving from an independent to dependent life style and, perhaps, most problematic of all, facing the reality of death. In choosing counsellors I look for mature people (they are mostly women) round about middle age who have had enough therapy to know something of their strengths and weaknesses, who have coped with crisis in their own lives and are not likely to turn away from talk about death.

Our first client died after the third session. He was 90 and in a nursing home where the counsellor visited him. She was shaken but had to accept that in working with this age group death must be an occupational hazard. Later, she took on a client in his mid-sixties – 'young' by SAGE standards. He had Parkinson's Disease and was anxious to fit in what achievements he could before becoming more disabled. After eighteen months, some of his ambitions, including a television appearance, have been realised. Other clients include a war veteran, who has, this year, for the first time since the war, been back to Germany. He found that he could let go of his hatred towards the whole German race and stop blaming the young for the sins of their fathers. This visit has enabled him to make peace with the German nation and himself.

Through a third party, we recently heard of an 82-year-old 'anorectic' who was starving herself to death. We responded at once but the referral had come too late to save her and soon after a visit had been arranged the counsellor heard that she was in a coma and expected to die within hours. Dying was what she wanted and fasting has been described as 'a gentle death' (Albery and Elliot, 1997, p.14). Animals do it. Among the Hindus it is accepted as a natural preparation for dying. It seems as if this lady, whom we never managed to see, had made her choice and would have stuck to it despite any persuasion from well-meaning outsiders.

SAGE has met with some enthusiasm but also prejudice and suspicion. Because launching the service – probably without enough publicity – has not brought floods of clients but only 20 in nearly two years, we get told that older people have been brought up to keep a 'stiff upper lip' and not show their feelings, that they like to keep 'themselves to themselves' and will find it impossible to accept such a newfangled enterprise. We might attract a few women but never any men. As it has turned out, at least half our clients have been men. My answer to the sceptics is that, speaking for my own generation, we have indeed been brought up not to talk about ourselves but many of us have changed as we grew older and adapted ourselves to a more open-minded world. The old can learn from the young just as much as the young from the old – or, perhaps, more.

When I first began practising as a psychotherapist I found myself working mostly with young students who could not afford the fees of more experienced practitioners. When an 80-year-old was referred to me I wondered how different working with her would turn out to be. I was also somewhat awed by learning that she had already undergone psychoanalysis with a famous name more than forty years earlier. As I listened to her and tried to respond, I was acutely aware of a life experience that would not be mine for another thirty years or so and that she was at a stage which I anticipated, if at all, with apprehension. I felt pushed forward in time to confront my own dread of dying, for, although we seldom talked directly of death as our inevitable end, its shadow was always on the horizon. During our years of being together we both faced major bereavements. When my husband died I was grateful for her empathy, though also aware of how helpless she felt in her longing to look after me and her struggle to avoid 'breaking the rules' by reversing our roles. In the transference I was always more mother than daughter and with this one hiccup that is how we continued to relate. The eventual ending of therapy was, to her, as threatening as death itself and it became almost impossible to set a date. Each time I tried she took refuge in forgetting until, at last, as part of our work on mourning and letting go, both of significant others and of parts of herself, she was able, though very painfully, to make a voluntary end before being forced into it by age and decrepitude. At our last session, although starting with denial, she was able to admit that as long as she could keep coming to see me she could postpone old age and dying. So, in ending therapy she faced death, even though, eventually, she escaped again into forgetfulness and dementia. I kept enough in touch to learn of her loss of independence through a family decision on residential care, first in a retirement home and later in a nursing home. This was something she had dreaded, but now, if still alive, I doubt if she knows where she is.

George Pollock (1987), a psychoanalyst from Chicago, has done research on the losses of old age and how earlier traumas, if not worked through, can exacerbate the pain of later life bereavement:

> It has become evident that a very crucial element for successful ageing is the ability to mourn prior states of the self. When one can accept ageing and its changes and mourn for the past the result can be a liberation, a freeing of energy for current living, including 'planning for the future'. (pp. 12–13)

Pollock describes psychotherapy as a 'humanizing force' that keeps us in touch with ourselves. What we forget and push away comes alive again, 'old emotional allegiances are revived, passions and rages reawakened, overgrown paths are walked on anew' (p.21). Working through the past, understanding it and letting it go is what he calls 'The Mourning-Liberation Process'. What liberates is talking about oneself, which, in an older person's culture, may have been so discouraged that therapy provides the first opportunity to do so. It is generally recognised today that those who are acutely bereaved need 'to talk and talk and talk'. Being old is a continuous state of bereavement in need of catharsis: 'By working with transferences, fantasies, dreams, symptomatic acts – the entire spectrum of what we see in psychoanalytic treatment – the patient develops insight, identifies with the analyst, and change occurs' (p.24).

Neither Life Review nor Mourning-Liberation are techniques that I have used consciously, and yet both seem to have spontaneously occurred and the older a person gets the more there will be to work through. Certainly in America, and, perhaps, more slowly in the UK, the very old (as well as the not so old) are being offered psychotherapy and being seen to benefit.

'Where is my mind? 'wrote a poet of 94. She thought her memory was failing and she was going mad:

> Give me grief, despair,
> A hopeless hope – anything but this void
> I wander in, only my body sovereign,
> Eating, sleeping, living the empty
> Daily round.

She wrote to a psychoanalyst whom she had met in the past, when she was teaching children and he was a child analyst. In her letter she told him that she felt bewildered and disorientated, had dizzy spells and a fear of falling. These symptoms had come on soon after her husband's death. Could he take her on as a patient? She did not think she needed prolonged therapy. Earlier in her life she had had a bad experience with an analyst so she did not want a stranger. She was quite aware that treatment would limit the friendship they had enjoyed up till now: 'Her turning to me and being in such acute distress made me feel I should honour her request' (Settlage, 1996, p.550).

Initially he saw her for psychotherapy over a period of three months and did not feel that her advanced age made the treatment different from that of other adults. She was reacting strongly to the death of her husband, whom she had looked after through his last illness. 'Instead of "grieving as would be appropriate", she saw herself as being in a self-centred martyrdom' (p.550). Both the analyst and her doctor wondered whether dizziness and failing memory were due to organic causes. But her memory returned after she admitted not wanting to remember her husband in his state of physical and mental decline. She, at first, denied having been angry during that time but then remembered, and brought to the next session, a poem she described as 'laced with anger'. Treatment then focused on the anger she had repressed from childhood, at not being acceptable to her parents, and how this was now being expressed in physical symptoms. Her dizziness soon disappeared. Instead of the variety of symptoms presented at the beginning, and the guilt that went with them, she became able fully to mourn her husband's death.

At the age of 99 she asked for analysis. Again, she had physical symptoms. 'My palpitations must be psychological, so I turned to you' (p.553). She was generally healthy and unimpaired mentally but had now become housebound, moving only between chair and bed during her daily routine. So she had to be visited at home and chose the study where she wrote her poems, rather than the living room, which was for meeting friends. In calling what followed 'psychoanalysis' and not 'psychotherapy', Settlage felt it met with the necessary criteria:

> Although the analytic couch and the usual frequency of four or five sessions a week were not employed, the treatment had the hallmarks of psychoanalytic work: free association, the use of dreams, transference, transference interpretations, resistance to the exposure of repressed mental content, insight, the resolution and working through of intrapsychic conflict and change in psychic structure. (p.558)

Some might claim the same for psychoanalytic psychotherapy or even psychodynamic counselling. There are obvious overlaps and a lot depends on what our training organisations allow us to call ourselves. What is impressive in this account is that a centenarian was able and willing to benefit from what she asked for and was given. The analysis continued for five years, ending when she died aged 104.

This time the focus was on death and her fear of it. Her doctor checked that there was nothing wrong with her heart but she had 'pounding palpitations' every time she woke from sleep. She had a habit of compulsive counting in multiples of three when she went to bed and when she woke up. She said it was like praying – 'to ward off evil'. With new insight she connected the counting with her pounding heart beats: 'Every time I wake up, I am reminded of my mortality, and my counting wards off the reality of death. After all, at my age death is always hovering in the wings' (p.553).

She had a fantasy of going on a trip with her daughter, although she was too physically frail for travelling. Some time later, she said: 'It is as if I go on after my death just like I imagined travelling with my daughter'.

In one of her dreams a man was asked: 'What is death?' He gave a vague answer. Still in the dream, she found herself saying: 'Death is giving!' Awake, she summed it up:

> Death really is a giving – a giving to the survivors and the survivors giving to each other. The gift is love. I do not want my death to be a burden to my family and friends. They should think of me as having joined the stream of life, as being with others who have died. (p.556)

Describing the very old, Settlage shows us their much diminished access to the external world, compared with the availability of all that is internal: 'The evocation of memories, fantasies and feelings compensates for the lack of external stimulation.' In this rich interiority there is a mysterious interaction of conscious and unconscious – 'the wellspring of creativity' (p.551). Writing poems had been, for this patient, 'like a breath of air'. She spoke of 'the therapy of writing'. She knew enough of Freud to attribute both her poems and her dreams to the unconscious. Both came spontaneously and unbidden. Her poems, she said, told her about herself and her roots. She was amazed at the explosiveness of what was hidden from consciousness. Through poetry she was able to work on those roots, to 'transform and transcend the losses of old age' (p.559). In analysis this work was extended to involve two persons instead of one.

I am reminded of Jung's 'transcendent function', the capacity of the human mind to form symbols. Art, whether in words, painting or music, shares what is subjective with those whom it reaches and in doing so transcends what would otherwise be only personal. Rosemary Gordon (1978) made a study of the creative process and linked it with our human knowledge that we must die, and the questions we are bound to ask about the meaning of our lives. It is her thesis that:

> those who would die well and those who would create well are people who must be capable of being open and available both to the life forces and the death forces ... they are people who can ... learn, acquire skills, concentrate and take account of both extra – and intra-psychic reality; and

they can also make themselves available to feelings of awe and wonder, which are the acknowledgement and experience of mystery. (p.165)

Settlage wrote that his 104-year-old patient was lucid when she died, that she accepted her mortality and was composing poems almost to the end. Helped, as she undoubtedly was, by her analysis, her dying and her creating could come together. She and her analyst were both intensely sad but she had lost her earlier depression and fear.

CHAPTER 8

A Time to Mourn

> To everything there is a season...
> A time to weep, and a time to laugh;
> A time to mourn, and a time to dance.
>
> Ecclesiastes, Ch.3, v.1

> Death is a lonely visitor. After it visits your home, nothing is ever the same
> again. There is an empty place at the table; there is an absence in the house.
> When someone close to you dies, it is an incredibly strange and desolate
> experience. Something breaks within you then, which
> will never be the same again.
>
> John O'Donahue (1997, p.252)

So much has been written about mourning as a psychological process that I
hesitate to add even more. I can only say that any packaging of experience
into a theory of stages (Kübler-Ross, 1970; Parkes, 1972, 1986), however
flexibly used, even if conceivably of help to students and counsellors coping
with loss for the first time, seems to bear little relation to the chaos of individual bereavement. What is expected to happen only too easily turns into what
ought to happen. A person's grief may even be measured in terms of how
many months or years it takes to 'get over' the loss and at what point grief
becomes pathological. I remember being 'cheered up' by the vicar of a
nearby parish (mercifully not my own) who tried to reassure me by stating,
authoritatively, 'it will take two years', and my irritated reply: 'Really? How
do you know?' It always strikes me that 'getting over' is not what one does
with loss. 'Getting on with it', 'getting used to it' or simply bearing and surviving it seem more realistic descriptions of what actually happens. As for

comforting the mourners, if these comforters are waiting for the stages they have been taught to expect, they may miss a bit of unique reality.

Assumptions are changing. At one time, according to a book of etiquette printed early this century, well-meaning friends would be advised to leave the suffering person alone in case the emotion spilled over and could not be contained: 'It is distressing alike to the visitor and the mourner to go through a scene of uncontrolled grief ... Even relatives should remember that the bereaved ones will want to be by themselves, and that solitude is often the greatest solace for grief' (Troubridge, 1926, pp.57–8).

That is a typically English reaction. In Latin and Middle-Eastern countries mourners have always been expected to lament openly. Orthodox Jews have the 'Shivah', a period of overt mourning in which a widow is encouraged to talk and show her feelings and is never left alone. I think most of us would put ourselves somewhere between these two extremes. Reaction against the 'stiff upper lip' can result in such recognition of one's right to grieve that tears are positively encouraged, as well as hugs from comparative strangers. In a Kübler-Ross workshop, at which I had hoped for some sort of comfort, I felt excluded by my inability to scream and express anger that I did not feel.

Assumptions and generalisations abound. Undoubtedly, there are still bereaved people – particularly of an older generation – who prefer to be left alone. Others want, above all, to be listened to and for permission to talk and talk, and repeat themselves over and over again, but not necessarily to be hugged.

The assumptions are changing again. Grief and mourning continue to be studied and there seems to be an increasing realisation of how much variation there is in the way people mourn:

> Counsellors who once were convinced that it was essential that grief be ex-
> pressed are now being urged to respect each individual client's way of cop-
> ing. Having been trained in listening skills, some must be wondering
> whether their overly specific model of how grief should be may have got in
> the way of listening to what some clients were really trying to tell them.
> (Walter, 1994, p.82)

It is hard for the comforters to get it right, though very important that the professionals do not pretend that they are the experts who are 'in the know' but have the humility to allow the mourners themselves to be their teachers.

Mourning on the Way to Death

In Chapter 1 I mentioned those who come into therapy when they are dying themselves. These people are mourning not the death of friends but of their own faculties, of the life they are about to leave, the end of their familiar bodies and their loving relationships with other bodies, the bidding goodbye to all those people – close and not so close – whose companionship gave meaning to their lives. All therapy is about loss or anticipation of loss and it is mourning, not denial, that brings benefit.

Parting from those we love is often gradual, with a lot of mourning occurring before death finally takes them away. Long illness or great age may set up barriers of forgetfulness or lack of interest, as though we are being excluded from a life we used to share. Personalities change. Sometimes, we feel betrayed. Anger gets caught up with guilt. Through reluctance to find fault with the dying, we blame ourselves. We may feel too ashamed to talk to anyone about how we feel. Shame sets us apart.

Louise was an only child who always had to carry the burden of her parents' expectations, as well as their disappointment when her first marriage failed and she married a foreigner and was living in another country when her mother got ill with cancer. Torn between loyalty to her husband and children and wanting to do the best for her mother, she managed a long visit to her parents' home, where her father was trying hard to nurse his wife and keep her out of hospital. The flat was small, so they lived in close quarters, Louise sharing a room with Mother and her bulky hospital bed while Father camped in the living room. Father took early retirement to look after his wife but when Louise was there his attempts were not appreciated as much as hers and all three were frustrated in their cramped space. The illness dragged on and Louise, though agonised for her mother, felt the pull of her three small children and decided that she must go back to them. Her mother's last words to her were: 'You know that you are killing me.' Three months later, Louise returned for her mother's funeral.

The strain of waiting for Mother to die caught up with her. She broke down and came near to suicide. Afterwards, she went into therapy, with the result that she took a counselling course and began a training in psychotherapy. While coping with her courses and trying to find the money for her own expensive therapy and supervision, her father began to go downhill. He came to stay with her for a time and then had a period of sharing his flat with his brother, Louise's uncle. This worked well until the uncle died.

Father had been diagnosed some years before with prostate cancer, but this was slow to develop. He also had diabetes and, now that he lived alone, was forgetful about taking his insulin. During telephone conversations his speech would be slurred and grow faint and Louise had to keep reminding him that it must be time for his next dose. She managed to visit him during the holidays but her husband seldom came with her and Father criticised him for his absence, regarding it as his duty towards both wife and father-in-law to accompany Louise and be there for both of them.

Louise worked hard during these visits to keep the flat clean and bring order into her father's life. She became aware that he was using her mother's money as well as his own but for some time she was puzzled about what he could be spending it on. It was only after the cancer got worse that she discovered there was another woman in his life. She felt betrayed by his lies and evasions and also by his reckless spending of money that should have come to her, and which she needed badly. For a long time anger and disillusion got in the way of what had once been a relationship of love and respect. Only in the last months of his life, when she hardly left his side, did she feel compassion. She had spent three months away from her home and her studies. Again there was conflict. She made arrangements to leave but Father deteriorated and she managed to put off her flight for 24 hours. Then, mercifully, he died during the night and she was able to be with him to the end. His was a protracted death. She told me that the death rattle lasted three weeks.

Louise flew back for her father's funeral, having meticulously made the arrangements by telephone. His only legacy to her was the flat, which she had to sell in order to make ends meet. So, as part of her bereavement, she no longer has a foothold in her own country. Some bitter feelings, still mixed with compassion, remain, together with love for both her parents and a deeper understanding of their complicated relationship. Her only cousin had also died, so, in her mid-fifties, there is nothing left of her original family. But she now has the compensation of two grandchildren and a hoped-for involvement in their future. She is still mourning the past and giving herself time to work through a lot of chaotic feelings so that, eventually, she may be able to transcend those violently opposed forces of love and hate which inevitably upset the balance of our lives.

The story of Louise is one of many. For those who find themselves last in a line there may be some relief that the deaths are over, leaving only their own to mourn when the time comes. And yet, one can never be sure. As with the two mothers whose tragedies I related earlier, deaths do not necessarily happen in orderly progression, the oldest going first. For those who lose their children the world is turned upside down, so that they murmur piteously: 'it should have been me'.

A variation on this theme is the story of a widow who found herself living for five years with her very old mother, mourning her husband's death and also the younger mother she used to have. While waiting for the second death, she both dreaded and guiltily longed for it. These mixed feelings tormented and, sometimes, shamed her, and she blamed herself for not being able to show the affection that her mother so obviously craved. She remained numb and unable to mourn appropriately, her only feeling a yearning for all that she had lost. When, in her late nineties, her mother peacefully died, the daughter's main reactions were relief and a sense of release. She now had the freedom to choose where and how to live without being held back by another person's need. As she embarked on the next phase of her life in a new place with new friends, she got used to being alone and found herself less lonely than during her mother's final years. The loss of her husband was not something she 'got over' but 'got on with' and slowly the pain became less sharp, making room at last for mourning her mother not as an old lady but as younger, happier and much loved.

Each Bereavement is Unique

My friend, Margaret, is allowing me to quote from an account with this title, which she began writing a few months after her husband's death. 'I am writing this for me. I have an aching need to get this down properly!' She also wrote it to try and explain why, although she cared deeply for Edwin, she found herself 'not devastated but astonishingly calm'. She had her own (unique?) trouble with those who wanted to comfort her: 'should I go through the signs of devastation in order not to distress them or do I try to explain to them that, for me, it has not been like that and risk shocking them?'

One of Margaret's many jobs had been nursing people with Alzheimer's Disease. When she began to notice tell-tale signs in her husband, she told herself: 'who better to look after him than me?' But she knew what hell the partners of Alzheimer's patients had to go through, some of which I have touched on in an earlier chapter.

At the beginning of his illness she and Edwin were able to talk about what was happening. There was heartbreak and desolation, but not all the time.

They made a resolution to find something of special interest for every week – a visit to the theatre, inviting friends, a picture exhibition or a country walk.

It had been Edwin's idea to walk the South Downs Way, a small stretch at a time, starting from different points. It was a Saturday afternoon in early spring and the sun was shining. They drove to the top of Cocking Hill and set off towards Graffham Down. She remembers every detail of that walk, their last together:

> When we needed to cross the road to the car, Edwin got it wrong. Even at the time I guessed that it was probably his Alzheimer confusion that caused it … I had no sense of danger as Edwin stepped into the road; there was a sudden panic in front of me as I saw him lunge forward to try to reach the other side and in almost the same second I saw his body flying high through the air in an arc. As he was in the air, in slow motion it seemed, I thought first, 'He can't survive this', and then, 'This is the end of the nightmare'.

She was surprised at how calm she was. During the next days, weeks, months people kept calling her wonderful, but that was not how she felt. Later, she wrote: 'On reflection it was astonishing that the sun got up and went down as usual' and 'I suppose that for the first four months I have been in automatic gear'.

She describes the post and how reading it – 'every letter and card was important' – helped give the day a new pattern: 'A vital part of my new start to the day was the post's clumping down to the mat in heavy batches. I made a drink and carried the drink and the day's batch back to bed'. Everyone wrote differently: 'Darling Margaret', 'Dear Margaret, Oh dear, Oh dear Margaret' and 'You will now have to walk the path of life without your dear one beside you. So be it – It's all in the order of things'. 'That's bracing', said her neighbour. She agreed, but liked it.

The post went on coming. Answering letters got her through the night. But there was so much of it that she was overwhelmed and, sometimes, wanted to curse it: 'Bloody post, why is it still coming?' Then, when she had her first morning without a letter or card, she said: 'Help! Post, where are you?' Missing it made her laugh. She needed some light relief. She treated her word processor as a friend: 'As my mind filled with thoughts, I told my machine what they were. I created 'Edwin's File' into which I wrote down the thoughts that came into my head before they slid out again'.

One of these statements made to the machine was: 'I haven't taken in yet that I'm alone. I still feel like Edwin's wife'. Reading this, I remembered my own bereavement and that my mourning was 'resolved' (if that is the word) when I became able to say 'I' instead of 'we'. It is a painful resolution, but necessary.

Margaret went on to write about the 'wrong kind of care' and how much more helpful it was when friends said that they had no words or did not know what to say, but showed their affection, than when they made confident assertions such as 'I know what it is like' and got it wrong, as, of course, they were bound to. No one knows *exactly* how another person feels. How could they?:

> Four words I have found especially difficult: 'You must be feeling...' That 'must' has seemed like a two-edged sword, a word of empathy and of insistence: 'If you are not, then you should be.' For much of the time I have not been missing Edwin greatly. Strange, I know. But, taking one day at a time, I have accepted each day as it really has been and not worried about how perhaps it should have been ... I could not wish Edwin back to continue to feel so desolate.

A year later she found herself saying: 'Oh Edwin, I would like you back!' It had taken her a long time to make that simple statement. She had been too close to his desolation. But now she was able to remember him at his best – his pre-Alzheimer self – and that was the person she was missing.

Margaret did not want counselling. She was determined to cope with her mourning in her own way. She needed to talk about Edwin to her friends and for them to listen without telling her what they thought she was feeling, and, thereby, imposing what she felt to be an *ought*. I think there is a lesson here for all those, professional and otherwise, who embark on what has come to be called 'Grief Work'. You may see repeating patterns, you may recognise stages, but it is by no means always helpful to point these out. It is a person's *uniqueness* that needs your response. As for interpretations – when in doubt, don't!

Funeral Options

When my father-in-law died my husband's stepmother asked him and me to arrange a Church of England funeral. 'He was Jewish', we protested. She made it clear that funerals were for the loved ones left behind and that *she* wanted a Christian burial. My husband told me that his father had said something like: 'just put me in the ground anywhere'. He had never taken an interest in synagogue or church and, as far as any of us knew, had no beliefs. So, reluctantly, we tried to please her. First, we asked a parish priest, whom we knew, whether he would conduct a not-too-Christian ceremony. At first, he warmed to the idea and we began choosing old testament readings. The next day he telephoned to say that he had changed his mind and found he could not bring himself to do it. One of the reasons he gave was that it would show disrespect for the old man. 'You should get a rabbi', he said firmly. But that was not what the stepmother wanted. She was a nominal Christian but out of touch with the Church. We felt uncomfortable. Eventually, we asked for the name of the chaplain on duty at the cemetery where she wanted him buried. We managed to see him and found he was quite used to the kind of problem we described. Together, we planned a simple ceremony, which had to be Christian but could be dominated by sonorous passages from Isaiah. We then combed London for a particular 'cello setting of a Jewish lament for the dead which had once been played to him on his birthday by a musician friend. The ceremony offended no one, though it puzzled a few. Many years later, when the stepmother died, we found ourselves in the chapel of the same cemetery for a service we had not arranged. I chiefly remember the small congregation struggling slowly through all five verses of 'Onward Christian Soldiers', because, said someone, it was her favourite hymn.

So – who do we perform these ceremonies for? And a further question: what are the options?

Traditionally, in all the major religions, what matters most is the destination of the soul. In the churchyard the body is committed to the ground, 'dust to dust', but 'in sure and certain hope of the resurrection to eternal life'. The congregation of family and friends may not believe what they are hearing. If asked why they have come, they may say something about paying their last respects or to support the next of kin; it is an ordeal that has to be gone through; holding a funeral is the 'done thing'.

In our pluralist society provision has to be made for Jews, Moslems, Sikhs, Hindus and Buddhists, who each have their special rites-of-passage in which what happens to the soul is the main concern. Ideas of reincarnation have caught on among many of those brought up (perhaps loosely) in a Christian tradition. Being born again in a different body on an already well-trodden planet may be more comforting, and, perhaps, more likely, than arriving in a nebulous heaven that we can no longer try and locate beyond the stars. No obvious provision is made for the majority of our population, who have more or less repudiated Church upbringing, have no expectations of eternal life, no belief in a God outside themselves, can discover no meaning or relevance in biblical words, yet, nevertheless, have an undefined feeling for the numinous, which they want to find some appropriate way to express. When it comes to burying their dead they will have to find that way for themselves, but, increasingly, they may find guidance through the testimony of those in their ranks who have already wrestled with the problem and come up with solutions.

Tony Walter (1994), writing as a sociologist, examines three cultural responses to death, which he names traditional, modern and late modern. Traditional death is rooted in community. In the past people travelled less, neighbours stayed put and relations were near at hand. More recently we have tended to move about and families have been dispersed. In modern death the public domain takes over and the dying patient becomes an object to be treated. Death is medicalised and taken out of the home. It is from corpses that students learn their craft: 'Not only are dead and dying bodies medicalised, but dead bodies enable the medicalisation of living bodies' (p.13). Young people dying of cancer or in catastrophes like Hillsborough catch the public eye and, as the young are likely to be involved in more social groups and have more friends than the old, their dying is less likely to be neglected. With so much media coverage, traditions are revived or changed. Flowers are left at scenes of disaster, both by friends and anonymous television viewers, a habit which reached its peak in the enormous spread of flowers for Princess Diana. The late-modern attitude joins our private to our public lives. Patients are listened to as persons and – to some extent – allowed to die in their own way, with palliative care very much to the fore:

> Life-centred funerals incorporate the personal style of the deceased into the mass throughput of the modern funeral home or crematorium. In bereavement counselling, the trained professional (representing the public sphere) acknowledges and affirms the feelings of the bereaved, but in doing so protects the public from these unruly feelings. (Walter, 1994, p.40)

Walter sees the late-modern attitude as still exerting control, though in a highly sophisticated manner. All three attitudes affect choice of funeral. There is no longer an orthodoxy in these matters, but most people seem unaware of having any freedom to choose.

What we mostly find ourselves doing is delegating responsibility to undertakers, who are now re-named funeral directors and are prepared to take over the direction of the whole show: 'The growth of professional services and escalating costs is directly related to spiritual and social impoverishment' (Gill and Cox, 1996, p.27). We are distressed and pressed for time; the general expectation is that the funeral will not be delayed for more than a week after a person's death. With relief, we hand over to the professionals both the body and ourselves:

> We end up having booked their cars and drivers and bearers, having bought the coffin from their (inevitable) limited stock, having handed over the body of the deceased, probably to be embalmed, to be prepared for the coffin and dressed in the garments they have in stock. (Gill and Cox, 1996, p.25)

All we have to do is pay the bill. If we are practising Christians, we will arrange the actual funeral service with a vicar who is known to us, but, even so, it is the funeral director who, with an air of authority, takes charge of the body and tells us what to do. Funerals are expensive and he will see to it that we are given our money's worth, even if, afterwards, we are left not sure that what happened was quite what we wanted or relevant to the wishes of the deceased.

Not everyone asks questions. The easy way is to trust a firm that may have handled family funerals in the past. The firm itself may be a family business and take a pride in handing down their skills from one generation to another. Graham Swift (1996), in his prize-winning novel, *Last Orders*, sums up this attitude:

> It's not a trade many will choose. You have to be raised to it, father to son. It runs in the family, like death itself runs in the human race, and there's comfort in that ... You can't run a funeral without pride. When you step out and slow-pace in front of the hearse, in your coat and hat and gloves, you can't do it like you're apologizing. You have to make happen at that moment what the bereaved and bereft want to make happen ... You can't run a funeral without authority. When people don't know what to do, they have to be told. (pp.78–9)

But people today do not necessarily accept what they are told, not only about the relevance of this 'traditional' funeral, invented by the Victorians, but about what happens behind the scenes. Many firms embalm the body as a matter of course unless specifically asked not to by the relatives, who are unlikely to refuse what they had no idea was on the agenda. Replacing blood with formaldehyde and a pink dye to make the corpse look less dead is not hygienic but poisons the earth or atmosphere, so is not ecologically sound. Television programmes have now invited us to observe what is done to the corpse after we have handed it over – to see the embalmers at work, to follow what happens when there has to be a post-mortem, to venture behind the curtains of the crematorium when the coffin has slid from view, the charging of the cremator, the raking of the ashes and the further process of reducing and refining them for scattering or burial. These programmes are not for the squeamish but they may answer a few of our queries and, perhaps, shock us into some degree of choice or participation.

Something has to be done with a dead body: 'a funeral is the last statement about a person, an ultimate affirmation of human dignity' (Walter, 1994, p.180). But there is no law that imposes a religious ceremony, or any ceremony at all. If a person is buried on private land, there is no necessity for a coffin – a shroud or blanket will do. A tree may be planted instead of a stone memorial. What we do for our favourite dogs is, legally, no different for favourite humans. The only laws are: getting a death certificate from a doctor, taking this to the Registrar in order to obtain a further certificate before burial or cremation is allowed and then registering the grave and the name of the person who has been buried. The grave must then be dug to a required depth. DIY funerals are acceptable if these formalities are observed. Having carried out our mandatory duties, we can be flexible and imaginative about the rest. The choice need not be between the extremes of using a funeral director or managing the whole thing ourselves but in deciding just how much professional guidance we need and how much we feel able to organise with friends and family joining in to provide transport and carry the coffin (if there is one) to the grave. We may decide to decorate, or even to make, the coffin ourselves. A new option, or, perhaps, the revival of an old tradition, is the Woodland Burial that is offered by some local authorities and private cemeteries. These are places where trees will be planted, wildflowers encouraged to grow and a habitat created for wildlife.

Whatever ritual we, the mourners, decide to enact, our aim will be to give our loved one a dignified send-off. Whether or not this has been discussed before he dies, so that the ceremony will be one of his choosing, we hope that what we do would meet with his approval. So, whether or not we believe there is a soul to pray for, the funeral day is a special time for saying goodbye to that person and celebrating the life that has just ended. But funerals are also therapeutic for the mourners. The day may be dreaded – perhaps, we hope to control our tears, though, in a late-modern ceremony, emotion will be encouraged.

Therapy, says Tony Walter (1994), may be a by-product through catharsis of ritual but it is not what funerals are for: 'Without a corpse to dispose of and a soul to release, funerals wouldn't happen. If all you want is therapy for the living, then you need not a funeral but a therapy session instead' (p.179). And another comment: 'Ritual action round the body and within the community is replaced by talk in a group of strangers facilitated by a psychotherapist' (p.178).

In late-modern, or post-modern, society we are intent on approaching death each in our own way. Therapy groups and self-help groups may facilitate our choices of how to die and how to mourn, or they may isolate us in artificial groupings. Community spirit flourishes naturally when people suffer together, when families rally round one of their kin with terminal cancer, when friends are dying of AIDS, or when we encounter, in the face of accident, sickness or deprivation, the revival of a neighbourliness which seemed almost to have died.

As a psychotherapist, I have helped individuals to mourn in their own way and I have sought therapeutic help in my own mourning, but, eventually, we have to get on with the family and friends that we happen to have, even if we do not always meet with perfect mutual understanding and sympathy. There is no 'one way' to mourn but plenty of ways to contribute and also to learn and go on learning from other people's experience.

CHAPTER 9

On the Edge

...We are such stuff
As dreams are made on, and out little life
Is rounded with a sleep.

Shakespeare, *The Tempest*, IV, 1

I saw Eternity the other night
Like a great Ring of pure and endless light,
All calm as it was bright;
And round beneath it, Time, in hours, days, years,
Driven by the spheres,
Like a vast shadow moved, in which the world
And all her train were hurled.

Henry Vaughan, *The World*

Dreams of Death

When we sleep our ego loses its tenacity and is no longer in control of our thoughts. At some imperceptible moment, unless we are severely insomniac, there is a letting go of the edge of consciousness and we are taken over by that archetypal mode of being in which personal and collective are confusingly enmeshed and the dreams that emerge startle, and sometimes discomfort us, into dismissing and disowning them. Insomnia may be one of our defences and so, of course, is forgetfulness, or, if we are in therapy, remembering so much detail that both patient and therapist become too overwhelmed to make any attempt at understanding.

But there are some dreams that refuse to be ignored. Laura, who had a life-long horror of death, recorded in her eight-year-old diary a dream that she remembered from more than a year earlier, in which an angel visited her with the news that she would die at some time in the year that had just begun (the dream was in the Christmas holidays, just after New Year). Laura pleaded with the angel and eventually elicited from him that typically adult response 'we'll see about it', which, in her experience so far, had usually resulted in forgetting and lack of action. Laura did not forget her dream. Although life went on as usual and she lived it happily enough from day to day, the memory threw a shadow over the nights. At first, a year seemed a long time, but, as it got near to ending, her nightly fears increased so that, eventually, on New Year's Eve, she panicked and refused to go to sleep unless her mother stayed beside her. The excess of emotion did, in fact, wear her out and she was asleep long before midnight, when her mother got worried enough to check that she was still breathing.

When, many years later, Laura was in therapy for the first time, this dream was not believed. No child of that age, she was told, could possibly have that sort of dream. But Laura had her diary entry to prove it. Nevertheless, the dream was not explored. What was, perhaps, unusual was her exact memory for dates, so that she could say exactly what happened to her, as well as what was going on in the outside world, during every year of her life. The habit was an attempt to control time, which, like a tidal wave, seemed to bear down on her, increasing in power and speed as she got older.

In later life Laura had recurring dreams of having her head cut off. None of these executions were deserved. She was always led as an innocent victim to the block or guillotine. Sometimes, it was not she who was to be beheaded but a child or a delicate young man, whom she was cradling in her arms and doing her best to protect. These dreams were brought to her second (Jungian) analyst, who listened with interest and suggested that the child and also the masculine animus figure were both aspects of herself. Towards the end of her analysis she had what they both considered a 'big' dream. She had kept her habit of diary writing and recorded every dream that she remembered, so I can describe it in her own words:

> An innocent man was brought on a cart to his execution. I was going to stay and watch. Then it was suddenly I who was to lose my head. The Devil, like a little imp, was dancing round and wanted me to play with him. Then the voice of God boomed out of the sky. The voice said, 'yes', and the crowd answered, 'yes', all except the Devil, who said 'no' and seemed to be urging me also to say 'no'. I brought the Devil a plate of food. I knew he would hand it back for me to eat, but I knew that would be wrong. He turned into a huge,

dark, grinning man, who snatched the food and gobbled it up. People cheered and I thought that was because the Devil had saved my soul by not letting me eat with him. The voice of God boomed, 'yes', and, this time, I answered, 'yes'. The executioner seemed to be on my side but I knew he would go ahead and kill me. I didn't even try to escape. As I bowed my head on the block and waited for the axe, I had a memory of this happening to me before, although I thought this odd – how could I die more than once? I thought I remembered a quick pain and a blackout. I tried to think pleasant thoughts – fields in sunlight, a tree-lined road. I expected an accusation or some prayers. I wished the executioner would hurry. Then God's voice boomed, 'now', and the executioner began slowing sawing through my neck. But I woke up before it hurt.

Laura remembered a ballet on the theme of Faust, which she had seen as a small child but had screamed so loudly that she had to be taken out of the theatre. Her fear of death had begun at this time. She had been appalled at the idea that she might be asked to sell her soul. In this dream she had tried to make friends with the Devil and, in not eating with him, it seemed that her soul was saved. It was he who ate the forbidden food and she was able to say 'yes' to God. The executioner, in sawing through her neck, was dehumanising her, treating her like meat. But the greatest fear was losing her head. 'What does that mean?', said her analyst. Suddenly, she understood. Her fear of death had to do with letting go – losing her ego. This was something she needed to dream over and over again – a repetition remembered, this time, even while dreaming it – before the realisation dawned on her. To die would be to lose her ego, that small conscious bit of herself, seemingly located in her head, the only bit with which she could identify.

I was interested to read Rosemary Gordon's (1978) description of a psychotic patient whose dreams were full of graveyards and rotting leaves. Unlike Laura, this patient wanted to get rid of her ego:

> Death tends to be experienced as the loss of the personal, the separate ego
> ... awareness and fear of death must reside in the ego-system and it is this
> system that death demands as a sacrifice. One way of cheating death is by
> failing to have an ego available for sacrifice. (p.87)

This patient laments: 'If only I could stop knowing and thinking, if only I could be unconscious, then I could kill myself and then I would feel no guilt about it' (p.88).

We often hear reports of dreams that seem to foretell a person's death or turn out to have been dreamed on the night that someone is dying far from home. In a book that my great grandmother wrote about her family, I found one of these reports:

> I was walking in a large green field. The sky was cloudy, and its dark hue was reflected in a river which flowed below the field, and further on fell into the Firth of Forth. As I walked by the side of the river, I observed a vessel in full sail coming from the sea. It came rapidly along and passed me. It also looked dark and black from the sombre tint of the sky. But just after it passed, a faint, sickly ray of sunshine glanced upon the stern and I read these words 'from St. Vincent'. I instantly felt heart-struck and exclaimed, 'That vessel brings me fatal tidings.' I then awoke. I had not recovered from the unpleasant shock of this dream when the letter-bag was brought to me, being seven in the morning. (Dundas, 1891, pp.163–4)

The dreamer, if I have calculated correctly, was my great, great, great grandmother! Her husband died of a fever while fighting the French in the West Indies. The date was 1794. When she tore open the letter, she was, at first, relieved. The death reported was that of a friend of her husband's. Later, she discovered, 'Alas! It was himself! Through some unaccountable error the mistake was made in the names' (p.164).

Jung (1975) keeps reminding us of the historicity of the unconscious. We tend to regard our dreams less as 'historical regressions' than 'anticipations of the future':

> For everything that will be happens on the basis of what has been, and of what – consciously or unconsciously – still exists as a memory-trace. In so far as no man is born totally new, but continually repeats the stage of development last reached by the species, he contains unconsciously, as an *a priori datum*, the entire psychic structure developed both upwards and downwards by his ancestors in the course of the ages. (pp.279–80)

There is no time in the unconscious. What was and what will be come together in our dreams. Age and gender can shift in the course of one dream. The dead and the living can converse with each other.

After his wife's death, Jung (1967) saw her in a dream which was 'like a vision'. She was in her prime, about 30: 'Her expression was neither joyful nor sad, but rather, objectively wise and understanding, without the slightest emotional reaction, as though she were beyond the mist of affects' (p.327). Through this dream she seemed to be giving him a portrait of their marriage, how their relationship began, its development over 53 years, and her death: 'Face to face with such wholeness one remains speechless, for it can scarcely be comprehended' (p.327). In dreams such as these one is aware that letting go of the ego does not mean falling into chaos. There is a hidden order in the dream images calling out for our attention and understanding.

How does a dying person dream? James Hall (1991) suggests that 'the unconscious mind, as reflected in dreams, views death with much less concern than does the waking ego' (p.311).

Marie-Louise Von Franz (1980) dips into history to show us a series of dreams by the early Christian martyr, Perpetua, who was put to death in Carthage in 202 or 203 AD. The story of her life was written at the time – possibly by Tertullian – but she recorded, in her own hand, a sequence of four dreams that she had had during the weeks leading up to her death. She was 22 and mother of a baby son who was brought to her in prison for breast-feeding. There is no mention of her husband but her father, a convinced Pagan, did all he could to make her recant. One of her brothers also became a Christian. Von Franz looks at the dream images from a psychological, rather than theological, stance and tries to show what insights they give of 'the unconscious spiritual situation of the time':

> We find archetypal images constellated in them which we also encounter in the literature of that epoch, when the *weltanschauung* of antiquity was dissolving and the Christian conception of the world was breaking through. They appear here spontaneously in an unusual person, in an unusually tragic moment of her life, and lay bare the whole deep conflict of that time. (p.9)

Perpetua asks God for a 'vision' and then dreams of a ladder that reaches to heaven but is so narrow that only one person at a time can climb it. On each side there are all sorts of sharp instruments – swords, lances, daggers and spears – so that a careless climber could easily be torn to pieces. Beneath the ladder is a dragon. Sarturus, one of her fellow martyrs, climbs the ladder first and, when he reaches the top, speaks to her: 'Perpetua, I am holding thee, but see that the dragon does not bite thee'. She answers: 'He shall not harm me, in the name of Jesus Christ' (p.11). She then treads on the dragon's head and goes up the ladder. She arrives in a garden, where a white-haired shepherd is milking sheep. He welcomes her and gives her a piece of cheese, which she receives with folded hands and eats. All around her, people say: 'Amen'. She wakes up and tells this dream to her brother 'and from that time we began to put no more hope in this world'.

In interpreting this dream Von Franz is convinced that it is genuine: 'Had the visions been invented for the sake of edification, the author would most certainly have made use of exclusively Christian motifs' (p.15). In fact, all the dreams recorded by Perpetua contain archetypal images which would have been common among Pagans, Gnostics and Christians of that time. The first dream seems to have come in answer to a question – was she destined to be martyred? To call for dreams in this way was customary among Pagans as well as Christians. The ladder, besides recalling Jacob's dream, figures both in the Egyptian mysteries and the cult of Mithras. It can be seen as a means of ascending to a higher state of consciousness. The ladder can only be climbed singly and there is no turning back. The dream shows instruments of torture, representing martyrdom of a different kind from Perpetua's actual fate in the arena. By this, we see that the dream's truth is mythological rather than factual:

> It is as though the dream were intent on representing the real and deeper meaning of the event threatening the dreamer in the outer world in order thereby to prepare her for her inescapable fate. Therefore it displays the archetypal background of this fate. (p.20)

Sarturus can be seen as an animus figure representing a masculine component of her nature that leads her away from her exclusively feminine existence as wife and mother. The dragon she no doubt interpreted as symbolising the Devil, the tempter in the Garden of Eden. But in pre-Christian times the serpent was understood more ambiguously as an 'unconscious nature spirit, as the wisdom of the earth' (p.23). In Perpetua's dream the dragon might stand for the danger of slipping back into Paganism, a weakness that she overcomes by trampling it underfoot. To reach her destination she does not journey over the earth but ascends to an extra-mundane paradise 'beyond the material world and the cosmos' (p.27). The 'Good Shepherd' who welcomes her is an archetypal image in both Christianity and Paganism. She accepts his cheese made with milk instead of the bread and wine of the Christian sacrament. In many of the ancient mysteries it is milk that nourishes the spiritually reborn. Consciously, Perpetua had turned away from the gods of antiquity, but their archetypal images are still strong in the unconscious.

After being condemned to death, Perpetua has two dreams of her little brother, Dinocrates, who died as a child of seven in great pain from cancer of the face. In the first of these dreams there is a distance between them. The child is thirsty but not tall enough to reach a basin of water that is too high for him. Perpetua wishes she could help him. In her next dream Dinocrates is clean and well-clothed, with only a scar where the cancer had been. He is drinking water from a golden flask that never empties. He then goes off to play.

These two dreams are more personal. Von Franz suggests that Dinocrates embodies a spiritual content in Perpetua herself and his suffering is also her own. Memories of their shared childhood are of a time before baptism with 'living water', a time when the redeeming truth was still out of reach. The 'distance' between them means that, consciously, she has moved away from Paganism and refuses to be influenced by her father. Unconsciously, the world of her childhood still clings to her. These dreams have links with the ladder dream in that there are obstacles in the way of high consciousness. First, it is the dragon as instinctual reaction, then the family life of her childhood. In the three dreams there is a reaching for something higher, the attainment of milk as heavenly food and then water from the 'fountain of life'.

Finally, we come to the dream that Perpetua recorded on the night before her death. The deacon, Pomponius, comes to the prison door dressed in a festive toga. He takes her hand and leads her through a rough and pathless country. They come to the amphitheatre, where a huge crowd awaits the promised spectacle. He tells her not to be afraid; he will be fighting with her. Then he leaves and she waits for the wild beasts. Instead, a huge Egyptian 'of horrible appearance' comes, with his attendants, to fight her. Her own attendants are there to wash and rub her with oil. She is undressed and changes into a man. Next comes a helper, a 'man of miraculous size', towering above them all. He wears a festive tunic and shoes of gold and silver. He carries a rod and seems to be a trainer of gladiators, a Lanista. He also has a green bough on which hang golden apples. He declares that if the Egyptian wins, he will kill Perpetua with his sword, but, if she is the one to triumph, he will give her the green bough. The Lanista withdraws and her fight with the Egyptian begins. He tries to seize her feet but is overthrown and she treads on his head. She receives the bough and begins to go towards the gate of the pardoned. 'And I awoke and understood that it was not with the beasts, but against the Devil that I should have to fight, but I knew the victory would be mine' (p.14).

What actually happened next day was that Perpetua was led into the amphitheatre singing psalms and was immediately knocked down by a mad cow. She seemed in a trance but the crowd, impressed by her courage, 'pardoned her to the extent that she should be put to death by the sword' (p.15). This was done, at first clumsily but then she seized the sword herself and pointed it at her throat, showing her killer how to do his work.

Von Franz comments that this dream may at first seem to be 'a simple statement of the dreamer's actual situation' (p.44). Then she proceeds on a lengthy amplification. Psychologically, prison and isolation from the world is necessary for initiation into the ancient mysteries and 'often an initial symbol of the process of individuation in the dreams of modern people' (p.45). Initiation takes place under the guidance of a spiritual leader. The deacon, Pomponius, whom Perpetua knew in her waking life, takes charge, much as Saturus did in her first dream. He leads her to the place of martyrdom and assures her that he will fight with her, but it seems he is only with her as an unconscious, spiritual power. His place is taken (surprisingly) by a Lanista, a Director of gladiators, who promises her the bough of the Tree of Life. The path to the amphitheatre has been hard, for, however saintly she may prove to be, Perpetua would not go to her martyrdom without any doubt or dread. The deacon has acted as a 'guiding Christian animus' (p.48). To arrive in the amphitheatre is to step into a magic circle, a mandala, a symbol of the Self, and this embraces the total personality, conscious and unconscious. It also contains the opposing forces of Paganism and Christianity. In this enclosure the final contest takes place. Perpetua expects the wild beasts and that the fight will be similar to the one with the dragon. Instead, she meets the Egyptian, the most powerful symbol of ancient Pagan wisdom. Her dream reveals 'that the central conflict does not consist solely in overcoming the animal instincts but implies a fight against the spirit of Paganism, against the Pagan experience of the spirit projected into nature, against the spirit of the earth from which the Christian endeavoured to tear himself free' (p.52).

The Egyptian seeks to undermine her by trying to seize her feet. He stands for the Paganism of her father, who flung himself at her feet to plead with her 'not to destroy us all' (p.54). In this dream she identifies completely with the animus and turns into a man. In undressing she divests herself of her unconscious animal nature and her feminine ego-consciousness.

A surprising figure is the trainer of gladiators, straight out of the Pagan world, who, in her dream, becomes Perpetua's spiritual guide and the one to reward her with the bough of golden fruit, which is an archetypal image famous in ancient myth. The bough gives the promise of eternal life and also the means of passing over into the kingdom of the dead, a descent into the unconscious. The bough corresponds to the milk of the first dream and the water of life given to Dinocrates. The flask from which he drinks and the fruit of the bough are both gold, symbolic of the highest value. These dreams, and others like them, 'reveal the whole unconscious situation of humanity at that time, Pagan as well as Christian, and show the conflict which the Christians experienced in endeavouring to tear themselves free from the spirit … In truth, viewed from the psychological standpoint, the martyrs appear in many respects as the tragic, unconscious victims of the transformation which was then being fulfilled deep down in the collective stratum of the human soul' (p.75).

The symbols in these dreams are universal and the same images repeat themselves through the centuries. Only the language in which we describe them varies. The fight between 'goodies' and 'baddies' continues but the monsters these days are likely to be aliens from another planet. Space travel may replace ladders but we still yearn to ascend to a better world, just as we hope to find our lost Eden, not in the past but the future. At the end of the second millennium of our era, as at the beginning of the first, we feel ourselves to be in a state of transition, eager for new truths yet still shaped and moulded by the old mythologies.

Views from the Edge

In spite of what Hamlet said about 'the undiscovered country from whose bourn no traveller returns', there have been hints all through history that some of us, at times of accident or severe medical crisis, experience what it is like to die and come back to tell the tale. Plato tells us the story of Er, who returned to life when already on his funeral pyre and recounted what he had seen in the realm of the dead, where souls chose their destinies for the next round of earthly life (many of them unwisely) before drinking the water of forgetfulness and being 'carried up to their birth, this way and that, like shooting stars.' (Plato, 1908, p.370). A Christian story is told by the Venerable Bede, in the eighth century, of a man who was pronounced dead but suddenly sat up in the presence of his weeping family and vowed to amend his future life. Tall stories, we may say, but perhaps based on rumours of truth.

Until recently, scientists have found these Near Death Experiences (NDEs) impossible to accept and patients have tended to keep their stories to themselves for fear of being considered crazy. But as methods of resuscitation improve more NDEs get reported and researchers are getting pushed into finding the area worth studying. Doctors, whose whole training and outlook is contained within scientific paradigms, start out with scepticism and expectations of discovering simple physical explanations, but, in fact, the more they probe, the more baffled they become.

The following is a typical NDE:

> I was floating in what seemed to be a tunnel; dark but not frightening at all. I could see a light at the end and I felt as though I was being pulled towards it. I had to go – there was no alternative. But still I wasn't frightened. Rather the reverse. I had the most wonderful feeling of peace … The light at the end got brighter and brighter, but it didn't hurt my eyes … I felt I was being drawn into it and the feeling was … pure bliss and love. There was someone there in the light waiting for me. And then suddenly I was pulled back … slammed into my body again. (Fenwick, 1997, p.6)

Typically, this experience had started with the patient, out of his body, watching from the ceiling what the doctors were doing, 'scurrying round' the body on the bed.

To identify a 'typical' NDE the researchers have needed to hear a great many descriptions – in Peter Fenwick's case, over 300 – and allow for cultural differences in language before it has been possible to list some essential features common to them all. For most people, there is peace, joy and bliss. Pain is left behind with the body while the 'person' rises in the air and looks down (though being out of the body does not apply in every case). Next, there is a tunnel with brilliant light at the end; often, the light acts as a magnet, drawing the person into itself. There is some sort of presence, described as a 'being of light' and called God, Christ, prophet or angel by those brought up in monotheist religions. The presence is welcome and loving. At this point some sort of barrier is encountered, marking a point of no return. This may be a closed gate or wall, or some figure who bars the way. There is a glimpse of another country, usually an idyllic garden or meadow, brilliantly coloured and filled with light. There may be a meeting with dead relatives. Sometimes, there is a flash-back of the person's life or of events still to be lived through and indications that there may be more work to be done before entry is allowed. A decision is involved whether to stay or go back. There may be a longing not to leave such a beautiful place. Then comes a rapid return to the body – often arriving feet first – and the resumption of heaviness and pain. Afterwards, the experience is clearly and permanently remembered with none of the elusiveness we associate with dreams. Almost everyone, after an NDE, loses all fear of death.

It would be strange – and I think unbelievable – if all the NDEs reported were unfailingly blissful. There must surely be a shadow side to the experience but, although this is obviously true, not many distressing NDEs get reported. It is, of course, easier to spread good news than bad and none of us readily speak evil of ourselves. So it could be a sense of shame that silences those who have caught glimpses of hell, the sinners' destination. What reports there are seem to fall into three categories.

First, there are people who describe the tunnel, the light and the presence just as in those happier reports, but the interpretation is different. Here is a child's account: 'That night I was picked up, unwillingly, by a lady wearing a long, green, flowing robe, mediaeval style. She carried me in her arms down a long, dark, green, mouldy type dirt-walled tunnel swiftly taking me somewhere I did not want to go' (Evans-Bush and Greyson, 1996, p.215). Or this, from an adult woman:

> I found myself growing more and more afraid as the speed picked up and I realized that I was headed towards that pinpoint of light at the end of the tunnel … I decided then and there that I would go no further, and I tried to backpedal, stop and turn round again, but to no avail. (p.217)

It strikes me that those who fight so hard for control must find it very hard to die. But, sometimes, these frightening experiences resolve in letting go and, after a struggle, bring the joy and peace already described.

Second, there is an experience of emptiness and loss of meaning:

> A small group of circles appeared ahead of me … The circles were black and white and made a clicking sound as they snapped black to white, white to black. They were jeering and tormenting … The message in their click-ing was: your life never existed. Your family never existed. You were al-lowed to imagine it. You were allowed to make it up … There was never anything there. That's the joke – it was all a joke. (p.219)

Years later, this patient was looking through a book and found a picture of those circles. She flung the book across the room in disgust. So the circles were real; they had been seen by someone else; she could no longer pretend they were imaginary. Very much later still, she learnt that the circles repre-sented the yin and yang of Eastern tradition and believed that the book was probably Jung's *Man and his Symbols*.

The third category is just as negative but more graphic. There is a wailing and gnashing of teeth, grotesque sub-human creatures, tormented and tormenting. Such NDEs leave a bitter aftertaste.

As a neurophysiologist and neuropsychiatrist, Peter Fenwick (1997) tries to find a scientific explanation. He would expect all thoughts and feelings to result from neuronal activity in the brain: '"Mind" is merely a product of the brain; it certainly cannot act at a distance from it, or independently of it' (p.197). Our models of the world are created in our brains from the messages that come in coded pulses via the sense organs. The codes are neutral. Whether we see, hear or smell depends on which area of the brain they reach. This can be proved by brain-scanning techniques and applies to imaginary sights and sounds as well as those from the world outside us. In dreams the brain continues to build models, not with external data – although a little can slip through – but with emotion and memory carried internally. In deep unconsciousness there can be no model building, no experiencing, no memory. Yet NDEs are remarkably lucid and clearly remembered. How?

Fenwick looked into the various ways in which changes in body chemistry can cause brain dysfunction and altered experience. He also considered the psychological content of the NDE and how its meaning may depend on the personality and culture of the person concerned. He explored whether NDEs were induced by drugs, oxygen starvation or too much carbon dioxide. Could they be categorised as hallucinations? But none of these explanations was satisfactory: 'Brains which are disorganized so that consciousness is lost do not produce coherent hallucinations. One is again driven back to asking how lucid experiences can arise in the disorganized brain of an unconscious person' (p.217).

A partial explanation for blissful states is that they may be due to endorphins, the brain's natural pain-killing drugs. NDEs occur when people are in great pain or stress, situations in which endorphins are likely to be produced. Most people, as they get near to death, are found to have raised endorphin levels, but comparatively few have NDEs. Research also shows a link with right-hemisphere activity, which may account for feelings of unity, loss of boundaries, altered perceptions of time and certainty that the NDE is 'more real than everyday life'.

NDEs have a lot in common with mystical experience and the brain activity involved is probably the same in both cases. Melvin Morse (1990) writes:

> I feel that just understanding near-death experiences will be our first step at healing the great division between science and religion ... Educating phy-sicians, nurses and ourselves about what people experience in those final hours will shatter our prejudices about the way we think about medicine and life. (p.93)

And another voice:

> The psychologist cannot definitively answer the question of whether con-
> sciousness is literally able to move out of the body into another realm of re-
> ality. But given that these are all equally unprovable assertions, to insist on
> a purely organic explanation of these events is to abandon true openness in
> the face of an unanswerable question. (Corbett, 1996, p.215)

When science can take us no further, we are left with the possibility of soul
and the question that I raised when writing about the dying brain and what
happens to identity in dementia. Does the mind (or self) exist independently
of the brain? In trying to find an answer we must look a little harder for a definition of who we are – both in life and in death.

CHAPTER 10

Who Dies?

Ah, what a dusty answer gets the soul
When hot for certainties in this our life!

George Meredith, *Modern Love*, p.458

First, we must address the question who lives? If someone asks who we are, the simple answer is to say one's name. This appellation, given, inherited and ours from birth, is how we are recognised by others and through which we relate to them. 'Doth any here know me?', cries King Lear, 'who is it that can tell me who I am?' Stripped of title and unrecognised, he hovers for the rest of the play on the edge of madness. We need our names and titles as reference points, and we hope to be remembered by them after we die. When Lear's fool comes up with the answer 'Lear's shadow', he is presumably seeing his master as less than his former authoritative self. In archetypal terms, we may see Lear as tragically possessed by his shadow and impelled to act out the dark side of his nature.

A new patient sits in front of me. I already know her name but not much else. I hesitate to ask a lot of questions. I want to hear in her own words who she is, or who she thinks she is, or how she has been labelled in her family. Perhaps she sees herself as simply mother, looking after a lot of helpless children and not attending to herself. Or she presents as a permanent child, not respected for having grown up and for owning her own thoughts and opinions. What I would most like to give this person is help to live with more of herself than the one aspect she seems able to comprehend.

So, who are we? What is that 'myself' which I name and hang on to with love, with hate and love-hate? In childhood I learnt that I was a 'child of God', 'a temple of the Holy Spirit'. Then I read Freud and learned about ego, id and superego. Later, I turned to Jung and the labels changed again. It is with this Jungian terminology that I find myself more or less at home, and this has something to do with my own ageing and that of my patients. Jung's language seems to me to cover, fairly adequately, the whole course of life; and death is not excluded. However, if I possibly can, I avoid jargon of any kind. In asking who dies, the ego, the self (or Self), some definitions seem to be called for. But that does not mean the question is answerable.

Ego

Using my own words, I would say that my ego is what I think I am, a defini-tion of my sense of 'I-ness'. I find it hard to say 'ego' without talking about 'ego-consciousness', since the whole point of ego is that it is conscious. I think this is a simplification of what Jung meant. He had his own kind of jar-gon and had more difficulty than Freud ever did in finding the words to convey his meanings. I am aware, of course, that the person I thought I was as a child is not quite the same as the person I am (or *think* I am) now, and yet I have a conscious sense of continuity. My consciousness has expanded to admit a whole lot of new information. Sooner or later it will contract. But my ego is not the whole of what I am and this is where Jung differed from Freud, for whom the ego was all-important. For Jungians, the ego is born out of unconsciousness: 'It is just man's turning away from instinct – his opposing himself to instinct – that creates consciousness' (Jung, 1977, p.388). In his essay on 'The Stages of Life', he asks:

> How does consciousness arise in the first place? Nobody can say with cer-tainty; but we can observe small children in the process of becoming con-scious … In the early years of life there is no conscious memory; at most there are islands of consciousness which are like single lamps or lighted objects in the far-flung darkness. (p.390)

These islands need to be connected. New perceptions must be linked in memory with what went before, in order to build 'very important series of contents belonging to the perceiving subject himself, the so-called ego' (p.390).

The ego, inevitably, brings problems. How much easier to stay in an instinctual paradise! The conflict is the same as that described by Becker (1973) between the animal and the symbolic, and presents difficulties at every stage. In old age we may hope to have integrated some of the raw material of the unconscious into consciousness. But what then?

Ego-consciousness was needed for living in this world, for attaining our share of wisdom and creating some small thing of value, or, at least, some image of what we thought we were, for another generation – who will probably see it differently from what we intended.

But I doubt if there is anything immortal about this ego and, perhaps, our supreme task is to relinquish, with a good grace, this small portion of what we are when we die.

Self

Some Jungian writers differentiate between the personal self, with a small 's', and the big, transpersonal Self written with a capital letter. The 'small s' self is not the ego but it needs the ego to become incarnate in our lives. Since Fordham (1976) revolutionised Jungian thinking – in London at least – we have begun to see self as potentially active from birth. By a process known as deintegration, parts of the self emerge in response to the infant's readiness and the mother's containment. As these pieces cohere, the ego is formed. The self in this context is an archetype and, perhaps, deserving of the big S, though I see no sign of Jung himself making this distinction, so neither shall I! Deintegration followed by reintegration (Fordham's categories) are pro-cesses that begin in infancy and alternate with each other throughout our lives, but never more than a part of self becomes conscious.

Anthony Stevens (1982) uses the capital S and affirms the importance of our sense of identity. He remembers, aged four or five, becoming suddenly quite certain of his own existence: "'This is me," I thought, "all me; and it's been here all the time.'" (p.140). This, he records, was the way the self gave itself conscious recognition through the ego.

Casting my own mind back, I can remember no moment of sudden enlightenment but I recognise the feeling of having been here 'all the time'. The concept of a beginning and end to my 'I-ness' seems to have been added later.

In that it transcends consciousness, Jung relates the self archetype to God. In doing so he makes it clear that God, in himself, is imageless but, through the ages, we have personified him and can relate to his image in the same way that our remote ancestors peopled the earth with many gods who were their unconscious projections made conscious through bodily image. Jung's archetypes – for instance, anima, animus, child, wise old man – show how inherent it is in humans to make images: 'The archetype is essentially an unconscious content that is altered by becoming conscious and being perceived, and it takes its colour from the individual consciousness in which it happens to appear' (Jung, 1975, p.5).

Self and ego need each other but there is tension between them. The self pushes the ego to actualise more and more of its unlived potential and produces disturbing dreams and troubled thoughts. 'This', says Stevens (1982), 'is the secret of man's "Divine Discontent." For all of us much more is "planned for" than we can ever hope to realise in conscious reality: our lives are crowded with lost opportunities' (p.142).

Since it is self that gives birth to ego, the suggestion seems to be that there is a 'divine spark' in each of us. Inevitably, the question arises: can self ever die?

Body, Soul and Spirit

'I pray God', wrote St Paul to the Thessalonians, 'your whole spirit and soul and body be preserved'. What did he mean by this tripartite division of what we are?

In this scientific age we know a lot about bodies, how they are born, develop, combat disease, decline and fall apart. We know – or can find out – how the brain functions and that it needs to be intact if we are to be fully alive. But 'soul' and 'spirit' are elusive entities and even the Church, to whose idiom we presume they belong, seems to mix one with the other. In *The Oxford Dictionary of the Christian Church* the entry for soul reads: 'No precise teaching about the soul received general acceptance in the Christian Church until the Middle Ages'. And, of St. Paul: '…in his language he is not entirely consistent and spirit sometimes denotes the principle of supernatural life in contrast to the natural life of the soul, and on other occasions signifies the higher powers (intellect and will) as opposed to the lower faculties (emotions etc.)' (Cross, 1971, p.1273).

I was brought up to believe I had an immortal soul and that was the part of me that would never die. I was also taught about the Resurrection of the Body, which, if believable, sometimes made me wonder why I needed a soul as well. I was given the image of a pure white soul that got blackened by sin but that confession and absolution cleaned it up again. With a child's concrete thinking I envisaged a white lining under my skin and wondered how big a hole the surgeon's knife had torn in it when, early in life, I had my appendix taken out. I clung to the idea of immortality and was much moved by Hans Andersen's 'Little Mermaid' and her heroic, but hopeless, attempt to get herself a soul and live for ever. Psyche, I learnt later, was another word for soul, with interesting Pagan resonances since Psyche was loved by Eros and made immortal by Zeus.

Turning again to the Church dictionary, spirit has several definitions, one of them being the Third Person of the Trinity. Or:

(1) The intelligent and immaterial part of man or the human soul in general, whether united with the body in life or separated from it in death, and especially that aspect of it which is concerned with religious truth and action and is directly susceptible to divine influence.

(2) An order of being which is superhuman in the sense that it is not subject to the limits of time, space and a bodily frame. (p.1281)

None of these definitions is precise and the words tend to be used interchangeably. In asking 'who dies?', the only conclusive fact is that bodies die; we have seen it happen. Psyche, soul, spirit, self, ego, conscious, unconscious – all these are invisible and intangible, so what proof is there that any of them exist?

And yet, says Jung (1977), 'We are steeped in a world that was created by our own psyche' (p.384). These words were written as an answer to the materialists, who would deny the reality of anything not directly perceived by the senses. He reminds us that:

consciousness has no direct relation to any material objects. We perceive nothing but images, transmitted to us indirectly by a complicated nervous apparatus ... What appears to us as immediate reality consists of carefully processed images ... In order to determine, even approximately, the real nature of material things, we need the elaborate apparatus and complicated procedures of chemistry and physics. These disciplines are really tools which help the human intellect to cast a glance behind the deceptive veil of images into a non-psychic world. (pp.383–4)

He argues that 'the psychic alone has immediate reality' (p.384). In a few sentences he turns modern science on its head. Psyche comes first – and is boundless. Material reality is only a fraction of the whole. As in all his writings, Jung makes no theological or philosophical claims but delineates only what he observes happening: 'I am inclined in all difficult questions to let experience decide' (p.320).

Jung gives intimations rather than definitions. Sometimes, the words 'soul' and 'spirit' seem to be indistinguishable. Always, they are elusive. The soul needs no space. It has no body:

Bodies die, but can something invisible and incorporeal disappear? What is more, life and psyche existed for me before I could say 'I' and when this 'I' disappears, as in sleep or unconsciousness, life and psyche still go on as our observation of other people and our own dreams inform us. Why should the simple mind deny, in the face of such experiences, that the 'soul' lives in a realm beyond the body? (p.348)

He does not dismiss the idea of the soul's immortality but he commits himself to no certainties: 'I must confess that I know as little what "spirit" may be in itself as I know what "life" is. Thus, instead of "life" I must speak of the living body, and instead of "spirit" of psychic factors' (p.320). And, in a later paragraph, 'Life and spirit are two powers or necessities between which man is placed. Spirit gives meaning to his life, and the possibility of its greatest development. But life is essential to spirit, since its truth is nothing if it cannot live' (p.337).

It would be easy to get lost between these shifting meanings. But, sometimes, we can choose working models. Keeping close to the theology I was taught in childhood, I find it natural to see soul as personal, that which gives meaning to an individual life, and, perhaps, also that part of us which is able to live symbolically. Lionel Corbett (1996) distinguishes soul from spirit thus: 'The soul then is an aspect of consciousness that extends, or incarnates, into the human being; consciousness as spirit extends far beyond the individual' (p.118).

Individuation

Analysis, according to Jung, was not just a branch of medical practice. Patients were inclined to stay on with him long after being relieved of their symptoms. What they were looking for, and what he found himself responding to, was how to become 'a psychological "in-dividual", that is a separate, indivisible unity or "whole"' (Jung, 1975, p.275). What he termed 'individuation' is the conscious quest to realise our unconscious potential or, in words that I have already used, the coming into being of the self through the ego. Although those who feel this pressure may not be in the majority, individuation is not just for the intellectually or spiritually élite, nor is it ever an achieved, final state.

Anyone who experiences *vocation*, in the sense of being called to some special task or way of life, can be said to have felt the urge towards individuation. To follow a vocation is a choice in so far as it can be rejected. James Hillman (1996) believes that we are, each of us, accompanied through life by a personal 'daimon', a spirit like a guardian angel, to be our guide – or we may experience it as a destiny to be seized. The call comes from outside ourselves in that it *happens* to us and it may be so strong that any real choice is negated and we feel compelled to follow where the daimon leads. Hillman refers to the myth of Er (already mentioned) which tells how:

> We elected the body, the parents, the place and the circumstances that suited the soul and that, as the myth says, belongs to its necessity. This suggests that the circumstances, including my body and my parents whom I may curse, are my soul's choice – and I do not understand this because I have forgotten. (p.8)

Plato tells the myth to remind us of this forgotten choice, made by our souls before we were born, and Hillman believes that 'the myth has a redemptive, psychological function' (p.8).

Jung thought that individuation belonged to the second half of life and he gave, as one of his illustrations, the case history of a 55-year-old American lady who, though highly academic, had 'got stuck', as she herself realised, in a one-sided masculine (animus) version of herself. She began, for the first time in her life, to paint from imagination and because she knew nothing about artistic technique, produced a series of mandala paintings that revealed strikingly some of what was happening in her unconscious psyche. Painting and interpretation represented an unfinished journey, which went on for more than ten years. Some of the paintings were seen by Jung only after the patient died and he did not claim to have understood them all, though it was noticeable how the patterns became more balanced and harmonious as the patient progressed. Jung saw these paintings as representing the initial stages of individuation:

> It would be desirable to know what happened afterwards. But, just as neither the philosophical gold nor the philosopher's stone was ever made in reality, so nobody has ever been able to tell the story the whole way, at least not to mortal ears, for it is not the story-teller but death who speaks the final 'consummatum est'. (Jung, 1977, p.348)

Can We Still Believe in an After-Life?

Of all the questions posed in this last chapter, I have arrived at the one which is probably the most impossible to answer. All I can do is quote a diversity of views, without imposing too many speculations of my own in realms on which I can claim no expertise. But the temptation to explore issues of ultimate concern may prove impossible to resist, in which case I shall try to ground my hazy conjectures in acceptable theory. There will be no attempt at scientific proof, nor at merely rational thinking, since, according to Jung and his followers (and that includes me), such speculation belongs to psychic, rather than factual, reality.

It seems to me – though I suspect all such generalisations – that humankind is divided between those who are concerned, over-awed and, often, frightened by death and its aftermath, and those 'healthy-minded' individuals who confine their thoughts and fears to what they can see, touch and hear in the world around them. I have already written about fear. There is also hope. And some people are more hopeful than others.

Biblically (1 Cor.Ch.13), hope is listed together with faith and love, with love as the most important. For a full and happy life it is best to have all three, and it seems evident that a bad start in life reduces faith (or trust), the capacity to love and, in all likelihood, hope as well, though some manage to cling to a hope-against-hope which, however fragile, saves them from despair.

An ultimate hope that reaches beyond death has a long history. It seems that dismissing such hope as wishful thinking is a relatively modern assertion which began with the supremacy given to reason in the so-called 'Enlightenment' and, more recently, the discoveries of science.

Our distant ancestors buried their dead with food for their journey into another world, as well as possessions and ornaments belonging to their past. The Egyptians continued such traditions with additions of their own. In many cultures there was ancestor worship and festivals held at the tombs of the dead, who were thought to participate. Hope of a future life persisted into Greek civilisation and Plato taught his disciples that the human soul continued after the body died. Socrates, talking to his friends before his execution, declared that death was either a state of nothingness or the migration of the soul to another world. He could accept either alternative, to sleep, undisturbed by dreams, or to 'converse with Orpheus and Musaeus and Hesiod and Homer ... What infinite delight would there be in conversing with them and asking questions!' (Livingstone, 1946, pp.46–7).

Two of the major world religions, Christianity and Buddhism, support these hopes, but life beyond the grave is envisaged by each very differently. Stephen Levine (1982) writes about death from the Buddhist point of view in a book with the same title as I am using for this chapter, *Who Dies?* But whereas I have been struggling with self and ego, he has a simpler answer – there is no self to die!:

We think we are our thoughts. We call our thoughts 'I'. In letting go of thought, we go beyond ourselves, beyond who we imagine we are. Behind the restless movement of the mind is the stillness of being, the stillness that has no name, no reputation, nothing to protect. It is the natural mind. (p.21)

He emphasises the impermanence of mood and awareness. We do not own our own thoughts, or even our bodies: 'Let "who am I?" become unanswerable, beyond definition. Become that space out of which all things originate and into which all things recede' (p.183). Everything we think we are is illusion and we have to let it go. A Zen master was able, quite sincerely, to say to a terminally ill patient: 'Don't worry. You won't die'.

Levine describes the *bardos* in the Tibetan Book of the Dead. Buddhist monks and pious lay people learn to meditate on these states of transition from life and, through death, to life again. There are bardos of emergence, of roaming and of dissolution. Beginning with Birth, then Life, the Moments before Death and the Moments after Death, we come round to the Bardo of the Moment before Birth, which is one of dissolution and choosing the next stage of incarnation. So we are reminded again of the Er legend and the persistence of the belief in reincarnation through different cultures.

Children of my generation were brought up to sing 'There's a home for little children above the bright blue sky'. Was it believable? I think we were inclined to put this view of heaven in the same doubtful category as fairies, Father Christmas and, possibly, the gospel story of angels talking to shepherds and God born in a manger. Doubt breeds more doubt and, however much we may want to believe, one questionable fact leads to another, so that we may, by the time we get into our teens, find ourselves throwing away the whole religious package.

I wondered, on my only visit to a spiritualist church, whether the congregation had ever grown out of their early childhood credulity and also, with a sudden rush of paranoia, whether the Medium would spot my disbelief and ask me to leave. He brought greetings of warmth and love from the spirit world but no details of what the place was like. At the end of the service he picked out certain people so that he could display his fortune-telling skills and I was impressed by his clairvoyance, though unconvinced that he was inspired by anything more than his own intuition. The little spiritualist literature that I have seen portrays another world, not dissimilar to our familiar planet, where dead friends meet together and enjoy themselves. Through an expert Medium, at a service or seance, they are said to give advice to those not yet dead. Perhaps the banality of the proceedings is due to the limitations of language, which can only speak of the unknown in terms of the known, and, as in the near-death experiences, what happens depends on cultural expectations.

The passive recipients of the Medium's message do not have the benefit of the *actual experience* to amaze or enlighten them. There is emphasis on healing and some of the communications that I heard given to individuals, and the obvious understanding of their plight, may indeed have been therapeutic, but questions of life after this life got the vaguest and most unsatisfactory answers. I can only speak for myself in saying that I am none the wiser and, although naturally curious, prefer it this way. If there is anything ahead of us other than final extinction, I like to think of it as the ultimate surprise.

Jung had an abiding interest in the paranormal and was aware of his own psychic powers. On a visit to Freud in Vienna he tried to have a discussion on precognition and parapsychology but Freud dismissed what he called 'occult' phenomena as nonsense. Jung felt a curious sensation in his diaphragm, whereupon there was a loud noise from the bookcase, which alarmed them both. Jung called this an example of 'a catalytic exteriorisation phenomenon' and warned Freud that the noise would be repeated, although he had no idea why he knew. Sure enough, a moment later, the noise came again. Freud was aghast: 'This incident aroused his mistrust of me, and I had the feeling I had done something against him' (Jung, 1967, p.179). It was after his break with Freud that Jung became almost overwhelmed by unconscious contents, which kept appearing to him in powerful dreams and waking fantasies. 'Philemon' became a ghostly guru and represented 'a force which was not myself' (p.207) and which seemed to come from the 'objective' or 'collective' psyche. In Jung's autobiography, *Memories, Dreams, Reflections* (1967), he describes many occasions of being haunted, including an incident, shared by his family, which began with a frantic ringing of the doorbell which was heard by everyone in the house and was followed by an invasion from the spirits of the dead.

Through all these experiences Jung was able never to lose touch with 'this world' made up of his family and his profession. This gave him a secure base to which he knew he could always return and be assured that he was 'an actually existing, ordinary person' (p.214).

These were the experiences which enabled Jung to be sure of a psychic reality beyond our narrow ego-consciousness and to speculate on its continuance after the individual deaths of our bodies. He writes with authority born out of his experience: 'When I speak of things after death, I am speaking out of inner prompting and can go no further than to tell you dreams and myths that relate to this subject' (p.335). He continues cautiously: 'Although there is no way to marshal valid proof for continuance of the soul after death, there are nevertheless experiences which make me thoughtful. I take them as hints and do not presume to ascribe to them the significance of insights' (p.343).

If we assume that life continues in some mysterious 'there', he concludes that, since 'there' can have no location, the only way of continuing is in the psyche, which is free from the limits of space and time. There is no concrete proof, only a possibility. He wonders about the continuing psyche being conscious of itself and, like Peter Fenwick more than 30 years later, is astonished at what happens when the cerebral cortex, the seat of consciousness, has stopped functioning. He himself had a near-death experience that gave him feelings of bliss. He mentions cases of severe brain injury, or syncope, during which there can be both dreaming and perception of the outside world – some sort of consciousness in seeming unconsciousness but against all odds.

Jung did not particularly want life after death but recognised that, in most cases, 'the question of immortality is so urgent, so immediate, and also so ineradicable that we must make an effort to form some sort of view about it' (p.332). In fact, he suggested that it is everyone's duty to get hold of some conception, or create an image, of life after death, just as our ancestors have done since human beings began. He reminds us that:

> Day after day we live far beyond the bounds of our consciousness; without our knowledge, the life of the unconscious is also going on within us. The more the critical reason dominates, the more impoverished life becomes; but the more of the unconscious and the more of myth we are capable of making conscious, the more of life we integrate. (p.333)

Following Jung, Von Franz (1986) writes with conviction:

> ...the unconscious psyche pays very little attention to the abrupt end of bodily life and behaves as if the psychic life of the individual, that is the individuation process, will simply continue. In this connection, however, there are also dreams which symbolically indicate the end of bodily life and the explicit continuation of psychic life after death. The unconscious 'believes' quite obviously in a life after death. (p.viii)

I have always been puzzled about the ultimate aim of individuation but that may be because of a certain blindness in myself that makes me see life as a linear progression from birth to old age, rather than taking seriously the phrase 'life cycle'. Also, without meaning to, I seem to be thinking of an ego-process instead of a movement in the much less easily defined 'self'. So, it comes as a shock to read, in the above passage, that individuation 'will simply continue' after the body dies. In old age, it seems to me, there is a need to surrender what it has taken a life-time to acquire – a store of knowledge and, one hopes, quite a bit of wisdom, not all of which we will be able to hand on to those who come after us. There is a lot to surrender since we cling to earth and hardly dare peep over death's horizon, but if part of what we are is not doomed to total extinction, there may be some undreamed of change working through us quite outside our conscious will – not a change that I can *make* happen but something that happens to me. And, if any of this proves to be true, dying will be, in the words of Peter Pan, 'an awfully big adventure'.

At Christian burials we hear the words: 'in sure and certain hope of the resurrection to eternal life'. Some Christians prefer the concept of resurrection to that of the soul's immortality. Paul Tillich (1974), the existentialist theologian, goes so far as to say that belief in immortality is an escape from facing death. It is a way of 'continuing one's finitude, that is one's having to die infinitely, so that the actual death will never occur' and 'it makes endless what, by definition, must come to an end' (p.164). I suppose many Christians find consolation in whatever picture of heaven has been presented to them, not so much sitting on clouds and playing harps as 'a new heaven and a new earth' where 'God shall wipe away all tears from their eyes' (Rev. ch 21, v.1–4). But the stoic in me believes in facing my body's death as the end, even though a hope refuses to go away that in being able to accept an end without fooling myself I may somehow be rewarded!

Hope, I feel, is a necessity to keep us going in the face of life's 'slings and arrows', so why not an ultimate hope, not just for ourselves – we cannot live in isolation – but for all people at all times? The resurrection of our bodies, though factually impossible, has been a powerful symbol right through Christian history and has inspired artists from medieval times to Stanley Spencer. We would rather be psychosomatic persons than disembodied souls and I sometimes wonder if these resurrection symbols are an attempt to heal the split between these two.

But I can see a way in which even the Resurrection of the Body might make sense if instead of putting events into history, we could transcend time as measured by clocks and calendars – and experienced through life as robbing us of our youth and vitality – and accept eternity as another dimension. This is something of which poets down the ages have had intimations: 'He who kisses a joy as it flies', writes Blake, 'lives in eternity's sunrise'.

Nathan Field's book, *Breakdown and Breakthrough* (1996), is sub-titled 'Psychotherapy in a New Dimension':

> What I argue for is the recognition that four dimensionality exists, that we are encompassed by it as the fish is encompassed by the sea, and that the change of perspective brought about by our awakening to it not only alters our view of life, but enables us to enlist its healing power. (p.73)

In our clinical work he draws attention to transitions from 'disconnectedness to connection' and 'peak' moments of 'stillness, silence and intense mutuality'. As in prayer or meditation, the therapy situation can facilitate experiences where time seems to stop and what he calls 'another dimension' breaks through.

To be able to enjoy a new heaven or a new earth, Alan Watts (1954) insists that we need to forget:

> To be entranced eternally the blessed would have to forget eternally, so that the dance of omnipotence would not wear out the floor of memory with its tracks ... Not to forget is to die since what we call physical death is above all else the destruction of a system of memories, of an 'I'. (p.227)

So, once again, as in the legend of Er, we must drink the waters of Lethe. And Wordsworth seems to agree:

> Our birth is but a sleep and a forgetting.
> The soul that riseth with us, our life's star,
> Hath had elsewhere its setting
> And cometh from afar.

Remembering and forgetting belong to time and, in our time-limited existence, we do not want our memories to be taken away. There are no words for a timeless state, only glimpses.

I would like to end with an emphasis on time as circular. Why else did Jung keep drawing mandalas? There is no beginning and no end to a circle. It is Alpha and Omega.

I leave the last word with another poet, thus completing the quotation begun on my first page:

...And the end of all our exploring
Will be to arrive where we started
And know the place for the first time.

Eliot, *Little Gidding*

Love and Death in Psychoanalysis
The Guild of Psychotherapists'
Summer Conference, July 1998

An example of death coming out of the closet, and being spoken and written about, shows in the title of this conference. It was not of my choosing but, when chosen, I offered to help run it.

The Guild is not, strictly speaking, a centre for psychoanalysis, though some of its members would claim that that is what they are, in fact, practising. However, as one of the first to qualify, I could argue that psychoanalysis was not what the founder members had in mind. The Guild was envisaged as a fellowship of people sharing the same interests and wanting to practise what were termed 'ordinary' human skills in the one-to-one situation of psychotherapy. Learning would take place through the apprenticeship of beginners to experienced therapists from varying schools of analytic thought. As the name suggests, the model came from the guilds of workers in mediaeval Europe, whose aims – quoting Collins Concise Dictionary (1989) – were 'mutual aid and protection, and to maintain craft standards'. What has emerged in the course of twenty years is a training body and membership for those practising psychotherapy in any of its analytic forms. Whether Freudian, Kleinian, Lacanian or Jungian, we acknowledge our differences and are prepared to learn from and be enriched by each other.

The theme of Love and Death arose from last year's topic – Origins and Identities – and, in some subtle way, has evoked as next year's title – Speaking the Unspeakable.

When we all met in a large group, with no specific theme, at the end of the first day, one sensed unspeakable pain behind the actual words that slowly emerged. The discussion focused on suicide and the feelings of anger and betrayal that would inevitably follow among both patients and colleagues when a therapist opted for this way out. Some of us in the group spoke out for suicide as any person's ultimate choice, but this was questioned as irresponsible in a profession such as ours.

We also spoke of some practical arrangements that should be made by all of us in case of sudden death. These involve leaving a list of current patients with a trusted colleague whom we can rely on to inform, and, perhaps, see, those listed and, when possible, suggest an appropriate re-referral. We would also recommend that a colleague should undertake to dispose of any notes or confidential papers concerning patients.

Love was the theme as well as death – love that leads to conception and birth, life that leads irrevocably to death. Our speakers were poetic and creative, drawing on literature and mythology as well as clinical case material. To illustrate the substance of what was said, I have permission to publish an edited version of one of the conference papers.

From Oedipus' to Dido's Lament: A Matter of Love and Death

Repetition Compulsion and Other Forms of Remembering

As it must have done for all of you, the title of this conference raised many questions and associations for me – about love, about death, and about their relation to each other. How do love and death come together in this conference title?

They have their place as observable phenomena, with visible consequences in the outer world. But the 'Psychoanalysis' of this title focuses my thinking most particularly on the function of love and death in the inner world of the individual. It leads me to ask: what are their signifiers in psychoanalysis and culture generally? Does culture too have an inside or inner world in which love and death operate? Are the terms love and death explored metaphorically in our culture? Are love and death themselves signifiers, and, if so, of what?

The title of the conference connected with my thoughts about some work with a patient. Also, I had discovered the composer Purcell, and, in particular, his portrayal of the love and death of Queen Dido in the opera *Dido and Aeneas*. The themes of this seventeenth-century opera – from such a different world – seemed to connect with reflections on my clinical work. It enticed me into exploring other operatic treatments of myths and the discovery of Love and Death as recurring themes. In particular, I became interested in operatic treatments of that fundamental Freudian myth of King Oedipus – both by Stravinsky and Enescu – and that led me back to Sophocles' Theban plays.

Oedipus, it seems to me, is the story of the beginning of a life and its consequences, a story of parental anticipation and the withdrawal of love. I see in Oedipus premature disillusionment and negative anticipatory identification of the parents, a type of psychic death. Out of his beginning he starts his inexorable journey to the crossroads where father waits to be murdered (indeed provokes the murder), the Sphinx waits to be defeated and mother waits to be married. Then comes a process of unravelling, of remembering. That is the story of Sophocles' first Theban play and of Stravinsky's opera, a detective story that exposes the parental anticipation to fulfilment of prophecy, to exploration and illumination. A cruel decree, issued by the gods, is brought to completion by Oedipus' parents and by Oedipus himself. We see him driven to explore, to remember and reveal all.

If Oedipus deals with beginnings and their consequences, Dido tells of the end of a life. In Purcell's opera, as in Virgil, we are told little, if anything, of the earlier life of this African queen. Instead, we have a story of adult object relations, with Dido as an exemplar of the effect of premature disillusionment on adult relationships. Dido, against her better judgement, is persuaded to love Aeneas. They love. He leaves her to found Italy. She sings her Lament and then – again as if by necessity – she dies.

On the face of it, it is the loss of love that leads to death. The parents withdraw love from Oedipus when they attempt to sacrifice him. Aeneas abandons Dido and their love leads to Dido's death.

But here, in this conference, it is love (not the loss of love, but love) and death that are conjoined. 'That sweet little word "and"', as Wagner's Isolde says to Tristan. Love is one thing and death another but bring them together in one expression – 'love and death' – and the effect on the hearer is quite different. Now there is an interplay between them. There is no pathology in play. It is creative. In that interplay between the two, a third area is created from which new thoughts, feelings and images are generated. The word 'play' changes its meaning. We know that words do this. They are plastic in the dance of meaning. I feel on the edge of a split between idealisation and denigration, an idealisation of play, and of love as creative, and a denigration of death as destructive, but this would be to forget the interplay of creativity and destructiveness in the soul, in therapy and in our culture.

Love can certainly be hateful in its destructiveness. Parents' love comes entwined with parents' anticipation and anxiety. In parental expectation of the unborn there can be violence, especially if a form of negative anticipatory identification is in place, a sense of a process disrupted, with none of the organic sense of completion experienced in a timely death. There is no space for a psychic beginning. Privation, neglect and absence of the good feel like an attack, arousing both violent emotions and physical sensations. The former must be repressed and the latter may become chronic. Distress becomes disease.

Oedipus was burdened with an intolerable burden of parental anxiety and a negative form of anticipatory identification. It heralded his birth into a premature death, signifying the unlived life of the parents, the parental complexes, fantasies and anxieties. For Oedipus, a certain psychic abandonment was followed by a literal, physical abandonment, with murderous intent. In the myth the love and the parental fantasies are split between two sets of parents – the parents who take him in and from whom he runs so as not to fulfil the dreadful prophecy of parricide and incest, and the parents who sacrifice him to their anxious expectation and on whom he visits, all unknowingly, their worst fears.

I had a patient on whom the weight of parental anticipation lay so heavily that there was no psychic space for her in her family of origin. There was no way for her to discover who she was. It seemed that love and death were clenched in a vice-like grip in the mother's affectional world, leaving no room for the daughter's separate, individual identity. She could never measure up to an uncle who had died as a hero in the war, his death making him eternal and invincible in her mother's eyes, nor could she become the son who could have been his replacement.

The force of negative, anticipatory identification leaves little space for the individual. It leads to a dismembering and to the individual feeling cast out, unmembered/dismembered. Oedipus is a pawn of the gods because of his predicted destiny to kill his father and marry his mother. Sophocles unfolds before us the reality of Oedipus' subjugation to fate. Yet Oedipus' heroic achievement is the discovery of the truth. A different version of the story is to be found in an opera by the Romanian composer Enescu. 'Oedipe' tells the story of Oedipus from his birth in Thebes to his death in Colonnus. In this version the hero defies the gods and refuses to accept his fate as the ultimate truth about his human state. And he succeeds. His ending in Colonnus is the death of a man who has come through the crisis and risen above his destiny. After the psychic death, the premature death which finds dreadful expression in his self-mutilation, his final death in Colonnus is a good death, a completion.

In the case of Oedipus, as with my patient, parental disillusion set in early. Within the womb of parental imagination a different creature was stirring from the actual infant who was born. Who can determine what is illusion and what is disillusionment? Illusion can be benign or malign in its effects, as can disillusionment. The benign side may be seen as 'the love side' of the equation and the malign as 'the death side', love as creative, death as destructive. I keep finding the terms love and death, benign and malign, creative and destructive less stable than they appeared to be. Shakespeare says in Sonnet CLI: 'Yet who knows not conscience is born of love'. I know what love is. It is recognisable; it makes for happiness and generativity, in contrast to death as murder, cancer, AIDS or some fatal accident. Death is inevitable but can sometimes be deferred. And what of psychic death? Is it recognisable? Is it always a bad thing? Does the word always have the same meaning, or does it function in different ways? Death, as completion, has an inevitability that seems appropriate, despite the psychic pain, even of a right death. If you are close to the one who has died, be it your parent, partner or friend – or to a cherished idea or fantasy – then it feels devastating and the feeling lasts a long time. And what about intolerable psychic pain, paralysis, fragmentation, loss of eros – all of which seem to deal several forms of death? They can be derived from love, from the wrong sort of love, from love misapplied or misused.

In mainstream life and culture certain forms of love and certain forms of death are accepted as having an inherent sense of fatedness – for instance, the romantic love and death of Dido:

> Aeneas has no fate, but you.
> Let Dido smile, and I'll defy
> The feeble stroke of Destiny.

Perhaps Love and Death is an image of completion or fullness, a process with love as the beginning and death as the ending. The process can be experienced as *dissolution of the body of love*, of love's body as well as the physical body, leading to despair or nihilism. It can be seen as love's dream destroyed, linked to the fear of envious attack and destruction, of absence, lack, privation. This is Dido's despair, love's engagement now viewed as having been merely an *interlude* and its sweetest joys as a *delusion*. In their final confrontation Aeneas offers to stay 'offend the gods, and love obey'. But Dido is set on death:

For 'tis enough whate'er you now decree,
That you once had a thought of leaving me.

And the chorus' comment:

Great minds against themselves conspire,
And shun the cure they most desire.

Viewed more positively, the two realities of love and death may be seen as opposite poles in dialectical relation, creating, in the tension between them, a field where love and death can play or interplay. (The Latin for 'I play' is 'ludo', so interplay and interlude are variants on the same theme). It is the play of love and death in the soul, and within the analytic temenos. Wagner's lovers, Tristan and Isolde, throughout their great love duet, play delightedly with the images of love and death. The play Oedipus Rex leads to the creation of light. 'Lux facta est', cries Stravinsky's Oedipus at the moment of illumination amidst a blaze of trumpets – the light is made! At the end of the play, Oedipus' blinding can be viewed as a terrible punishment inflicted by the gods or as a refusal to look once again on the truth. Or we may see it as connected with the seer Teresias, whose actual bodily blindness is a signifier of his gift of prophecy or true insight. Oedipus Rex is a tragedy of love and death and leads, with tragic necessity, to Jocasta's suicide and to Oedipus' self-blinding and exile. But light is made and the blinding and exile lead to Colonnus, where Oedipus finds peace. Dido's death seems a totally negative event brought about by a malevolent sorceress and by her own conspiring against herself and shunning the cure. But, at a mythic level as well as musically and dramatically, it is a necessity and brings the opera to completion. Her death is apparently spontaneous (there is no indication that she kills herself). 'Death must come when he is gone', she sings. So, instead of merely beginning and ending there is completion – Alpha and Omega.

There are two sides to love and death. One is healing and nourishing, the other wounding. Both may deal a blow to the ego. In our culture – in the Hebrew bible, in Christianity, in literature and music – the relationship between love and death is represented in different, often opposite, ways. Love can be a deadly passion leading to premature death, a destructive process, or it can be a coming together which generates a third. Death is a process of separation into constituent elements, as in the five Skandas of Buddhism, and brings an attendant anxiety about the perceived threat to stability, about loss, about dissolution. There is a positive view of love-as-death or love-in-death, a loving union in death's embrace, as at the ecstatic close of Wagner's Tristan *and Isolde,* for which most of the opera has been one longing, agonising wait. Tristan cannot die, despite his wounds, till Isolde joins him. Their love cannot find fulfilment, except in death.

Perhaps love and death, pathology and health are changing in their dialectical interplay – with each other and with the ego, or the self. Love and Death is an endless kaleidoscopic pattern of coming together, of coming to be, of bringing to life and of ending(s) as the patterns re-arrange themselves in a continuing dance of life and death, in the psyche as in life itself. Indeed, what meaning does death have apart from love? What is the meaning of love without death? The pattern changes; the meaning shifts, and, in the shift, there is life, engagement, love and also ending, loss, death. Perhaps both love and death move in cycles and, at different periods in the cycle, are seen to be very close to each other, sometimes even indistinguishable. Or maybe the dance, the play, the cycle of love and death are most usefully perceived as happening within the spatial metaphor of height and depth, as a dynamic process removed from the dualism of love and death.

There seems to be a relation of love and death to time and to remembering (re-membering). 'Remember me' is the climax of Dido's lament – 'Remember me, but ah! Forget my fate'. Disillusionment and re-membering are polarities. Premature disillusionment, with its shattering effect on the psyche, with its fragmentation and fragility, leads to a sense of dis-memberment. The spike that pierced the infant Oedipus' feet leads to the pin with which the adult Oedipus puts out his eyes. This image is of fragmentation, a pervasive, distressing, maddening sense of non-belonging, of being essentially excommunicated, cut off, exiled – not just from Thebes, but from the sacred life-blood of relationship and from the sacred communion of love, loving words and a sense of the loving, beyond or beneath words, which nourishes life.

Oedipus the King, the play by Sophocles and the opera by Stravinsky, both begin near the end of the story and are, therefore, about remembering. Psychotherapy never comes in at the beginning. Indeed, perhaps psychotherapy is the beginning of the end. Therapy, like love and death, has a peculiar relationship with time. It is certainly a process of remembering.

Patients reach us in a state of crisis, an outer crisis pointing to something gone awry within. Or something chronic has become unbearable – 'this can't go on' or 'I can't go on'. They come with a story, but not necessarily *the* story. My patient's *first* story was of love and death. She spoke to me about a dead cat and her love for him. This was a story of epic proportions which was told and re-told, spiralling between the poles of love and death, just as her feelings swung between the agonising poles of love and grief. She had found him on the street, a stray. He had been physically abused, with a missing limb and other damage. He had lived with her for years and they had loved each other until his death from a tumour about nine months before she came to see me.

Looking back, I can see how much this presenting story contains, at least potentially – almost like an initial dream. But at the time I was bewildered by this woman, so full of affects, who seemed like a wild, injured creature. For a long time I had to keep faith with the understanding, yet without knowing that in speaking of the cat she was speaking of herself, of her own lostness, mutilation and abuse. Only gradually did I learn the story of the girl who was not given the psychic space to be a girl, who could not measure up to the undead uncle or to the expected son that would have replaced him.

We come into the patient's life as though coming into a film halfway through. We struggle to understand what is going on. Both parties are in the dark. The patients come with some version of a life story, or a series of stories, strung along in a linear fashion, or memories clustered around some foundational event. Their stories assume mythic dimensions but they cripple psychic life, just as the spike pierced the infant Oedipus' ankles. Something remains to emerge – to be remembered – either a counterpoint to the tale told, filling in some gaps, or else another tale/tune altogether, full of dark discords, overturning everything, standing our notions on their heads. Then, with a bloodrush, 'Lux facta est'.

Some of the considerations in this paper, of the shifty, shifting nature of love and death, seem rather global in scope and, ultimately with relief, can be left as the province of theology or philosophy. Within the scope of this conference we can take a more boundaried approach. Psychoanalysis is primarily a craft, a process, and, secondarily, a reflection on the questions which the material raises. It is confined within the restriction and constriction of the analytic space or temenos. One party is given the impossible obligation of saying whatever comes to mind, the other is required to exercise a self-restricting discipline and to avoid premature anticipation based on one's own need and fantasy. The therapist becomes a disciple of the patient's unconscious. People enter a sacred space where they hope for an encounter with the god, a hearing, a cure, relief. One thinks of the ancient Greek culture of healing, with its overnight stay and the search for a healing dream. Or one may think of the alchemists' bath into which king and queen must be immersed; or of the Christian ritual of immersion, which betokens dying and rebirth; or of the theatre, with its cathartic function, as conceived by the ancient Greeks, and which operatic reformers, like Wagner and Gluck before him, attempted to reinvoke. These stories are – almost invariably – about love and death ambiguously intertwined. For me, the analytic couch also bespeaks this mystery of sleep, of death and love. The very act of lying down is full of reverberations. The posture is for sleep, for death, for making love and life, for being born or re-born. The couch is a place for re-membering, a place where premature deaths and destructive loves can be re-membered in a relationship which gives a different experience of love and death. It is a place where the patients' 'lament' can be heard and given its space, a place to lament, to cry out in grief, to be dismembered and remembered.

Perhaps the damage done to my patient was too terrible, the dismemberment too severe to be able to hope for a cure – for a completion. She had told me this herself. But in her growing ability to experience some psychic space and to sing her own lament in the therapy, to remember (and re-member) her own dismembered life of loves and deaths, it seems to me that there is something new, a possibility of discovery and letting go. She has started to write poems, in which she rages and laments and, sometimes, allows herself hope or wonder.

In the experience of Love and Death completion is never finally achieved. But the dead hand of malign anticipatory identification can, perhaps, give way to a living relationship of ego to self, self to other, self to the past and the beckoning future.

From splitting to paradox: Samsara is Nirvana. There is the paradox of life's ugliness and beauty, of analysis and integration, of transference, relationship and the analytic third and of blind seers. We move from dismembered to re-membered, remembering, forgetting, transitive, intransitive.

The individual is not her fate: 'Remember me', sings Dido, 'but ah! Forget my fate'.

Our job is to help people forget.

You can't forget until you have remembered, until you have *been* remembered – re-membered!

Laurence Roberts
July 1998

References

Anthony, S. (1971) *The Discovery of Death in Childhood and After.* Harmondsworth: Penguin.

Alvarez, A. (1972) *The Savage God.* London: Weidenfeld and Nicolson.

Albery, N. and Elliot, G. and J. (1997) *The Natural Death Handbook.* London, Sydney, Auckland and Johannesburg: Rider.

Becker, E. (1973) *The Denial of Death.* New York: The Free Press, Division of Macmillan Publishing Co. Inc.

Bertoia, J. (1993) *Drawings from a Dying Child.* London: Routledge.

Bettleheim, B. (1987) *The Uses of Enchantment.* Harmondsworth: Penguin.

Bienvenuto, B. and Kennedy, R. (1986) *The Works of Jacques Lacan: An Introduction.* London: Free Association Books.

Bismark, (1918) 'In conversation with Meyer von Waldeck, 11 August 1867.' In *Oxford Book of Quotations* (1998) Oxford: Oxford University Press.

Blake, W. (1977) *The Portable Blake.* London: Penguin, Viking.

Boothby, R. (1991) *Death and Desire; Psychoanalytic Theory in Lacan's Return to Freud.* New York and London: Routledge.

Bor, R. Miller, R. and Goldman, E. (1992) *Theory and Practice of HIV Counselling: A Systemic Approach.* London, New York: Cassells.

Brooke, R. (1915) *1914 and Other Poems.* London: Sidgwick and Jackson.

Brown, J. (1997) 'Response to Chris Purnell's article'. *British Journal of Psychotherapy 13,* 4.

Butler, R.N. (1963) 'The life review: An interpretation of reminicence in the ageing.' *Psychiatry 26,* 65–75.

Butler, R.N. and Lewis, M. (1974) *Life Review Therapy in Geriatrics,* 165–173.

Butler, M. and Orbach, A. (1993) *Being Your Age.* London: SPCK.

Clough (1862) 'The latest decalogue.' In *Oxford Book of Quotations* (1998) Oxford: Oxford University Press.

Corbett, L. (1996) *The Religious Function of the Psyche.* London, New York: Routledge.

Cox, M. and Theilgaard, A. (1994) *Shakespeare as Prompter, The Amending Imagination and the Therapeutic Process.* London: Jessica Kingsley Publishers.

Cross, F.L. (ed) (1971) *The Oxford Dictionary of the Christian Church.* London: Oxford University Press.

Crossley, M. (1997) 'The divided self: The destructive potential of HIV diagnosis'. *Journal for the Society of Existential Analysis 8,* 2, 73–94.

Donne, J. (1624) 'Devotions upon emergent occasions, meditation xvii.' In *Oxford Book of Quotations* (1998). Oxford: Oxford University Press.

Dundas, M.I. (1891) *Dundas of Fingask: Some Memorials of the Family.* Edinburgh: T and A Constable.

Eckstaedt, A. (1986) 'Two complementary cases of identification involving "Third Reich" fathers'. *International Journal of Psychoanalysis 67*, 3, 317–327.

Eigen, M. (1996) *Psychic Deadness.* Northvale, New Jersey and London: Jason Aronson.

Elliot, G. (1986) *Middlemarch.* (First pub.1871). Harmondsworth: Penguin.

Eliot, T.S. (1968) *Murder in the Cathedral.* London: Faber and Faber.

Erikson, E. (1974) *Childhood and Society.* Harmondsworth: Penguin.

Evans-Bush, N. and Greyson, B. (1996) 'Distressing near-death experiences'. In L.W. Bailey and J. Yates (eds) *The Near Death Experience, a Reader.* New York: Villard.

Fenwick, P. and E. (1997) *The Truth in the Light.* New York: Berkeley.

Field, N. (1996) *Breakdown and Breakthrough, Psychotherapy in a New Dimension.* London: Routledge.

Fordham (1976) *The Self and Autism.* London: Heinemann.

Foulds, G.A. (1976) *The Hierarchical Nature of Personal Illness.* London: Routledge.

Fox, J. and Gill, S. (1996) *The Dead Good Funerals Book.* Cumbria, England: Engineers of Imagination.

Freud, S. (1905) *On Psychotherapy, SE VII.* London: Hogarth.

Freud, S. (1915) 'The disillusionment of war.' In *Thoughts of War and Death, Civilisation, Society and Religion* (1991) Harmondsworth: Penguin.

Freud, S. (1984) *On Metapsychology.* Harmondsworth: Penguin.

Freud, S. (1991) *Civilization, Society and Religion.* Harmondsworth: Penguin.

Galbraith, J.K. (1969) 'Letter to President Kennedy, 2.3.62' in *Oxford Dictionary of Quotations.* Oxford: Oxford University Press.

Gallwey, P. (1997) Forward to 'Forensic Psychotherapy with a Potential Serial Killer'. *British Journal of Psychotherapy 13*, 4, 473–487.

Garfield, S. (1994) *The End of Innocence: Britain in Time of Aids.* London, Boston: Faber.

Gilbert, M. (1987) *The Holocaust, The Jewish Tragedy.* Glasgow: Collins (Fontana).

Gilleard, C.J. (1984) *Living with Dementia: Community Care of the Elderly Mentally Infirm.* Beckenham, Kent and Surrey Hills, NSW, Australia: Croom Helm.

Guibert, H. (1991) 'To a friend who did not save my life, Tr. Linda Coverdale'. *Oxford Book of Quotations.* Oxford: Oxford University Press.

Gordon, R. (1978) *Dying and Creating: A Search for Meaning.* London: The Society of Analytical Psychology, Vol. V.

Guntrip, H. (1971) *Psychoanalytic Theory and the Self.* London: Hogarth.

Hall, J.A. (1991) *Patterns of Dreaming: Jungian Technique in Theory and Practice.* Boston, London: Shambala.

Hillman, J. (1996) *The Soul's Code: In Search of Character and Calling.* New York: Random House.

Hillman, J. (1997) *Suicide and the Soul.* Woodstock, Connecticut: Spring Publications Inc.

Hinton, J. (1990) *Dying.* Harmondsworth: Penguin (first publn. 1967).

Hornbacher, M. (1998) *Wasted, A Memoir of Anorexia and Bulimia.* London: Flamingo, HarperCollins.

Ivan, L. and Melrose, M. (1986) *The Way we Die*. Chichester: Angel Press.

Jacoby, M. (1993) *Individuation and Narcissism: The Psychology of the Self in Jung and Kohut*. London, New York: Routledge.

James, W. (1974) *The Varieties of Religious Experience*. London: Collins (Fontana).

Jones, E. (1964) *The Life and Work of Sigmund Freud*. London: Pelican.

Judd, D. (1989) *Give Sorrow Words: Working with a Dying Child*. London: Free Association Books.

Jung, C.G. (1954) *The Development of the Personality, CW 17*. London: Routledge.

Jung, C.G. (1967) *Memories, Dreams, Reflections*. London: Collins (Fontana).

Jung, C.G. (1975) *Aion, CW 9II*. London: Routledge.

Jung, C.G. (1977) *The Structure and Dynamics of the Psyche, CW 8*. London: Routledge.

Jung, C.G. (1979) *The Spirit in Man, Art and Literature, CW 15*. London: Routledge.

Jung, C.G. (1990) *Symbols of Transformation, CW 5*. Princeton, NJ: Princeton University Press.

Keizer, B. (1996) *Dancing with Mr. D: Notes on Life and Death*. London: Doubleday.

Klein, H. and Kogan, I. (1986) 'Identification Processes and Denial in Shadow of Nazism'. *International Journal of Psychoanalysis 67*, 1, 45–52.

Kogan, I. (1995) *The Cry of Mute Children: A Psychoanalytic Perspective of the Second Generation of the Holocaust*. London: Free Association Books.

Kohon, G. (1983) *The British School of Psychoanalysis, The Independent Position*. London: Free Association Books.

Kübler-Ross, E. (1970) *On Death and Dying*. London: Tavistock.

Kübler-Ross, E. (1983) *On Children and Death*. New York and London: Macmillan.

Lacan, J. (1975) *Le Seminaire 20: Encore*. Paris: Editions de Seuil.

Lacan, J. (1988) *The Seminars of Jacques Lacan, Bk.1, Freud's Papers on Technique (1953–4)*. ed. J.A. Miller, Tr. J. Forrester. New York: W.W. Norton Co.

Laing, R. (1965) *The Divided Self: An Existential Study in Madness and Sanity*. London: Pelican.

Levine, S. (1982) *Who Dies? An Investigation into Conscious Living and Conscious Dying*. New York, London, Toronto, Sydney, Auckland: Anchor Books, Doubleday.

Lewis, C.S. (1966) *The Last Battle*. Harmondsworth: Penguin.

Livingstone, R.W. (1946) *Portrait of Socrates*. Oxford: Clarendon Press.

MacLeod, S. (1981) *The Art of Starvation, One Girl's Journey through Adolescence and Anorexia: A Study of Survival*. London: Virago.

Macquarrie, J. (1972) *Existentialism*. Harmondsworth: Penguin.

Magarshack, D. (1978) *Translator's Introduction to 'The Idiot' by Dostoievsky, F.* Harmondsworth: Penguin.

Mander, R. (1994) *Loss and Bereavement in Childbearing*. Oxford: Blackwell Scientific Publications.

May, R. (1969) *Existential Psychology*. New York: Random House Inc.

Meredith, G. (1862) 'Modern love' In *Oxford Book of Quotations* (1998) Oxford: Oxford University Press.

Milton, M. (1996) 'An existential approach to HIV related psychotherapy'. *Journal of the Society for Existential Analysis 8*, 1, 115–129.

Morse, M. (1990) *Closer to the Light: Learning from Children's Near Death Experience.* New York: Villard.

Negri, R. (1994) *The Newborn in the Intensive Care Unit.* London: Karnac.

Nuland, S. (1994) *How We Die.* London: Chatto and Windus.

O'Donahue, J. (1997) *Anam Cara, Spiritual Wisdom from the Celtic World.* London, New York, Toronto, Sydney, Auckland: Bantam Press.

O'Siadhail, M. (1998) *Our Double Time.* Newcastle: Bloodaxe Books.

Orbach, A. (1996) *Not Too Late: Psychotherapy and Ageing.* London: Jessica Kingsley Publishers.

Ostow, M. (1986) 'The psychodynamics of apocalyptic discussion of papers on identification and the Nazi phenomena'. *International Journal of Psychoanalysis 67*, 1, 277–287.

Owen, W. (1933) *The Poems of Wilfrid Owen, ed. E. Blunden.* London: Phoenix Library, Chatto and Windus.

Parfit, D. (1986) *Reasons and Persons.* Oxford, New York: Oxford University Press.

Parkes, (1986) *Bereavement: Studies of Grief in Adult Life.* London: Tavistock.

Pines, D. (1986) 'Working with women survivors of the holocaust: Affective experiences in transference and countertransference'. *International Journal of Psychoanalysis 67*, 3, 295–309.

Plato (tr. J. Llewellin Davies) (1908) *The Republic of Plato.* London: Macmillan.

Polledri, P. (1997) 'Forensic psychotherapy with a potential serial killer'. *British Journal of Psychotherapy 13*, 4, 473–487.

Pollock, G.H. (1987) *Treating the Elderly with Psychotherapy: The Scope for Change in Later Life.* Madison, Connecticut: Int. University Press, Inc.

Purnell, C. (1996) 'An attachment-based approach to working with clients affected by HIV and AIDS'. *British Journal of Psychotherapy 12*, 4, 521–50.

Redfearn, J. (1992) *The Exploding Self, The Creative and Destructive Nucleus of the Personality.* Wilmette, Illinois: Chiron Publns.

Reeves, R. (1998) *Personal Communication* - Letter to the Author

Rendell, R. (1995) *The Reason Why: An Anthology of the Murderous Mind.* London: Jonathan Cape.

Samuels, A. (1993) 'Jung, anti-semitism and the Nazis'. *The Journal of Analytical Psychology 38*, 4, 468–470.

Samuels, A., Shorter, B. and Plaut, A. (1986) *A Critical Dictionary of Jungian Analysis.* London: Routledge.

Sereny, G. (1998) *Cries Unheard: The Story of Mary Bell.* London: Macmillan.

Settlage, C.F. (1996) 'Transcending old age: creativity, development and psycho-analysis in the life of a centenarian'. *International Journal of Psychoanalysis 77*, 540–563.

Sourkes, R.M. (1995) *Armfuls of Time: The Psychological Experience of a Child with Life-threatening Illness.* London, USA, Canada: Routledge.

Stern, C. (1996) *Dr Iain West's Casebook.* London: Little Brown.

Stevens, A. (1982) *Archetype, A Natural History of the Self.* London: Routledge.

Storr, A. (1989) *Solitude.* London: Flamingo.

Swift, G. (1996) *Last Orders.* London: Picador.

Symington, N. (1993) *Narcissism, A New Theory.* London: Karnac.

Taylor, C. (1997) 'A Case of Murder'. In E. Weldon and A. Van Velsen (eds) *A Practical Guide to Forensic Psychotherapy.* London: Jessica Kingsley Publishers.

Teilhard de Chardin, P. (1979) *The Hymn of the Universe.* London: Collins Fount Paperbacks.

Tillich, P. (1974) *The Courage to Be.* London: Collins (Fontana).

Tolstoy, L. (1960) *The Death of Ivan Ilyid and Other Stories.* Harmondsworth: Penguin.

Tolstoy, L. (1975) *Anna Karenina.* London: The Folio Society.

Troubridge, Lady (1926) *The Book of Etiquette.* Kingswood, Surrey: The World's Work.

Van de Post, L. (1982) *Yet Being Someone Other.* London: Hogarth.

Vaughan, H. (1916) 'The world.' In *The Oxford Book of Mystical Verse.* Oxford: Clarenden Press.

Voluntary Euthanasia Society (1992) *Your Ultimate Choice, The Right to Die with Dignity, A Selection.* London: Souvenir Press.

Von Franz, M.L. (1980) *The Passion of Perpetua.* Dallas, TX: Spring Publications Inc.

Von Franz, M.L. (1986) *On Dreams and Death.* Boston: Shambala.

Von Franz, M.L. (1987) *Shadow and Evil in Fairy Tales.* Dallas, TX: Spring Publications Inc.

Walter, T. (1994) *The Revival of Death.* London, New York: Routledge.

Watts, A. (1954) *Myth and Ritual in Christianity.* London: Thames and Hudson.

Welldon, E. (1997) 'Forensic psychotherapy: The practical approach'. *A Practical Guide to Forensic Psychotherapy.* London: Jessica Kingsley Publishers.

Williams, J. (1991) *The Modern Sherlock Holmes: An Introduction to Forensic Science Today.* London: Broadside Books Ltd.

Willis, R. (1993) *World Mythology, The Illustrated Guide.* London: Duncan Baird.

Winnicott, D.W. (1960) 'Ego distortion in terms of true and false self.' In *The Maturational Processes and the Facilitating Environment.* (1976) London: Hogarth.

Winnicott, D.W. (1976) *The Maturational Processes and the Facilitating Environment.* London: Hogarth.

Winnicott, D.W. (1986) *Home is Where We Start From.* London: Hogarth.

Wordsworth, W. (1980) 'Intimations of immortality from recollections of early childhood.' In *The New Golden Treasury of English Verse.* London: Pan Books.

Subject Index

Author Index